AF322841

Challenges and Choices
Facing American Labor

Challenges and Choices Facing American Labor

edited by
Thomas A. Kochan

The MIT Press
Cambridge, Massachusetts
London, England

Third printing, 1986

© 1985 by
The Massachusetts Institute of Technology

All rights reserved. No part of this book may be reproduced in any form by any electronic or mechanical means (including photocopying, recording, or information storage and retrieval) without permission in writing from the publisher.

This book was set in Palatino
by The MIT Press Computergraphics Department
and printed and bound by Halliday Lithograph
in the United States of America.

Library of Congress Cataloging in Publication Data

Main entry under title:

Challenges and choices facing American labor.

  Includes bibliographies and index.
  1. Industrial relations—United States—Addresses, essays, lectures.
  2. Trade-unions—United States—Addresses, essays, lectures.
I. Kochan, Thomas A.
HD8072.5.C47 1985   331′.0973   84–19372
ISBN 0-262-11095-4 (H)
      0-262-61039-6 (P)

Contents

Contents vi

Foreword

This book is the result of a June 1983 conference at M.I.T.'s Endicott Conference Center. For two-and-a-half days, thirty-four union officials and twenty-three academics discussed a series of research papers from a three-year study, "U.S. Industrial Relations in Transition," sponsored by the Sloan Foundation.

The Sloan Project has examined a wide range of fundamental changes that have been occurring in industrial relations, especially in the United States. The project has operated at three levels. At the level of the small group and department where productivity is determined, special attention has been paid to quality of work life, worker participation, and alternative forms of work organization. At the plant or middle level of the system, the emphasis has been on concession bargaining and some significant changes that have been taking place in the structure of collective bargaining. At the highest, or strategic, level the important policy themes of the increasingly closer link between industrial relations and business strategy have been examined: the evolution of comprehensive personnel policies in unorganized operations and the involvement of workers and union representatives in the key business decisions of the corporation.

In planning the conference, we wanted an opportunity to discuss our emerging research findings with a cross section of leaders of local and national unions as well as representatives of the headquarters staff of the AFL-CIO. We viewed the occasion as a special opportunity for those of us at M.I.T., along with other academics, to engage labor leaders in a discussion of research that is examining some of the important issues and changes that are very much a part of the current industrial relations system. The conference met our highest expectations; the discussion was incisive and thought-provoking. It is for this reason that we decided to include in this volume as much as possible of the dialogue with the union officials.

We would like to thank all the attendees for their enthusiastic participation and, especially, the planning committee—Donald Ephlin, UAW; Rudy Oswald, AFL-CIO; Richard Prosten, AFL-CIO; Jack Sheinkman, Amalgamated Clothing and Textile Workers; and Lynn Williams, United Steelworkers. The conference would not have taken place without the careful planning and guidance of Carolanne Foilb, and these papers would not have been ready for publication without the excellent assistance of Nancy Mower and Michelle Kamin.

Thomas A. Kochan
Robert B. McKersie
Michael J. Piore

Challenges and Choices
Facing American Labor

1   U.S. Industrial Relations in Transition

Thomas A. Kochan and
Michael J. Piore

Industrial relations practices appear to have been changing in a number of important ways in the past few years. These changes have sparked a debate among practitioners, researchers, and policy makers over whether the nature and degree of change is only a temporary adjustment caused by the severity of the world economic crisis or a more fundamental structural change that will have lasting effects on the U.S. industrial relations system. For the past several years a number of us at M.I.T. and neighboring universities have been engaged in research designed to document and analyze the current state of industrial relations and the changes that are under way. The following chapters are based on this work and were first presented at a meeting with labor union leaders in June 1983. The purpose of this conference was to obtain a critical assessment of this research from active labor leaders and to explore with them the implications of our findings to date for the American labor movement.

The subject matter covered in the various studies is diverse, ranging from the evolution of the legal structure for union organizing and bargaining to technology and work practices on the shop floor to the strategies conceived at the highest levels of employer and labor organizations. It is not all conceived in response to a single set of problems, and we hope the reader will focus on each study and the discussion it generated. Nonetheless, two central themes appear to be emerging.

First, while the most visible examples of change in industrial relations may lie in the economic concessions and trade-offs that have occurred in collective bargaining negotiations in recent years, other, perhaps more important, changes are occurring more quietly, both above and below the level of collective bargaining. We believe an understanding of these changes and their long-run implications for industrial relations requires a broadening of the focus of industrial relations analysis and activity. That is, to understand what is happening in industrial relations today, we must also look at the strategic decisions made at the highest levels of the firm and at the organization of work and the participation of individual workers in the workplace.

Second, not all of the current changes are a product of short-run economic pressures. Rather, many are the result of pressures and trends that have been under way for some time. Throughout the 1970s, for example, the environment of industrial relations was slowly but steadily being altered as a result of the growth of competitive pressures within the U.S. and world economies, shifts in the demographic, industrial, occupational, and regional distribution of the labor force, the growing effectiveness of employers in remaining nonunion and the corresponding decline in union coverage in the private sector, and the emergence of new technologies and market structures. We will review these general trends and the current responses of employers and unions in the following sections.

Shifts in the Industrial Relations Environment

The most important environmental trend of the past two decades influencing the conduct of industrial relations has been the decline in union and collective bargaining coverage in the private sector. The factors responsible for this decline are diverse. The effects of structural (industry, region, and occupation) shifts in the American economy are reviewed by Henry Farber. His analysis shows that some, but clearly not all, of the changes in union coverage can be explained by these structural shifts. Paul Osterman's analysis of white-collar occupations complements the aggregate analysis by exploring some of the internal labor market features that make these jobs and occupations difficult to organize. Richard Freeman reviews the changing record of National Labor Relations Board elections and analyzes some of the reasons for the declining effectiveness of the election process as a means of obtaining new union members. The increase in employer aggressiveness, as indicated by the rise in the number of employer unfair labor practices since 1960 and the declining union win rates in elections, is clearly another part of the explanation of these trends.

Janice Klein and David Wanger explore another potential effect of the legal environment by tracing shifts in employer strategies in NLRB election campaigns to several key NLRB decisions and doctrines of the 1950s. Noah Meltz provides another perspective on American labor law by comparing it to the procedures governing union recognition in the various provinces of Canada. Meltz suggests that differences in laws and their enforcement, along with differences in political influence of the Canadian and American labor movements, help explain why Canadian union membership expanded during this period in contrast to the U.S. experience.

It should be noted that the recent changes in employer behavior do not represent a fundamental change in management philosophy. American employers have historically been philosophically opposed to unionism. The New Deal labor policies, however, followed by the rise of industrial unionism and the support given to collective bargaining principles by the War Labor Board, created a period from the mid-1930s through the 1950s in which most employers followed a pragmatic strategy of accepting unions and conducting their industrial relations within the framework of collective bargaining. A new managerial resistance to unions appears to have developed gradually in the 1960s and acquired speed and momentum in the 1970s. By the second half of that decade it had become a coherent, articulated strategy of what is now often referred to as "union avoidance."

While the Freeman and the Klein and Wanger chapters document the more aggressive union avoidance strategies associated with employer conduct in representation elections, the study by Anil Verma and Thomas Kochan describes another, perhaps more important, means by which employers avoided unions in the 1970s—the development and use of sophisticated human resource management systems at the plant level designed to reduce the incentives of workers to organize.

This strategy emphasizes (1) paying wages that are competitive in the local labor market, (2) maintaining flexibility in work organization, and (3) stressing high levels of communication, involvement, commitment, and motivation of individual workers. By emphasizing broad-banded job classifications, fewer work rules on work assignment and job transfers, and more active training programs, many large nonunion firms have been able to manage their internal labor markets so that fewer workers are separated involuntarily. The costs of labor are kept lower, and employers can better adjust to changing markets with more flexible technologies and work organization systems.

While part of the motivation driving these new human resource management strategies is to keep the firm unorganized, it is clear that they have become popular for other reasons as well. From the standpoint of the firm, they not only make good business and employee-relations sense but also appear to be well suited to changes in the nature of technology and the structure of product markets. This is the central message in the chapter written by Michael Piore. He and Charles Sabel conclude from their comparative research on technology and work organization that the world economy as a whole is moving away from market structures and technologies oriented toward long runs of standardized products. This movement is a result of three factors: (1) the saturation of the world market for consumer durable goods; (2) the diversion of investment away from standardized, mass-produced goods in favor of more specialized markets caused by the enormous instability and uncertainty of the economic environment of the 1970s; and (3) the growth of new computer-based technologies that reduce the cost of flexible production techniques. The net result of these market and technology shifts is that the forms of job-control unionism, as exemplified by comprehensive and detailed collective bargaining agreements and tight job classifications, become more costly and burdensome under flexible production systems. If this is true, then the more flexible forms of work organization found in the newer nonunion systems have a logic that goes considerably deeper than the union avoidance motive.

The Current Responses in Industrial Relations

The 1970s will go down in American labor history as a decade in which the pressures for change were building gradually within the unionized sector of the American economy but the parties to collective bargaining did not respond accordingly. Instead, the patterns of behavior built up during the post–World War II environment of economic growth and expansion of world markets continued to dominate the behavior of management and union officials and the process and results of collective bargaining. Consequently, during the 1970s a gap developed between the internal practices of management and unions and external environmental pressures.

If the 1970s were years of complacency in collective bargaining, the 1980s can be characterized as a time of turmoil, experimentation, and testing of new approaches in search of new ways of coping with an increasingly competitive environment. We will now turn to a discussion of the research that analyzes employer and union responses in the current period. In doing so, we will illustrate the value of examining current practices at three levels of industrial relations within firms and unions: (1) strategic decision-making levels, (2) collective bargaining, and (3) workplace or shop floor relations.

Changes in Corporate Industrial Relations Practice

Over the past twenty years many labor relations professionals within unionized corporations became increasingly isolated, conservative, and less influential. Because labor relations managers were primarily concerned with maintaining stable and peaceful union-management relations, they made no aggressive attempts to change work practices or to change significantly wage and fringe-benefit formulas or patterns. Nor did they readily accept the need to introduce direct strategies for involving workers and unions in efforts to improve the quality of work life and productivity that many others within and outside their firms were urging on them. They remained focused on traditional collective bargaining activities and responsibilities.

Meanwhile, the growth of government regulations, the increase in the demand for managers, professionals, and technical employees, and the increasing interest in union avoidance among top executives led to the development of a new set of human resource management specialists who were more conversant with different types of planning, behavioral-science-based innovations in work organization and personnel systems, and organizational-change techniques that now form the foundation of nonunion human resource management systems. Because of the importance of these functions to top executives, and because of the increasing importance of government regulations and tight labor markets for professionals, labor relations specialists have lost ground to the human resource management specialists. This gradual evolution has laid the foundation for the current transformation in the conduct of industrial relations that appears to be taking place in many firms.

The nature of this transformation can be seen in several ways. For example, the economic crisis facing many companies has strengthened the link between overall business policy and strategy and industrial relations and collective bargaining. Decisions regarding investment in different businesses or plants have traditionally been isolated from most of the industrial relations professionals within corporations. New demands for concessions from unions, however, coupled with countervailing union demands for greater information sharing, are forcing a closer link between investment (and other basic business decisions) and the industrial relations function. This in turn is calling on industrial relations and human resource management professionals to engage in more long-term planning and strategic analysis of alternatives for reducing labor costs and increasing productivity. Indeed, the drive for productivity improvement and labor-cost control is also forging a closer link between operating or line managers and labor relations and human resource specialists.

Thus, the techniques of strategic planning and analysis are now being introduced into the industrial relations function more directly. Also, a wider group of managers is increasingly part of the planning and development of strategy for contract negotiations.

Another development of significance has been the high level of visibility given to worker participation and involvement in Japan and in many nonunion companies. These models have caught the interest and attention of many top executives outside of the industrial relations function. This has led to an increase in corporate efforts to develop new patterns of communication and involvement with individual employees and in small groups both to improve employee commitment to the firm and to increase productivity. These efforts have again required industrial relations managers to develop new strategies not only for working with trade union leaders but for involving individual employees and bringing about higher levels of trust and involvement at the workplace. Again, the skills and techniques required to implement this strategy require active cooperation between organizational development specialists and traditional industrial relations specialists. In short, the role of industrial relations within many corporations is undergoing fundamental change. Companies are searching for new strategies that link their industrial relations performance to the larger business strategies of the firm and to efforts to reduce labor costs, increase productivity, and enhance the commitment and participation of individual workers.

Changes in Collective Bargaining

The major changes occurring in collective bargaining are easily summarized because of their high visibility. A comprehensive summary of the results of bargaining in key industries is provided in the study by Harry Katz. The rate of compensation increase in major collective bargaining agreements in 1982 was 3.6%, compared to an average of 9.8% for calendar year 1981. Furthermore, 43% of the workers covered under contracts negotiated in 1982 provided for no wage increase in the first year and 35% provided for no wage increase over the term of the agreement. Peter Cappelli and Robert McKersie take a closer look at the phenomenon that has become known as "concession bargaining."

Their analysis shows that the answer to whether temporary wage concessions produced significant improvements in employment security or restored the competitive position of employers varied greatly from industry to industry

Katz points out the large diversity in 1982 bargaining outcomes that these average figures obscure. Indeed, a larger-than-normal dispersion in settlement rates occurred in 1982. While industries under extreme duress negotiated wage freezes, deferrals, or wage cuts, other firms and industries under less intensive pressures settled at levels only marginally lower than those of earlier years.

Pehaps even more significantly, as Cappelli and McKersie and Katz point out, 1982 brought about a renewal of plant-specific bargaining over work practices, particularly over the scope of job definitions and classifications, rules governing the movement of people across jobs through bidding and posting procedures and bumping rights, general plant practices that affect the flexibility and the use of human resources, and payment for time not worked. These all represent efforts to gain control over manufacturing costs, reduce compensation differentials with nonunion competitors, and achieve greater flexibility in the allocation of human resources.

While these changes in bargaining outcomes are important, changes of equal and perhaps more long-lasting importance have occurred in the structure and process of negotiations in some key industries. In bargaining relationships facing the severest competitive pressures, there has been a shift away from long-standing pattern bargaining or centralized bargaining arrangements and an increase in emphasis on company or plant profits or financial prospects. In other cases employers have begun to communicate more directly with employees by providing information on costs, profits, and the state of competition. As one-time events, these changes are not likely to have lasting significance. Where, however, they are combined with continuing efforts to modify workplace practices and involve individual and small groups of employees more directly in problem solving at the workplace, they may produce new forms of plant-level industrial relations. Thus, we need to examine more carefully the changes in workplace relationships that are under way in some bargaining relationships.

Changes in the Workplace

The increase in the attention paid to the degree of involvement, commitment, and participation of individual workers and work groups in task-related decisions has resulted from both corporate strategy and efforts to bring about changes in work rules and practices at the plant level through collective bargaining. Indeed, while a number of quality-of-work-life (QWL) or related worker-participation efforts were started in the late 1960s and early 1970s, most of them deemphasized productivity issues and separated QWL efforts from the collective bargaining process and relationship. The study of worker-participation programs summarized by Kochan, Katz, and Mower, however, argues that current participation efforts are more directly addressing issues affecting work organization and productivity and in some instances are fostering innovations that are at variance with the provisions found in bargaining agreements. For example, where QWL programs grapple directly with production problems, they frequently get into issues involving the scope of jobs and provisions for moving workers across jobs. This leads to questions concerning the role of seniority, compensation and job evaluation systems, and the promotion, transfer, and bumping rights of different workers. Thus, QWL programs serve in some cases as another vehicle for employers to achieve the type of broad-banded jobs and higher degrees of flexibility in the assignment and utilization of people that are associated with the forms of work organization found in many newer nonunion firms.

Labor Union Responses

Most of the analysis so far has focused on changes in industrial relations resulting from proactive behavior on the part of employers. Union leaders, however, are responding to employers in a variety of different ways, some of which begin to expand their roles at the levels of industrial relations below and above collective bargaining. These new forms of union participation also represent potentially significant departures from traditional patterns and principles.

Traditionally, the main point of contact for unions in industrial relations has been at the middle of the three-tiered framework, where unions negotiate collective bargaining agreements with individual firms. The American collective bargaining system is predicated on the principle that "management acts and workers and their labor organizations react" to the effects of management policy either through the grievance procedure or by introducing new proposals in contract negotiation. However, we see considerable thought and experimentation being given to greater involvement by unions at levels both below and above the level of contract negotiations and administration.

At the lowest level of industrial relations—in the relationships among individuals, work groups, and supervisors—a number of unions are currently participating as joint partners with management in quality-of-work-life efforts. Kochan, Katz, and Mower review the effects of these programs on local unions and speculate on their implications for the labor movement. They note that these workplace participation efforts entail a mixed bag of risks and opportunities for local unions. Union leaders can play important roles in setting the stage for, designing, and administering participation programs and thereby attempt to integrate them into their representational role at the workplace. On the other hand, over time these efforts are likely to build higher commitment of the worker to the firm, challenge existing work rules, and fashion new work-organization arrangements. If this occurs, local unions will find it necessary to modify their traditional roles at the workplace and adjust to the increased flexibility and variation in practices that eventually result from greater worker involvement. Kochan, Katz, and Mower conclude that those unions that are most successful in handling these programs are the ones that integrate their QWL strategies into their broader bargaining and representational strategies.

While more union leaders are actively participating in these programs now than in the 1970s, many union leaders still remain quite skeptical. How labor leaders sort out or interpret these experiences will have an important bearing on the role unions will play in the workplace.

At the levels of strategic decision making, where employers make basic investment and resource deployment decisions, the emerging picture for union leaders is one of experimentation. McKersie reviews some of the activity at this level. He notes that although U.S. unions have been reluctant to follow the German model of formal representation on boards of directors, the American labor movement is now openly discussing the advantages and limitations of seeking to represent workers' job security and financial interests at the strategic level of the enterprise or industry.

In only a very limited number of actual cases (notably at Chrysler and Pan Am) are unions represented on company boards. However, there is considerable movement in some sectors toward a more uniquely "American" style of union influence in strategic decision making. Some union leaders are being brought into management councils for briefings and discussions about the direction of the business and its implications for the union's membership. More and more unions are now receiving information about financial performance, maintenance programs, and investment plans for specific plants. Other unions are demanding an earlier and more meaningful role in decisions involving the design and introduction of new technology. All of these represent a testing and gradual movement by some unions toward a greater involvement at the strategic level of business decision making.

John Joyce, president of one of the key U.S. building trades unions, provides an excellent perspective on these issues. Joyce's analysis, originally presented at an International Labour Organization Conference, serves as an instructive complement to this conference. It addresses many of the issues we have been studying concerning the appropriate mix of union strategies at the workplace, in collective bargaining, and in management decision making.

Lee Price's observations on the growing internationalization of the American economy serve as a useful reminder that the changes we have been studying at the microlevel of industrial relations are occurring in the context of a changing world economy. His study provides an overview of the shifts in the structure of the U.S. economy and raises concerns about their longer-run impacts on employment, income distribution, and the viability of current trade policies. The key implication of his analysis for collective bargaining is that labor costs have become a more important competitive factor as the relative costs of transportation and communication decline, the speed of technology transfer increases, and the skill levels of workers in developing countries improve.

Internal Contradictions in American Industrial Relations

Although some unions and employers are searching for new ways of relating to each other at different levels, the predominant pattern is one of internal contradiction. For example, many of the companies that have experienced significant diversification and growth from 1960 to 1980 are now following a very aggressive and sophisticated strategy of union avoidance at both the corporate level and in new plants; at the same time in older plants they are negotiating concessions from unions and encouraging the development of labor-management cooperation and worker participation. Thus the broad corporate strategies decided at the highest level of the firm contain many elements of a very adversarial approach, while these same firms may be seeking to overcome adversarial relationships at the level of the plant. Although only a few unions have been able to exert enough pressure to force these diversified firms to abandon their union avoidance strategies, many unions are cooperating with plant-level efforts at employee involvement. It is difficult, however, to see how long cooperation can last at the plant level and at the workplace in the face of a union avoidance strategy at the corporate level.

Conversely, in several companies that are more highly unionized and have accepted the reality that new facilities are likely to be unionized, there is greater recognition of and agreement among top management and union officials on key strategic issues and on the need for labor-cost moderation, but the level of conflict and distrust at the plant level between workers and plant management remains quite high. Thus, in some cases there is a higher level of institutional accommodation between the representatives of the company and the national union than among workers, local union leaders, and management representatives at the workplace.

Implications for Union Strategies

It is always easier to describe and interpret historical and current events than to predict their long-run consequences or their specific implications for the labor movement. Indeed, we find it neither possible nor appropriate to propose what we think are the "best" strategies for union leaders to follow in coping with these changes. Instead our purpose in this volume is to continue the dialogue begun at the conference over the strategic issues and choices facing the American labor movement. Perhaps the best way to end this introductory chapter then is to pose a series of strategic questions that the labor movement must continue to address if it is to strengthen its role in American society and in the workplace.

First, is the traditional system of collective bargaining able to cope with an increasingly competitive world economy? The old system achieved stability only by taking wages out of competition and achieving standard wages. The ability of collective bargaining to achieve this result appears to have broken down in most sectors of the economy.

Second, employer strategic decisions at the levels of the firm well removed from the collective bargaining table appear to be the driving forces affecting employment security of union members and the organizational security of unions. Does this call for a modification of the traditional view that unions do not want to participate in management decision making? If more participation or consultation is to be sought, what forms should it take, and can it be achieved within the confines of existing labor law?

Third, are the more varied and flexible forms of worker participation channels for extending industrial democracy to union members, thereby strengthening in the role of labor unions and improving the competitive position of unionized employers? Or will they inevitably weaken unions by reducing the perceived need for union representation and collective bargaining in the eyes of union members?

Fourth, how can the sophisticated and the aggressive union avoidance strategies of American employers be neutralized? Is it possible to organize new union members on a plant-by-plant basis under the current union representation election procedures in the face of employer opposition? Or will a wholesale change in organizing strategy and the law governing union representation be needed to change or alter significantly the membership trends of the past twenty years?

I

Challenges to Union Organizing

2 The Extent of Unionization in the United States

Henry S. Farber

Although it is well known that the extent of unionization in the United States has been declining for more than two decades, the reasons for this decline are far from clear. Some have argued that the decrease is due primarily to a shift in employment away from the historically heavily unionized industries, such as those in the manufacturing sector, toward the less unionized industries in the service sector. Others stress the movement in employment and population away from the historically heavily unionized North Central and Northeast regions to the less-unionized South. Still others have argued that at least part of these shifts in employment may be a result of unionization rather than a cause of its decline. The reasoning behind this argument is that as the American economy became more open to low-labor-cost foreign competition over the last two decades, the unionized firms, faced with "artificially" high labor costs, were at a competitive disadvantage. They had to leave the affected industries or shift production to a region where they could operate without labor unions.

It is not my purpose to analyze the reasons for the structural shifts in the U.S. economy; these shifts are taken as given. My purpose is to address three issues. First, how much of the decline in unionization can be accounted for by sectoral shifts in employment? Second, why are some sectors less unionized than others? The decline in unionization being taken as given, the cross-sectional differences in the extent of unionization are analyzed in detail. These differences are broken down into two components, one due to variation in worker demand for union representation and one due to variation in the ability of workers who want union jobs to get them. Third, can unions target successful organization drives on the basis of such characteristics as region, occupation, and industry?

Table 2.1
National union membership as a percentage of nonagricultural employment: By industry, selected years, 1956–78

| Year | Total | Private sector | | Government |
		Manufacturing	Nonmanufacturing	
1956	34.5%	51.3%	30.0%	12.5%
1960	33.2	51.1	28.8	12.8
1964	30.7	48.3	25.8	15.1
1968	29.8	46.6	24.4	18.2
1972	28.3	46.6	23.0	18.4
1976	26.6	45.1	21.0	20.3
1978	25.1	39.7	19.8	23.4

Source: *Handbook of Labor Statistics*, 1980, U.S. Bureau of Labor Statistics, Bulletin No. 2070; *Employment and Training Report of the President*, 1978.

Sectoral Shifts and the Decline in Unionization

The proportion of the nonagricultural labor force in the United States that is unionized has declined over the last twenty-five years from 35% in 1956 to barely 25% in 1978. Except for government, the unionized proportion of the labor force decreased in every major sector over this period. The broadest outlines of this pattern are documented in table 2.1, using Bureau of Labor Statistics data on membership in national and international unions in combination with labor force data on the number of workers on nonagricultural payrolls. For example, even within the manufacturing sector, one of the strongholds of the labor movement, the proportion unionized fell from 51% in 1956 to 40% in 1978. At the same time the proportion of nonmanufacturing private-sector employment unionized fell from 30% to 20%. The only major sector to show a gain was government, where the unionized fraction increased from 13% to 23%.

One consistent feature of the industrial distribution of unionization over time documented in table 2.1 is that the manufacturing sector is by far the most highly organized. On this basis, it has been argued that one explanation for the overall decline in the extent of organization is that employment in manufacturing has accounted for a progressively smaller share of employment over this period. The sectoral breakdown of employment (table 2.2) shows that the proportion of nonagricultural

Table 2.2
Percentage distribution of nonagricultural employment by industrial sector: Selected years 1956–78

| Year | Total | Private Sector | | Government |
		Manufacturing	Nonmanufacturing	
1956	100.0%	32.9%	53.2%	13.9%
1960	100.0	31.0	53.6	15.4
1964	100.0	29.6	53.9	16.5
1968	100.0	29.1	53.5	17.4
1972	100.0	26.0	55.9	18.1
1976	100.0	23.9	57.4	18.7
1978	100.0	23.7	58.4	17.9

Source: *Handbook of Labor Statistics*, 1980, U. S. Bureau of Labor Statistics, Bulletin No. 2070; *Employment and Training Report of the President*, 1978.

employment that is in the manufacturing sector fell from one-third in 1956 to less than one-quarter in 1978.

On one level it is clear that there must be more to the decline in unionization than a shift in employment away from manufacturing because the extent of organization has declined even within the manufacturing sector. On the other hand the industrial shift must account for some portion of the decline. One way to determine how much of the drop in unionization could possibly be accounted for by the shift away from manufacturing is to compute what the extent of unionization would have been in 1978 had the industrial composition of the labor force remained unchanged. More precisely, it is possible to compute the hypothetical overall extent of unionization as a weighted average of the 1978 sector-specific extents of unionization using as weights the 1956 sectoral employment levels rather than the 1978 sectoral employment levels.

On this basis the hypothetical 1978 extent of unionization is computed to be 26.8%. This is very close to the actual 1978 extent of unionization of 25.1%, and nowhere near the actual 1956 extent of unionization of 34.5%. Thus, it can be concluded that the shift in employment away from manufacturing can account for at most 1.7 percentage points (18%) of the 9.4 percentage point drop in the extent of unionization. Clearly, the explanation for the decline lies elsewhere.

Table 2.3 documents another dimension along which unionization in the United States has varied consistently over the past twenty-five

Table 2.3
National union membership as a percentage of nonagricultural employment by region: Selected years, 1956–78

Year	U.S.	Nonsouth	South
1953	32.6%	36.5%	17.1%
1972	28.3	32.9	14.4
1976	26.6	31.2	13.6
1978	25.1	29.6	12.8

Source: *Handbook of Labor Statistics*, 1980, U.S. Bureau of Labor Statistics, Bulletin No. 2070; Leo Troy, "The Growth of Union Membership in the South," *Southern Economic Journal* 24 (April 1958): 407–20.
Note: The South is here defined as Alabama, Arkansas, Florida, Georgia, Kentucky, Louisiana, Mississippi, North Carolina, South Carolina, Tennessee, Texas, and Virginia. The 1953 figures in table 2.3 are from Troy (1958) and are not directly comparable to those in table 2.1 for 1956, derived by the Bureau of Labor Statistics.

Table 2.4
Percentage of nonagricultural employment by region: Selected years, 1956–78

Year	U.S.	Nonsouth	South
1953	100.0%	80.1%	19.9%
1972	100.0	75.0	25.0
1976	100.0	73.7	26.3
1978	100.0	73.1	26.9

Source: *Handbook of Labor Statistics*, 1980, U.S. Bureau of Labor Statistics, Bulletin No. 2070; Leo Troy, "The Growth of Union Membership in the South," *Southern Economic Journal* 24 (April 1958): 407–20.
Note: The South is here defined as Alabama, Arkansas, Florida, Georgia, Kentucky, Louisiana, Mississippi, North Carolina, South Carolina, Tennessee, Texas, and Virginia. The 1953 figures in table 2.3 are from Troy (1958) and are not directly comparable to those in table 2.1 for 1956, derived by the Bureau of Labor Statistics.

years. The extent of unionization has always been substantially lower in the South than elsewhere.[1] While the extent of unionization dropped in all regions of the country between 1953 and 1978, it fell from 17% to 13% within the South and from 37% to 30% outside that region.[2] At the same time the regional distribution of employment (table 2.4) shifted toward the South. In 1953 only 20% of employment was in the South; by 1978 this had increased to 27%. These facts suggest that some portion of the decline in unionization can be attributed to the shift in employment toward the less-unionized South.

Once again, it is clear that the entire decline in unionization cannot be explained by a shift in employment toward the South because the extent of unionization decreased in all regions. On the other hand, the sort of hypothetical calculation that was carried out for industry can be performed on the basis of region. This should determine the extent to which the decline in unionization can be accounted for by regional shifts in employment. To this end, a hypothetical extent of unionization was calculated as the weighted average of the 1978 region-specific extents of unionization, using as weights the 1953 region-specific employment levels rather than the 1978 region-specific employment levels.

On this basis the hypothetical 1978 unionization rate is 26.3%. Once again, this is very close to the actual 1978 unionization rate of 25.1% and nowhere near the actual 1953 extent of unionization of 32.6%. Thus, it can be concluded that the shift in employment toward the South can account for at most 1.2 percentage points (16%) of the 7.5 percentage point drop in the extent of unionization. Overall, the shifts in the industrial and the regional composition of the labor force can account for at most 3 percentage points of the overall drop in the extent of unionization, and it is likely that they account for less than this amount, since the industrial and regional shifts are not independent.

Another major change in the labor force over the past two decades is the shift in occupational composition away from the relatively heavily unionized blue-collar operatives, laborers, and craftsmen toward the less-unionized white-collar occupations. In 1958 blue-collar workers made up 40.5% of the labor force; by 1977 this percentage had fallen to 34.4. Unfortunately, no time series data are available on the extent of unionization by occupation. Nonetheless, cross-section evidence from the May 1977 *Current Population Survey* suggests that at that time, 42.6% of blue-collar workers were unionized, compared to only 30.5% of the overall sample.[3] Although these figures are not directly comparable to those in tables 2.1 through 2.4, it is clear that blue-collar workers are substantially more likely to be unionized than are white-collar workers and that this could account for some of the drop in the extent of unionization.

Making adjustments for sample differences and assuming that the *relative* propensity for union representation among blue-collar and white-collar workers is fixed over time, the hypothetical 1977 extent of unionization computed as a weighted average of the 1977 occupation-specific extents of unionization, using as weights 1958 occupation-specific employment levels rather than 1977 employment levels, is

28.0%. Assuming a 1977 actual extent of unionization of 25.9%, it can be concluded that the shift in the labor force away from blue-collar occupations can account for at most 2.1 percentage points (21%) of the 9.8 percentage point drop in the extent of unionization.

The last major change that has been argued to have a major effect on the overall extent of unionization is the tremendous increase in the number of females in the labor force. In 1956 females made up 32% of the employed labor force, while in 1978 females accounted for 41%. Unfortunately, as with occupation, no time series data are available on the extent of unionization by sex. Nonetheless, cross-section evidence from the May 1977 *Current Population Survey* suggests that at that time, 20.6% of females were unionized compared to fully 38.1% of males.[4] Although these figures are not directly comparable to those in tables 2.1 through 2.4, it is clear that females are substantially less likely to be unionized than are males and that this could account for some of the drop in the extent of unionization.

Making adjustments for sample differences and assuming that the *relative* propensity for union representation among males and females is fixed over time, the hypothetical 1977 extent of unionization computed as a weighted average of the 1977 sex-specific extents of unionization, using as weights the 1956 male and female employment levels rather than 1977 employment levels, is 28.3%. Assuming a 1977 actual extent of unionization of 25.9%, it can be concluded that the increase in the labor force participation rate of females can account for at most 2.4 percentage points (24%) of the 9.8 percentage point drop in the extent of unionization.

These crude calculations suggest that the shift in the composition of the labor force away from blue-collar jobs and toward females is potentially more important in accounting for the decline in unionization than either the shift away from manufacturing or the shift toward the South. However, the importance of the result regarding females is probably overstated, because of the assumption that females' propensity to organize relative to males is fixed over time is not a very good one. This is for two related reasons. First, the occupational distribution of females has changed considerably over time as females have sought and won the right to hold a larger variety of jobs. Indeed, females are now much more likely to hold jobs once considered reserved for males and much more likely to be unionized. Thus, the findings with regard to sex and occupation are likely to be related.

The second reason is that the attachment of individual females to the labor force is changing. The traditional argument as to why females are relatively difficult to organize is that they have a weaker attachment to the labor force in the long run and hence less interest in investing in their jobs through collective bargaining. If nothing else, however, the tremendous increase in the labor force participation rate of females demonstrates their increasing attachment to the labor force.

None of this is meant to imply that many females are no longer segregated in low-wage and largely nonunion occupations. Clearly, the fact that the extent of unionization among females is substantially lower in 1977 than that of males make this an untenable position. However, it is not satisfactory as an explanation of the decline in unionization to say that the increase in the fraction of the labor force that is female is a causal factor.

Taken at face value, these results suggest that shifts in the industrial, regional, occupational, and sexual composition of the labor force can account for at most three-quarters of the decline in the extent of unionization over the past twenty-five years. Due to correlation among these dimensions, however, it is likely that these shifts account for a substantially smaller proportion of the overall decline.

In order to derive a rough estimate of the maximum potential effect of these structural shifts that takes account of the correlation among the various dimensions, let us look at the results of a regression analysis of the union status of individual workers. (The data and the analysis are described in detail in the next section, and the results are referred to here only as they relate to the argument at hand.)

The contribution of the shift in the structure of the work force in any particular dimension from the mid-1950s to 1977 on the extent of unionization can be estimated crudely, accounting for the correlations across dimensions, as the actual shift over this period in the proportion of the work force with a given characteristic (see tables 2.2 and 2.4 and the earlier discussion) multiplied by the regression coefficient (table 2.7, col. 1) on the variable representing that characteristic. This analysis relies on the rather strong assumption that for workers in any particular group the propensity to unionize in the mid-1950s was the same as that in 1977.

If this calculation is labeled the ordinary least squares (OLS) estimate, and the variable-by-variable-based results derived earlier the Simple estimate, the comparison is as shown in table 2.5.

Table 2.5
Decomposition of decline in unionization, mid 1950s–1978

	Percentage point drop	
Dimension	OLS	Simple
away from manufactuirng	1.0	1.7
toward south	1.2	1.2
toward white collar	1.2	2.1
toward female	0.5	2.4
Total accounted for	3.9	7.4

Note: The OLS estimate is computed as the decline in the proportion of the workforce with a given characteristic multiplied by the appropriate regression coefficient contained in the first column of table 2.7. The Simple estimate is computed based on the decline in the proportion of the workforce with a given characteristic using the proportion of that workforce with that characteristic organized in the mid 1950s. The actual decline in unionization over this period was 9.4 percentage points.

These results indicate that only about 40% of the almost 10 percentage point drop in the extent of unionization can be accounted for by gross shifts in these four dimensions of the labor force. These four dimensions are related, as can be seen by the fact that the sum of the individual effects (the Simple analysis) seems to account for over three-quarters of the decline. Most striking is the fact that the Simple estimate of the effect of the shift toward a more heavily female work force was estimated to be 2.4 percentage points but only 0.5 percentage point once the correlations with the other dimensions were accounted for. Note that larger effects of changes in industrial and occupational distribution would be found using either measure if finer gradations of industry and occupation were used.

Overall, these results suggest that industrial, regional, occupational, and sexual shifts in the composition of the labor force can account for at most 40% of the decline in the extent of unionization over the past twenty-five years. In addition, it is likely that at least some of the shifts in composition are the result of unionization rather than a cause of its decline. Therefore, a complete explanation of the decline must lie elsewhere.

Worker Preferences for Unionization and the Supply of Union Jobs

Taken as given in the previous discussion were the well-known cross-sectional differences in the extent of organization of workers. Particularly with regard to industry, region, and occupation, it seems natural that the less-unionized categories (nonmanufacturing, South, white-collar) represent fertile ground for new organizing efforts. Before evaluating this targeting strategy, it is necessary to investigate in more detail why the less-unionized sectors are in fact less unionized. In what follows, the results already found are investigated further by estimating a cross-section regression model of the union status of workers. Then the union status of workers is examined in the light of a simple theoretical framework and a set of data that allow the separate identification of workers' preferences for union representation and their ability to find a union job, supposing that they want one.

Data from the Quality of Employment Survey (QES) developed by the Survey Research Center at the University of Michigan are used in this analysis. These data provide information on the union status of workers and on the explicit preferences of nonunion workers for union representation. The QES contains data for approximately 1,500 randomly selected workers (both union and nonunion) on their personal characteristics and job attributes.[5] The particular sample used in this study was derived from the QES by selecting those workers for whom the survey contained valid information on the variables listed in table 2.6. After the deletion of self-employed workers, managers, and sales workers, the remaining sample contained 1,035 workers.

Table 2.6 contains descriptions of the variables used in the study as well as their means for the entire sample and for the union and nonunion subsamples. The base group for the dichotomous variables consists of white non-Southern male blue-collar nonmanufacturing workers who do not live in a state with a right-to-work (RTW) law. On average, the 38% of the sample who are unionized are more likely to be male, nonwhite, non-Southern, in a manufacturing job, and in a blue-collar occupation.[6] Unionization is here defined as working on a job covered by a collective bargaining agreement. The means for the QES subsample contained in table 2.6 are not directly comparable to the data on the trends in unionization previously discussed.

It is clear from the sample means (table 2.6) that the broad outlines regarding sectoral differences in the extent of unionization are reflected in the QES data. Given the potential correlation between certain of the dimensions, such as sex and occupation, a multivariate analysis will prove useful in analyzing this problem further. To this end, table 2.7 contains an ordinary least squares (OLS) analysis of the probability of union representation.[7]

Table 2.6
Means of data: Quality of employment survey, 1977

Variable	Description (Dichotomous variables =0 otherwise)	Combined Sample	Union Sample	Nonunion Sample
U	=1 if works on union job	.377	1.0	0.0
VFU	=1 if desires union representation	—	—	.361
NW	=1 if nonwhite	.128	.141	.119
Fe	=1 if female	.394	.297	.453
Blue	=1 if occupation is blue-collar	.449	.608	.353
Cler	=1 if occupation is clerical	.186	.100	.239
Serv	=1 if occupation is service	.147	.108	.171
Prof & Tech	=1 if occupation is professional or technical	.217	.185	.237
Man	=1 if industry is manufacturing	.287	.403	.217
South	=1 if worker resides in south	.354	.236	.425
RTW	=1 if worker in RTW state	.335	.223	.403
Unfair Sup.	=1 if supervisor unfair	—	—	.363[a]
Bad Pay	=1 if pay is not good	—	—	.420[a]
Bad Security	=1 if job security is not good	—	—	.264[a]
Unfair Promo.	=1 if promotions not fair	—	—	.499[a]
Sample size		1,035	390	645

a. These variables are based on a reduced sample of 531 nonunion workers for whom information on these variables was available.

The first column of table 2.7 contains a regression of the union status of individual workers on the sectoral characteristic of the workers, including race, sex, occupation, industry, and region. The coefficients can be interpreted quantitatively as the effect of the particular characteristic on the probability of union representation. The results are consistent with those discussed previously, and some interesting insights can be gained by examining them in more detail.

Blue-collar workers (the base occupation) are significantly more likely to work on a union job than are any of the other occupational groups. The magnitude of this effect is quite striking, with a base-group worker (white, male, blue-collar, nonmanufacturing, non-Southern) having a probability of union representation of .515 while an otherwise equivalent worker who is on a clerical job has a probability of union representation

Table 2.7
Estimates of OLS model of union status:
Quality of Employment Survey, 1977

Variable	(1)	(2)	(3)
Constant	.515	.429	.529
	(.0307)	(.0244)	(.0310)
NW	.0813	.0811	.0801
	(.0431)	(.0434)	(.0430)
Fe	− .0508	− .127	− .0425
	(.0330)	(.0299)	(.0330)
Cler	− .229	—	− .234
	(.0457)		(.0456)
Serv	− .158	—	− .161
	(.0479)		(.0477)
Prof & Tech	− .138	—	− .144
	(.0409)		(.0409)
Man	.109	.180	.107
	(.0354)	(.0322)	(.0353)
South	− .181	− .180	− .118
	(.0301)	(.0303)	(.0373)
RTW	—	—	− .107
			(.0378)
R^2	.113	.0890	.120

Note: The numbers in parentheses are standard errors. The dependent variable for this analysis takes on the value one for union workers and zero for nonunion workers. $N = 1{,}035$.

of .286 (= .515− .229). Similarly, an otherwise equivalent service worker has a probability of union representation of .357, and an otherwise equivalent professional or technical worker has a probability of union representation of .377.

It is interesting to note that there does not seem to be a significant correlation between sex and union status after controlling for occupation. The second column of table 2.7 contains estimates of the union status regression with the occupation variables omitted. In this formulation there seems to be a large (12.7 percentage points) and significant negative effect of being female on the probability of union representation. The fact that this effect disappears when occupation is controlled for explicity suggests that females are not significantly different from males with regard to union status, except that they are segregated into relatively less-unionized occupational groups.

As we saw in the previous section, on average workers in manufacturing industries are more likely to be unionized than are workers in other industries.[8] This is corroborated by the results in the first column of table 2.7 where it is estimated, after controlling for occupation, that manufacturing workers are approximately 11 percentage points more likely to be unionized than are nonmanufacturing workers. The estimates in the second column of table 2.7 suggest that this effect rises to 18 percentage points when occupation is not controlled for. Thus, a substantial portion of the overall relationship between manufacturing employment and union status is due to the fact that manufacturing employment is relatively concentrated among highly unionized blue-collar workers.

With regard to region, the results verify that workers in the South are significantly less likely to be unionized (18 percentage points less) than workers elsewhere. Some have argued that this is the result of the presence of right-to-work (RTW) laws in many of these states. The third column of table 2.7 contains estimates of the model augmented by an RTW variable. The RTW variable has a significant negative coefficient, and, while the South variable still has a significant negative coefficient, its magnitude is reduced by one-third (to 12 percentage points). Overall, these results suggest not only that RTW laws are indeed correlated with less unionization but also that in the South there is less unionization even after controlling for the presence of RTW laws. Thus there must be other factors that inhibit unionization in the South.[9]

The last dimension considered here is race. It is clear from table 2.7 that nonwhites are significantly more likely to work on a union job than otherwise equivalent whites. The magnitude of this effect is not influenced by the inclusion of the occupational variables. Thus, this relationship is not caused by the possibility that blacks are segregated into particular occupations.

In order to gain further insight into the cross-sectional differences in the extent of unionization, it is useful to decompose these differences into two components. The first is variation in worker preferences for union representation. The second, recognizing that some workers who desire union representation are frustrated in realizing their desire, is variation in the supply of union jobs relative to demand. This potential frustration suggests that there are queues for vacancies in existing union jobs.[10]

The important implication of this decomposition for the analysis here is that on the basis of union status alone it is not possible to determine whether a nonunion worker is nonunion because he did not desire a union job or because he desired a union job but was not able to get one. It is obvious that these two very different reasons for nonunion employment will suggest very different strategies for union organizing activity. Other things being equal, it will clearly be much easier to organize workers who are nonunion in spite of a desire for union representation than it will be to organize workers who are not interested in union representation.

Given that there may be workers who desire a union job but who are frustrated in their attempts to be hired by a union employer, it is necessary to develop a measure of worker preference for union representation as distinct from their actual union status. The QES contains sufficient data to develop just such a measure. The crucial bit of information is the response to the question, asked only of nonunion workers, "If an election were held with secret ballots, would you vote for or against having a union or employee association represent you?" This latter variable, termed VFU, is interpreted here as the current preference of a worker for union representation on his current job, and it is a measure of the demand for union representation by the worker.[11] The combination of this information with the information on union status is sufficient to identify the demand for union representation of all workers and the supply (availability) of union jobs relative to this demand.

Table 2.8
Estimates of OLS model of preference for union representation: Quality of
Employment Survey, 1977

Variable	(1)	(2)	(3)
Constant	.642	.583	.657
	(.0317)	(.0250)	(.0320)
NW	.251	.257	.250
	(.0445)	(.0446)	(.0443)
Fe	.0199	− .0290	.0289
	(.0340)	(.0306)	(.0340)
Cler	− .166	—	− .171
	(0.472)		(.0470)
Serv	− .0547	—	− .0582
	(.0494)		(0.493)
Prof & Tech	− .114	—	− .122
	(0.423)		(.0422)
Man	.0934	.139	.0911
	(.0365)	(.0331)	(.0364)
South	− .121	− .119	− .0522
	(.0310)	(.0311)	(0.385)
RTW	—	—	− .117
			(.0389)
R^2	.0742	.0609	.0822

Note: The numbers in parentheses are standard errors. The dependent variable takes on
the value one for all union workers and for those nonunion workers who answered the
VFU question affirmatively. The dependent variable takes on the value zero for those
nonunion workers who answered the VFU question negatively. N=1,035.

While not without its problems, the VFU measure can serve as an
indicator of the preferences of nonunion workers for union representation. In the absence of analogous information regarding the preferences
of union workers, it will be assumed here that all union workers in
fact desire union representation.[12] Thus, in our QES sample all union
workers and those nonunion workers who answered the VFU question
affirmatively are categorized as desiring union representation.

In order to determine how worker preferences for union representation
vary by sector, table 2.8 contains OLS estimates of a model of worker
preferences. This is similar to the analysis in table 2.7 except that the
dependent variable is now an indicator of worker preferences rather
than an indicator of actual union status.[13] Some of the patterns that

were found with the union status model are also found here. In particular, it is found that nonwhites and manufacturing workers are more likely to desire union representation.

On the other hand, a number of interesting contrasts are apparent when one compares the estimates of the union status and the union preference models. First, there seems to be no difference between males and females in their preference for union representation regardless of whether or not occupation is controlled for. This is evidence against the conventional wisdom that females are less interested in union representation because of a weaker long-term commitment to the labor force.

A second contrast is that white-collar workers are not uniformly less likely to desire union representation. It is true that clerical workers and professional and technical workers are significantly less likely than blue-collar workers to desire union jobs, but no distinction can be made between service workers and blue-collar workers in this dimension. This suggests that the lower extent of unionization found for service workers must be due to some factor other than a lack of interest.

A final contrast is that there seems to be a lower demand for union representation among Southern workers until the presence of RTW laws is accounted for. It seems that the demand for union representation is lower in states with RTW laws, but it is not lower simply on the basis of region.[14] (Of course, it is true that many Southern states have RTW laws so that the demand for union representation *is* lower in the South.) What this suggests is that the lower extent of unionization found in the South even after controlling for the presence of RTW laws (see table 2.7) must be due to some factor other than less demand by workers.

In order to investigate further the nature of these other factors affecting the extent of unionization independent of worker preferences, the analysis turns to sectoral differences in the likelihood that a worker who desires union representation will actually be hired by a union employer. To the extent that such differences are found they must reflect differences in the degree of *frustrated* demand for union representation which in turn reflect differences in the supply of union jobs relative to sectoral demand. This analysis can be carried out in a straightforward fashion by creating a sample which consists only of those workers who desire union representation. As before, this sample consists of all of the union workers plus those nonunion workers who answered the VFU question affirmatively—623 workers in all.

Table 2.9
Estimates of OLS model of union status conditional on desiring union representation: Quality of Employment Survey, 1977

Variable	(1)	(2)	(3)
Constant	.807	.724	.815
	(.0400)	(.0310)	(.0402)
NW	− .0699	− .0866	− .0686
	(.0489)	(.0491)	(.0488)
Fe	− .111	− .187	− .104
	(.0424)	(.0383)	(.0426)
Cler	− .228	—	− .235
	(.0636)		(.0637)
Serv	− .203	—	− .207
	(.0609)		(.0609)
Prof & Tech	− .111	—	− .117
	(.0565)		(.0565)
Man	.0608	.145	.0609
	(.0455)	(.0392)	(.0454)
South	− .199	− .197	− .153
	(.0400)	(.0400)	(.0502)
RTW	—	—	− .0789
			(.0513)
R^2	.135	.112	.139

Note: The numbers in parentheses are standard errors. The dependent variable takes on the value one for all union workers and zero for all nonunion workers. The sample is restricted to all union workers and those nonunion workers who answered the VFU question affirmatively. $N = 623$.

Within this limited sample, analysis of the union status of workers amounts to an analysis of the (inverse) degree of frustration of worker preferences for unionization and thus of the supply of union jobs relative to demand. Table 2.9 contains OLS regressions of union status estimated over the subsample of 623 workers.[15] It is worth noting that there is substantial variation across groups in the degree of frustrated demand (supply constraints). The estimates contained in the first column of table 2.9 suggest that a base-group worker (white, male, blue-collar, manufacturing, non-Southern) who desires a union job has a probability of .8 of actually working on a union job. At the other extreme, a black southern female clerical worker who desires a union job has a probability of only .2 of actually working on a union job.[16]

The first specific result of interest from table 2.9 is that females who desire union jobs are significantly less likely to be unionized whether or not occupation is controlled for. Thus, in conjunction with the results found in tables 2.7 and 2.8, it can be concluded that the observed lower extent of unionization among females is due to their inability to find union jobs rather than to any preference against union representation. It must be pointed out that the nature of the restriction on the ability of females to find union jobs is not clear from this analysis. One possibility is that it is due to a reluctance on the part of unionized employers to hire females. Another is that the distribution of jobs available to females is predominantly nonunion and is not adequately controlled for by the included occupational variables.

A second result is that all three non-blue-collar occupations have a supply of union jobs that is significantly more constrained relative to demand than that for blue-collar workers. This difference is largest for clerical workers (23 percentage points) and smallest for professional and technical workers (11 percentage points). In conjunction with the results reported in tables 2.7 and 2.8, it appears that the lower extent of unionization among clerical workers and professional and technical workers is due to a combination of less demand for union representation and a supply of union jobs that is constrained relative to even this lower level of demand. At the same time, the lower extent of unionization among service workers is due almost entirely to supply constraints. Once again, it is not clear what these supply constraints are, but one possibility is that it is more expensive to organize among white-collar workers, perhaps because of employer resistance.

A final result is that the supply of union jobs in the South is significantly (20 percentage points) more constrained relative to demand than elsewhere. This result is not qualitatively affected by the presence of the RTW variable. In fact, we find only a small effect of RTW laws on the supply of union jobs relative to demand. In conjunction with the earlier results (see tables 2.7 and 2.8), it appears that the lower extent of unionization in the South is the result of lower demand for union representation in that region (largely correlated with RTW laws) and a supply of union jobs that is constrained relative to this lower level of demand.

To summarize these rather complicated results, three analyses were carried out. First, variation in the union status of workers was investigated, and the standard set of results was found. Nonwhites, blue-collar workers, and manufacturing workers are more likely to be unionized. Southern workers are less likely to be unionized. No systematic relationship with sex was found after occupation was controlled for. Second, and in order to investigate these findings further, variation in worker preferences for union representation (as distinct from union status) was investigated. It was found that nonwhites and manufacturing workers are more likely to desire union representation. At the same time, clerical workers, professional and technical workers, and Southern workers are less likely to desire union representation. No systematic correlation with sex was found whether or not occupation was controlled for. Finally, variation in the ability of workers who desire union representation to find union jobs was investigated. It was found that females, non-blue-collar workers, and Southern workers who desire union jobs are more likely than others to be frustrated in their desire for union jobs.

Overall, it can be concluded that the lower extent of unionization among females and service workers is due largely to a relative inability to find suitable union jobs. On the other hand, nonwhites and manufacturing workers are more likely to be unionized due to a greater desire for union representation. For Southern workers, clerical workers, and professional and technical workers, the lower extent of unionization is due to a combination of less preference for union representation and a relative inability to find union jobs.

Implications for Successful Targeting of Organization Activities

The results just reported suggest that demand for union representation is more likely to be frustrated among a number of groups, including white-collar workers, females, and Southern workers. It might seem reasonable to focus organizing efforts on these groups. It also might seem reasonable that fertile ground for organizing are those sectors that are least organized (e.g., the South, females, white-collar workers) since these sectors have a large group of unorganized workers. However, neither of these strategies is likely to be particularly effective. A successful strategy for organizing campaigns requires focusing on nonunion workers who are more likely to desire union representation, and appropriate targets cannot be identified from either frustrated demand or the extent of organization. For example, while it was found that there is a lower extent of unionization in the South and that demand for union representation is more likely to be frustrated in the South, it is not clear that a nonunion worker selected at random from the

South is more likely to desire union representation than a nonunion worker selected at random in the North. The South has a higher proportion of nonunion workers than other regions, but it is not clear that a higher proportion of Southern nonunion workers desire union representation.

There is a theoretical reason why it might be expected that nonunion workers who are members of less-unionized groups are not likely to differ from other nonunion workers in their desire for union representation. This is based on the process by which unions have made their organizing decisions in the past, leaving out a population of nonunion workers who are relatively homogeneous in their preference for unionization regardless of their observable characteristics. The argument, with supporting empirical evidence, is as follows.

Past organizing activity has taken place on some rational basis where the unions involved took into account the cost of organizing particular workers along with some measure of the workers' interest in union representation. The latter is important in assessing the probability of winning a representation election given the uncertainty of the outcome inherent in any organizing campaign.[17] With limited resources for organizing it makes the most sense to attempt first to organize those workers who show the greatest interest in unionization, other things being equal. Assuming that unions make decisions on a national basis, this suggests that there will have been relatively more organization among those groups most favorably disposed toward unionization.

Consider, for example, regional differences. In the long run there has been more organization outside the South partly because Southern workers are less favorably disposed toward unions. However, even within regions there are large differences among workers regarding their preferences for union representation. Thus, outside the South the unions have organized their best prospects, and the remaining nonunion work force outside the South is composed of those workers in that region who are least interested in unionization. Within the South, the more limited organization activity has also been concentrated among the best prospects, leaving a relatively large nonunion sector composed of those workers within the South who are least interested in unionization. Overall, a union deciding on how to allocate its organizing dollars between nonunion workers in different regions has organized more in the North because the expected payoff was higher there, but the nonunion workers left unorganized in the North should have about the same degree of interest in unionization as the nonunion workers in the South. If this were not the case, the union would have been better off organizing among the nonunion workers with the highest demand for union representation.

To summarize, given unmeasured differences among workers in their preference for union representation, in the long run the unions have organized those nonunion workers most favorably disposed toward unionization. This selection process has left a nonunion work force that is not only less interested in union representation but is relatively homogeneous in its interest in unionization across different observable regional, demographic, and occupational groups.

A final point before turning to the empirical evidence: in the 1930s and 1940s, when virtually all workers were nonunion, it was easy to target those workers who would be most interested in unionization on the basis of broad observable characteristics. However, forty or fifty years later it is difficult to target successfully on this basis, particularly by selecting those groups that are largely nonunion. The question to be asked in evaluating this latter strategy is, "If these workers are interested in unionization, why aren't they already organized?" Put another way, if these workers (say Southern, white-collar) were easy to organize, they would have been organized already.

In order to investigate differences among groups of nonunion workers in their preference for union representation, the response to the VFU question by the sample of 645 nonunion workers from the 1977 QES described in table 2.6 is analyzed. This is a direct measure of the desire of these nonunion workers for union representation on their current job, and it should be indicative of the level of demand for unionization among nonunion workers of different characteristics. The first three columns of table 2.10 contain OLS estimates of the determinants of VFU over the nonunion sample for the three sets of variables used in the analyses of union status and worker preferences presented earlier.[18]

The results in the first column are rather striking. The only variable that shows a statistically significant relationship with nonunion preference for union representation is that for nonwhites, and this is a group that is more rather than less unionized overall. In addition, the magnitude of the effect is rather large. White nonunion base-group workers are predicted to have a probability of desiring union representation of .28 while otherwise equivalent nonwhites have a probability of desiring union representation of .62. All of the other coefficients are small in magnitude ($<.07$), and only that for females is even marginally statistically significant at conventional levels.

Table 2.10
Estimates of OLS model of preference for union representation among nonunion workers: Quality of Employment Survey, 1977

Variable	(1)	(2)	(3)	(4)
Constant	.280 (.0416)	.276 (.0318)	.293 (.0424)	.116 (.0497)
NW	.341 (.0577)	.352 (.0572)	.341 (.0576)	.294 (.0614)
Fe	.0683 (.0424)	.0717 (.0373)	.0742 (.0425)	.0702 (.0447)
Cler	− .0180 (.0563)	—	− .0237 (.0563)	− .00046 (.0586)
Serv	.0580 (.0609)	—	.0543 (.0609)	.104 (.0645)
Prof. & Tech	− .0265 (.0516)	—	− .0340 (.0518)	− .0418 (.0544)
Man	.0658 (.0482)	.0612 (.0449)	.0632 (.0482)	.0389 (.0498)
South	− .00877 (.0374)	− .00634 (.0373)	.0360 (.0467)	.0256 (.0394)
RTW	—	—	− .0757 (.0473)	—
Unfair Sup.	—	—	—	.0155 (.0424)
Bad Pay	—	—	—	.125 (.0436)
Bad Security	—	—	—	.0967 (.0482)
Unfair Promo.	—	—	—	.151 (.0444)
R^2	.0689	.0655	.0726	.161
N	645	645	645	531

Note: The numbers in parentheses are standard errors. The dependent variable takes on the value one for those workers who answered the VFU question affirmatively and zero for those who answered negatively. The sample is restricted to nonunion workers.

Particularly interesting are the results for the regional and occupational variables. The estimated effect of Southern residence on nonunion preferences for union representation is virtually zero. Thus, it is not true that Southern nonunion workers, despite their relatively large numbers, are likely targets for a successful organization effort. On the other hand, as Kochan (1979) pointed out, neither is it true that Southern nonunion workers are *less* favorably disposed toward union organizing efforts than nonunion workers in other regions. The estimates in the third column of table 2.10 include the RTW law variable, and the effect of Southern residence is still insignificantly different from zero. More interestingly, in RTW states the probability that a nonunion worker desires union representation is weakly significantly negative. In other words, nonunion workers in states with RTW laws are less likely to desire union representation. This suggests that states with RTW laws may be unfavorable places for unions to target their organization efforts.[19]

With regard to occupation, the results in table 2.10 show that there are no significant distinctions in the preferences of nonunion workers for union representation. Nonunion white-collar workers are neither more nor less likely than nonunion blue-collar workers to desire union representation. Thus, an organization campaign focused on white-collar workers is neither likely to be more successful nor doomed to failure. It is interesting to note that when occupation is not controlled for (the second column of table 2.10), the results suggest that nonunion females are slightly, though significantly, more likely to desire union representation. Thus, targeting on females, or more particularly female occupations, may be slightly more successful in organizing than a random strategy.

Overall, the results are rather discouraging from the union movement's point of view. On average, nonunion workers of almost any description have a probability of desiring union representation of about .3. The major exceptions to this are nonwhite nonunion workers who have a probability of desiring union representation that is almost twice as large. However, nonwhites do not represent a substantial focus for new organizing activity. This is partly because they are already relatively highly organized and partly because it is not generally feasible to target organization drives by race.

Whether substantial new organization is likely, given these results, depends in part on how the 30% of nonunion workers who desire union representation are distributed. If they are scattered randomly across establishments, it is difficult to see how the unions will win very many elections. If, on the other hand, they are concentrated in a smaller number of establishments, then they may be organizable if these establishments can be identified. What is needed are some criteria for determining if the workers in an establishment are interested in unionization.

One potential dimension along which workers vary and which has not been investigated above is job satisfaction. Some earlier research using these data from the QES and data on the outcomes of NLRB-supervised representation elections concluded that workers who were concerned about various aspects of the job, including job security and fairness of treatment by supervisors, were more likely to vote for union representation.[20] In order to investigate this issue more generally, data on four job dissatisfaction measures were available for 531 of the 645 nonunion workers in the QES sample analyzed in this study. These include measures of dissatisfaction with fairness of supervision, adequacy of pay, adequacy of job security, and fairness of promotion procedures. Their means are presented in table 2.6.[21]

When the OLS analysis of nonunion worker preferences for union representation is augmented by these measures, the results (the fourth column of table 2.10) are quite striking. While none of the results with regard to demographic characteristics are changed, three of the four measures of job dissatisfaction have strongly positive effects on the probability of desiring union representation. The only measure that does not seem important relates to fairness of supervision. Quantitatively, a nonunion worker who feels his pay is not good has a 12.5 percentage point higher probability of desiring union representation. If he feels that his job security is not good, he is 10 percentage points more likely to desire union representation; if he feels that promotions are not handled fairly, he is 15 percentage points more likely to desire union representation.

Overall, if a nonunion worker is unhappy about his job in all three of these dimensions, his probability of desiring union representation is fully 37 percentage points higher than an otherwise equivalent satisfied nonunion worker. The average dissatisfied white nonunion worker's probability of desiring union representation is .49 while for a satisfied worker this probability is only .12.

These numbers suggest two things. First, and optimistically from the union movement's point of view, is that if the unions can target their organizing activity on nonunion workers who are dissatisfied with their jobs and if these workers are concentrated in a limited number of establishments, then the unions will probably meet with increased success in organizing. Second, and less optimistically from the union movement's point of view, is that a viable strategy for nonunion firms attempting to remain nonunion is to resolve these job satisfaction issues on their own.

Summary and Conclusions

Three issues were addressed in this study. First, the ability of sectoral shifts in employment to account for the decline in unionization over the past twenty-five years was investigated. The evidence suggests that the simple explanation for the decline, that employment has shifted away from the manufacturing sector and toward the South, cannot account for a large percentage of the drop in unionization. Other factors, such as the increase in white-collar and female employment, are also considered as potential explanations for the decline in unionization. Overall, these factors can account for at most 40% of the decline in unionization. Thus, a considerable fraction of the decline still remains to be accounted for.

The second issue addressed took as given the decline in unionization and attempted to understand the cross-sectional differences in the extent of unionization. It was argued that these differences can result either from variation in worker preferences for union representation or from variation in the ability of workers who desire union representation to find union employment. Data from the Quality of Employment Survey (QES) were used to investigate variation in worker preferences for union representation as distinct from the ability of interested workers to find union jobs. Explicitly recognized was the possibility that all workers who want union jobs may not be able to get them, resulting in queues for vacancies in existing unionized establishments.

Compared to a base group of white male blue-collared non-Southern nonmanufacturing workers, it was found that the lower extent of unionization among females and service workers is due largely to their relative inability to find union jobs despite a preference for union representation. On the other hand, it was found that nonwhites and manufacturing workers are more likely to be unionized, having a greater desire for union representation. The lower extent of unionization among Southern workers, clerical workers, and professional and technical workers was found to be due to a combination of less preference for union representation and a relative inability to find union jobs.

The final issue addressed relates to the ability of unions to target organization drives effectively on the basis of such characteristics as region, occupation, and industry. It was argued that such a strategy will be successful only to the extent that nonunion workers in particular regions or industries with particular demographic characteristics are more likely to desire union representation. It was further argued, based on past organizing strategies of the unions, that the remaining nonunion work force is likely to be relatively homogeneous in its desire for union representation, so that strategies of targeting organizing efforts on the least-unionized sector will not be especially effective. Empirical evidence, based on explicit measures from the QES of nonunion worker preferences for union representation, was presented in support of this conclusion. This evidence suggests that there are no significant differences on the basis of occupation, industry, or region in the preferences of nonunion workers for union representation. Thus, it can be concluded that a strategy of targeting organizing activity on the less-unionized sectors (the South, nonmanufacturing, white-collar) is not likely to be very effective. On the other hand, it is not likely to be particularly ineffective either.

Some rather discouraging lessons regarding prospects for the American labor movement are clear from the empirical analysis. First, the overall level of preference for union representation among the nonunion work force is relatively low, with a "typical" nonunion worker having a probability of desiring union representation of only approximately .3. Clearly, if the nonunion workers who desire union representation are not concentrated in particular establishments but are instead spread randomly throughout the nonunion work force, then unions are going to have problems winning very many representation elections. Related to this, the results support the hypothesis that targeting organizing activity on easily identifiable groups is not likely to be successful. Essentially, there are so few significant differences within the nonunion population in preference for union representation that no simple targeting rules are apparent.

One dimension along which significant differences do arise and that is potentially useful as a targeting device is job satisfaction. The empirical results clearly suggest that nonunion workers who are dissatisfied with a number of aspects of the job, including pay, job security, and the handling of promotions, are substantially more likely to desire union representation. An unfortunate feature of this finding from the union movement's point of view is that a viable strategy for nonunion firms attempting to remain nonunion is to resolve these job satisfaction issues on their own. This would reduce the threat of unionization in these firms to quite low levels. In this situation the task of the union movement is to demonstrate to potential members that it can provide services (levels of benefits and job satisfaction) that employers cannot or will not provide on their own. This is clearly a difficult task and one of the great challenges facing the American labor movement.

Notes

The research reported here was supported by Grant No. SES-8207703 from the National Science Foundation and by a grant from the Sloan Foundation to the Industrial Relations Section of the Sloan School of Management at M.I.T. The author also received support from the Sloan Foundation as an Alfred P. Sloan Research Fellow.

1. The definition of the Southern region as used in this section includes the following twelve states: Alabama, Arkansas, Florida, Georgia, Kentucky, Louisiana, Mississippi, North Carolina, South Carolina, Tennessee, Texas, and Virginia.

2. Care must be taken in interpreting movements over time in the regional breakdowns of the extent of unionization because consistently derived data on the regional extent of the unionization were not available until recently. The 1953 data reported here were derived from Troy (1958) in a fashion not directly comparable to the Bureau of Labor Statistics numbers reported for the later years. In fact, 1953 was selected because it is the only year earlier than 1965 for which a regional breakdown of union membership is readily available, and the list of states included in the definition of the South in note 1 is that used by Troy.

3. These figures are based on a sample different from the figures in tables 2.1 through 2.4. The sample of 28,827 workers excluded managerial, self-employed, construction, and sales workers. On this basis the overall extent of unionization was 30.5% as compared with a 1976 figure compiled by the Bureau of Labor Statistics, and used in the earlier analysis, of 26.6%. (See table 2.1.) Farber (1984) discusses the sample from the *Current Population Survey* in more detail. Freeman and Medoff (1979) discuss the problems in generating comparable estimates of the extent of unionization.

4. See note 3.

5. See Quinn and Staines (1979) for a detailed description of the survey design.

6. The definition of the South used with the QES data is that defined by the Bureau of the Census: Alabama, Arkansas, Delaware, District of Columbia,

Florida, Georgia, Kentucky, Louisiana, Maryland, Mississippi, North Carolina, Oklahoma, South Carolina, Tennessee, Texas, Virginia, and West Virginia.

The "blue-collar" occupation used with the QES data consists of craftsmen, operatives, and laborers. This is not meant to imply that all workers in other categories are white-collar workers. For example, there may be quite a number of blue-collar service workers.

7. Ordinary least squares is not the best technique to use for analysis of a model where the dependent variable can take on only discrete values. The parameter estimates will be unbiased, but the standard errors are likely to be misleading. A much better model would be a probit or a logit model. Neither of these is presented here because the coefficients cannot be interpreted as the quantitative effect of the relevant characteristic on the probability of union representation without a confusing transformation. All of the results presented using OLS in this study have been verified using a probit model, however, with regard to both the magnitude of the implied effect on the probability of union representation and the statistical significance of that effect.

8. Of course it is true that there is substantial variation within the nonmanufacturing sector in the extent of unionization as there is also substantial variation within the manufacturing sector. This variation is not treated explicitly here in order to focus on the broadest dimensions along which unionization varies.

9. See Ellwood and Fine (1983) for an interesting analysis of the effects of RTW laws on organizing activity. Farber (1984) presents a detailed analysis of the effects of RTW laws on the extent of unionization and on the interaction of these laws with regional differences in the extent of unionization.

10. Farber (1983) presents a detailed development of this model including a rationale for the existence of the queue along with a more sophisticated estimation strategy than that set forth below. See also Abowd and Farber (1982) for a related model and set of estimates.

11. Fully 36% of the nonunion sample responded yes to the VFU question so that there is substantial variation in the response.

12. Farber (1984) discusses the potential problems with this approach in some detail. He also presents an alternative approach that makes a less stringent assumption regarding the preferences of union workers. While estimation of this alternative formulation is beyond the scope of this study, Farber (1984) found virtually identical results using the approach used here and the alternative.

13. The dependent variable equals one if the individual desires union representation, and this is the case if the individual is unionized of if he is nonunion but answered yes to the VFU question. The dependent variable equals zero otherwise.

14. Farber (1984) discusses the interpretation of these sorts of results with particular emphasis on the role of RTW laws.

15. The dependent variable equals one if the individual is working on a union job, and zero otherwise. Note that all workers in this subsample of 623 workers who are not working on a union job answered yes to the VFU question.

16. The probability of such an individual desiring a union job is predicted to be .63 on the basis of the estimates contained in the first column of table 2.8.

17. This uncertainty is emphasized by considering the fact that unions currently win less than half of the representation elections supervised by the NLRB. For example, in fiscal year 1979 unions won only 47% of the 7,266 representation elections held. If there had been no uncertainty regarding the outcome, the unions would not have even attempted the 53% of elections that were eventually lost. (See National Labor Relations Board 1979.)

18. This analysis is very similar to that presented by Kochan (1979) using the same data. His results are identical to those presented here in all relevant respects.

19. Note that this may not be a result of the RTW laws, but merely a reflection of less preference for union representation causing the RTW laws. See note 9.

20. Kochan (1979) presents evidence using the QES on the relationship between job satisfaction and preference for union representation. Farber and Saks (1980) investigate individual voting behavior in thirty-three NLRB-supervised representation elections held in the early 1970s. A number of other factors in addition to those mentioned here were considered.

21. These measures are generally four response scales to a statement of the following sort regarding the worker's current job: "The pay is good." The possible responses are: 1 = not at all true; 2 = a little true; 3 = somewhat true; and 4 = very true. if the individual responded 1 or 2, he was coded as being "dissatisfied," and "not dissatisfied" otherwise.

References

Abowd, John M., and Henry S. Farber. "Job Queues and the Union Status of Workers." *Industrial and Labor Relations Review* 35 (April 1982).

Ellwood, David T., and Glenn Fine. "Effects of Right-To-Work Laws on Union Organizing." National Bureau of Economic Research Working Paper No. 1116 (May 1983).

Farber, Henry S. "The Determination of the Union Status of Workers." *Econometrica* (September 1983), Vol. 51, 1417–1437.

Farber, Henry S. "Right-to-Work Laws and the Extent of Unionization." *Journal of Labor Economics* Vol. 2 (July 1984).

Farber, Henry S., and Daniel H. Saks. "Why Workers Want Unions: The Role of Relative Wages and Job Characteristics." *Journal of Political Economy* 88 (April 1980): 349–369.

Freeman, Richard B., and James L. Medoff. "New Estimates of Private Sector Unionism in the United States." *Industrial and Labor Relations Review* 32 (January 1979).

Kochan, Thomas A. "How American Workers View Labor Unions." *Monthly Labor Review* (April 1979): 23–31.

National Labor Relations Board. *Annual Report*, 1979. Washington: Government Printing Office, 1979.

Quinn, Robert P., and Graham L. Staines. *The 1977 Quality of Employment Survey: Descriptive Statistics with Comparison Data from the 1969–70 and the 1972–73 Surveys*. Ann Arbor: Institute for Social Research, 1979.

Troy, Leo. "The Growth of Union Membership in the South." *Southern Economic Journal* 24 (April 1958): 407–420.

U.S. Bureau of Labor Statistics. *Handbook of Labor Statistics*, Bulletin No. 2070. Washington: Government Printing Office, 1980.

U.S. Executive Office of the President. *Employment and Training Report of the President*. Washington: Government Printing Office, 1978.

<h1>3</h1>

Why Are Unions Faring Poorly in NLRB Representation Elections?

Richard B. Freeman

Since the 1950s private-sector unions have experienced a substantial decline in the number of workers organized through National Labor Relations Board (NLRB) representation elections. In the mid-1950s through the mid-1960s unions were victorious in over 60% of NLRB elections, organizing 0.5 to 0.75% of the work force annually through the election procedure (see table 3.1). In the early 1980s unions were winning a bare 45% of elections and engaged in so few elections that just 0.14% of the unorganized work force became organized via NLRB elections—a percentage less than that needed for unions to maintain their share of the work force, much less to grow proportionally with it. The decline in union success in NLRB elections, coupled with a "natural" attrition of membership, underlies the precipitous fall in union density in the United States—a fall that contrasts sharply with increases in unionism in most other Western countries, including Canada.

What has caused this drop in union success in NLRB elections? Is this lack of success due to changes in the structure of the economy, such as the rise of white-collar employment, the growth of the Sunbelt, and the increased proportion of women in the work force? Is it due to failings by the unions, who have fallen down on the job of organizing the unorganized? To a decline in workers' desire for unions? Or to the increased strength and effectiveness of managerial opposition? How important is the 1970s recession in the decline?

This chapter seeks to answer these questions. It offers a critical review of existing research on union success or failure in NLRB elections and presents the results of new calculations designed to cast light on the factors at work. After a brief examination of the "body" of the poor performance of unions in NLRB representation elections, the chapter examines four "suspects": changes in economic structure, worker attitudes, changes in union organizing efforts, and changes in

Table 3.1
From NLRB elections to new union representation

	Workers in union victories as percent of private wage and salary workers	Elections ÷ private wage and salary workers (in thousands)	Workers eligible per election	Workers won as percent of workers eligible
	(1)	(2)	(3)	(4)
1950	2.0%	.152	157	84%
1955	1.0	.108	121	73
1960	0.7	.152	76	59
1965	0.7	.161	70	61
1970	0.6	.146	75	52
1975	0.4	.136	71	38
1980	0.2	.104	54	37
Log change				
1950–1980	−2.30	−.38	−1.07	−.82
1965–1980	−1.25	−.44	−.34	−.50

Source: "Private Wage and Salary Workers," U.S. Department of Labor, *Employment and Training Report of the President* 1981, p. 155, with private household workers excluded from the calculation. Elections, workers eligible per election, workers won as percent of workers eligible, from National Labor Relations Board, *Annual Reports*, various editions.

management opposition to unionism. Then it considers briefly the role of labor law in the decline in union success in NLRB elections.

The Body: Poor Union Performance in NLRB Relations

Table 3.1 summarizes the phenomenon under study. Column 1 shows the precipitous drop in the number of workers won by unions per private nonagricultural employee from 1950 to 1980, while columns (2)–(4) decompose the number of workers won to highlight the nature of the decline.

The decomposition in (2)–(4)) is:

Workers Won by Unions	= Elections	× Workers in NLRB Election	× Workers Won
Private, Wage and Salary Workers	Private, Nonagricultural Wage and Salary Workers	Elections	Workers in NLRB Election

The first term, which has received relatively little attention in popular discussion and professional analysis, represents the extent of organizing activity. The second term in the decomposition measures the average size of an NLRB election won by unions. The third term is the proportion of workers in elections won by unions; it has been at the center of many studies of declining union success in NLRB elections.

All three components of the decomposition equation show declines in union success: the number of elections has not kept pace with the growing work force; the average size of union victories has fallen; the proportion of workers in representation elections won by unions has fallen.

How important is each of these trends in the overall decline?

A crude decomposition is to take the logs of the principal variable—workers in union victories as a percent of private wage and salary workers—and the logs of the terms in the decomposition. From 1950 to 1980 the dominant terms are workers eligible per election and the win rate, workers won as a percent of workers eligible. From 1961 to 1980, which begins in a more "normal" period of unionization than 1950, all three terms have a substantial magnitude (see table 3.1).

Decomposing the number of workers treats each component as a separate entity. While for some purposes this is fruitful, it should not be taken as the last word. The three components of workers won/ nonagricultural labor force are undoubtedly interrelated: when the rate of successful elections falls, unions are likely to cut back organizing efforts; similarly, when a typical union victory garners fewer members than in the past, the return on effort will be lower, also contributing to potentially fewer election campaigns. Continuing research will, it is hoped, further illuminate the structure of the relations among the components of union gains by NLRB elections.[1]

From Workers Won in NLRB Elections to Union Density

Surprisingly, while there are numerous studies of how unions fare in NLRB elections, there has been virtually no work relating NLRB election results to the decline in union density in the United States. Organization of members through NLRB elections is, of course, not the only determinant of unionization in the United States. Indeed, in some years, changes in union membership or in union density have changed quite differently from what one would expect, given members organized through NLRB elections.

Between 1960 and 1961, for example, unions won over 218,000 members through NLRB elections, but union membership fell by 746,000. Between 1967 and 1968 unions won 271,695 members through NLRB elections, but union membership rose by 549,000. Despite increased membership from 1967 to 1968, however, the proportion of workers organized remained virtually constant.[2] Union membership also changes because of cyclical and secular changes in employment in already organized plants; organization of workers outside of NLRB elections (as in construction, where unions organize employers by convincing them that the union represents local craftsmen and can provide the employer with skilled workers for jobs); and because of plant shutdowns. The union share of the labor force changes not only when union membership changes but also when nonunion employment changes. Because some union (as well as nonunion) plants close down every year, and new plants are "born" nonunion, there is a normal decline in membership each year, which requires a certain amount of new organization by unions simply to maintain their share of the work force.

To examine the linkage between NLRB election results and changes in density, I have found the following "stock-flow" equation to be useful:

$$\text{Union density in year } t = \frac{\text{Gains in membership from NLRB elections}}{\text{Work force in year } t} - \lambda \left[\text{Union density in year } t-1\right]$$

where λ is the *net* attrition rate for the union density—that is, the rate at which union density would decrease ($\lambda > 0$) or increase ($\lambda < 0$) in the absence of NLRB elections. According to this equation, the pattern of change in the union share of the work force depends on the relation between the net attrition of the union share of the work force and the rate of new organization through NLRB elections. When the rate of attrition multiplied by the existing union share exceeds the proportion of the work force newly organized by NLRB elections, the union share will fall over time. When the rate of attrition times the share is smaller than the proportion newly organized, the union share will rise over time. When organization by NLRB elections just balances out the attrition, the union share will be constant.[3]

I have made several estimates of the magnitude of the attrition rate using variants of the "stock-flow" equation. My estimates suggest that the rate is on the order of 3% per year. That is, in the absence of new organization of workers through NLRB elections the union share of the work force in the United States tends to decline by roughly 3% a year.[4] If in one year 35% of the work force were organized, this proportion would decline to 34% (= 35% × (1 − .03)) in the following year.

With a 3% rate of attrition, the late 1970s–early 1980s level of new organization of workers through NLRB elections portends a disastrous decline for unionism. If unions continue to win just 0.3% of the work force in NLRB elections (see table 3.1), the steady-state share of the work force that will be organized will fall to a bare 10% of the non-agricultural work force. If the unions organize 0.6% of the work force through NLRB elections, as they did in the 1950s, the union share would stabilize at 20%.[5] In short, while other factors help determine union density, union success or failure in NLRB elections is an essential component in what is one of the most important changes in the U.S. labor market in recent decades, the decline in the proportion of private sector workers organized. Now, what factors have caused the decline in union success in NLRB representation elections?

The First Suspect: Changing Economic Structure

The first and simplest explanation of the decline in unionism is that it resulted from broad economic changes, which reduced the proportion of the work force in groups traditionally highly unionized and increased the proportion in groups traditionally nonunion. The explanation is simple because it ties the decline to the changing structure of the economy with no need to bring in changes in union or management behavior or the desires of workers for unions. It is a "technocratic" explanation, and technocratic explanations are invariably the easiest and least controversial. As Henry Farber shows (chapter 2, this volume), however, structural changes cannot account for the majority of the overall decline in unionization observed. Indeed, my own analysis of the effects of structural shifts on the decline in membership growth through the election process reinforces Farber's conclusion. That is, structural shifts in the labor force account for very little of the decline in union success in NLRB elections. Although the proportion of workers in some categories that are likely to vote union, as indicated in the 1977 Quality of Employment Survey, decreased (notably the blue-collar workers), the proportion of workers in other categories likely to vote for unions has increased (younger, black workers).[6]

Structural factors contribute only marginally to the decline in the union share of votes in NLRB elections, but they may contribute more to the declining number of election campaigns conducted by unions. (I have not yet analyzed this possible route of impact.) Barring an enormous influence of structural changes on numbers of elections (or on size of winning units, which seems a priori implausible), I conclude that structural changes in the economy are not the *prime* cause of declining union success in NLRB elections.

So, what is?

Second Suspect: Union Organizing Efforts

How have union organizing efforts changed over time? How much, if any, of the decline in private-sector unionism can be attributed to a decline in union organizing activity?

Paula Voos of the University of Wisconsin has analyzed these questions in some detail. She has developed estimates of the resources unions allocated to organizing activity based on the financial records of twenty different international unions. While her estimates are by no means perfect, they provide a useful indication of the trend in organizing activity. Voos's figures show that while unions have maintained roughly the same real expenditures per member for organizing, their effort has not kept pace with the growth of the work force, so that real expenditures per nonunion worker have actually declined by some 30% (see table 3.2). To see if this decline contributed to the falling union success rate, I made use of Voos's estimates of the impact of resources on unions' success in organizing their jurisdictions. According to her econometric analysis, a 10% increase in dollars spent per potential union member raises the proportion for whom the union wins representation rights by 7%. Using this figure, I estimate that the decline in union organizing effort contributed substantially to the 1950s–1970s drop in the proportion of nonagricultural workers newly organized through NLRB elections. In the early 1950s, unions organized roughly 1.0% of the work force annually through elections; in the early 1970s, they organized roughly 0.3% of the work force annually through elections. Voos's figures suggest that the decline in organizing effort reduced the proportion of newly organized by 21%, or 0.2 point of the 0.7 point drop.[7] While crude, these figures indicate that possibly as much as a third of

Table 3.2
Organizing efforts by twenty major U.S. unions, 1953–74

Year	Expenditures in millions of current dollars	Real expenditures utilizing wage deflator	Real expenditures per member of these unions	Real expenditures per nonunion employee
1953	$21.1	$34.4	$3.91	$1.03
1955	22.6	34.4	3.72	1.02
1960	28.1	35.2	3.94	.95
1965	33.2	35.9	3.79	.83
1970	49.5	41.7	4.15	.81
1974	64.4	41.3	3.94	.71

Source: Paula Voos, "Labor Union Organizing Programs, 1954–1977," Ph.D. diss., Harvard University, 1982.

the decline in union success through NLRB elections is linked to reduced organizing activity.

Another related statistic can be brought to bear on the issue of union organizing effort and electoral success. In some NLRB elections more than one union contest the right to represent workers. In this situation organizing effort is undoubtedly much higher than in elections that pit unions against management only. In 1980 the victory rate in elections with two or more unions on the ballot was 74.2%, compared to a rate of 47.4% when only one union was seeking representation rights. Before the unification of the AFL and CIO, employers would often express a desire to work with unions associated with one federation rather than the other ("The CIO is too leftist," "The AFL is too corrupt or is too craft-oriented"). After unification, the number of elections with two or more unions on the ballot fell, from 23.7% of NLRB elections in 1953 to 6.2% of elections in 1980, implying less choice for workers (and employers) among unions and less organizing activity per election.[8] All else being the same, the drop of 17.5 percentage points in the proportion of elections with two or more unions on the ballot would, at 1980 rates of victory, reduce the proportion of elections won by unions by 5 percentage points or a quarter of the actual drop in the proportion of elections won by unions, an estimate surprisingly close to that obtained from Voos's analyses.[9]

All told, reduced organizing activity appears to have contributed to the decline in union representation.

Managerial Opposition

While trade union organizing effort per nonunion worker has fallen, managerial opposition to unionism has increased by leaps and bounds. In the 1950s many managements did relatively little to discourage their workers from unionizing—after all, did not the law specify that the decision was for the workers to make? In ensuing decades, however, management has come to contest hotly nearly every significant NLRB election. Labor-management consultants, whose modus operandi is defeating unions in certification elections, are routinely brought in to run antiunion election campaigns. Because these consultants rarely comply with the Landrum-Griffin Act by reporting their activities to the Department of Labor, solid estimates of the number and receipts of such firms are unavailable.[10] That they have grown to become an important part of the labor relations scene is, however, incontestable.

What is the nature of the modern "union-prevention" business?

Management opposition to union organizing drives takes three basic forms. The first, sometimes called "positive labor relations," attempts to beat unions at their own game by offering unorganized workers most of the benefits of unionism—high wages, good fringe benefits, seniority protection, and the like—with none of the associated costs. This approach is described in more detail by Anil Verma and Thomas Kochan (chapter 5, this volume).

A second employer strategy is to conduct tough legal campaigns to convince workers that their interests might be better served by voting against unions. A typical campaign might involve

• Frequent written and verbal communications with workers, particularly by their immediate supervisors;

• predictions about the possible dire effects of unionism on worker well-being;

• presentation of information about strikes designed to frighten workers—unionism will bring active conflict to the firm;

• delay of the representation election, on the (correct) assumption that the greater the time between initial petitions for an election and the holding of the election, the more likely it is that union fervor will fall;

• efforts to obtain voting districts more favorable to management.

A third way to try to defeat unionism is to break the law, in particular to identify and fire leading prounion workers.

Figure 3.1 Employer unfair labor practices against unions, and number of NLRB representation elections, 1950–1980. Source: National Labor Relations Board, *Annual Reports*, 1950–1980.

Beginning in the 1960s the relative number of illegal activities committed by managements, after declining for years, rose at phenomenal rates (figure 3.1) From 1960 to 1980 the number of *all* employer unfair labor practices charges rose fourfold; the number of charges involving a firing for union activity rose threefold, and the number of workers awarded back pay or ordered reinstated to their jobs rose fivefold. By contrast, the number of NLRB elections barely changed in the same period. Despite increasingly sophisticated methods for disguising the cause of such firings, more employers have been judged guilty of firing workers for union activity in 1980 than ever before.[11] If one divides the number of persons fired for union activity in 1980 by the number of persons who voted for a union in elections to obtain an indication of the risk faced by workers desiring a union, one gets a remarkable result: one in twenty workers who favored the union got fired. Assuming that the vast bulk of union supporters are relatively inactive, the likelihood that an outspoken worker, exercising his or her legal rights under the Taft-Hartley Act, gets fired for union activity, is, according to these data, extraordinarily high.

One reason why firing workers for union activity has become increasingly popular is that the penalties for such activities are slight. Employers who are found guilty of firing union workers are forced to reinstate the workers and to pay them limited back pay (the wages they would have received minus whatever income they received from the alternative to the job), often several years later. In addition the employers must post a notice that they will not engage in such illegal activity again. Such notices are jocularly referred to as "hunting licenses" which, rather than convincing workers that management will forego such tactics in the future, warns them of how far management is willing to go to defeat unionism. Another reason for growing illegal management opposition: it is an exceedingly effective way to chill an organizing campaign.

How Much Does Management Opposition Contribute to Union Decline?

There are a wide variety of studies of the impact of managerial opposition on NLRB elections. Some studies compare success rates across elections where management employed different tactics; others analyze the determinants of the vote of individual workers (reported after the secret-ballot election); others relate management activity in a geographic area to union organizing success in the area; while yet others study changes over time. Despite considerable differences among studies, however, virtually all tell the same story: managerial opposition to unionism, particularly illegal campaign tactics, is a major, if not *the* major, determinant of NLRB election results.

Table 3.3 summarizes extant studies, divided between those focused on legal management opposition and those focused on illegal opposition. The studies of legal opposition show that:

1. The amount of company communication influences the election results, with unions winning most elections in which management opposition is light but less than half of those in which opposition is severe (studies 1, 2, 4, 6, 11, 12).

2. Union success is lower the longer the time delay between the initial petition and the actual holding of the election (studies 3, 6).

3. Elections to which companies accede readily to the election district proposed by the union (consent elections) produce greater chances of wins than elections in which the company battles the election district

Table 3.3
Studies of how company opposition affects union success in NLRB elections: Legal Opposition

Study	Finding	
1. National Industrial Conference Board study of 140 drives attempting to organize white collar unions, 1966–67.	Percentage of wins for union depends on amount of company communication:	
	written or no communication	85%
	meetings with workers	51%
	meetings and written communication	39%
2. AFL-CIO study of 495 NLRB elections in 1966–67.	Percentage of wins for union depends on extent of company opposition:	
	no opposition	97%
	some opposition	50%
	wages increased	37%
	surveillance of union, firing	43%
3. Prosten, analysis of probability of union win in 130,701 elections in 1962–77.	Percentage of wins falls with time delay between election and petition; is lower in stipulated than in other elections.	
4. Lawler, 155 NLRB elections, 1974–78.	Percentage of election wins for union falls if company hires consultant:	
	if no consultant	71%
	if consultant	23%
5. Drotning, 41 elections ordered void and rerun by NLRB.	Nature of employer's campaign influences voting average number of employer communications per election:	
	union losses	12.5%
	union wins	8.6%

Table 3.3 (Continued)

Study	Finding	
6. Roomkin-Block, 45,155, union representation cases, 1971–77.	Percentage of wins for union falls with delay between petition and actual election:	
	election 0–1 months	50%
	2 months	45%
	3 months	41%
	4–7 months	30%
	8–12 months	30%
7. Seeber and Cooke, proportion of workers voting for union representation by state, 1970–78.	One percentage point in proportion of elections to which employers "consent" to the election district changes the percentage point of union success by one-half.	

Legal and Illegal Opposition

Study	Finding	
8. U.S. General Accounting Office, analysis of 400 8(a)(3) illegal firings or other discrimination for union involvement cases—368 representation elections.	Unions were more successful in campaign in which no employer discrimination occurred than in those that involved an unfair-labor-practice charge.	
	Success rate:	
	no violation	45%
	violation	38%
9. Aspin study of 71 NLRB elections in which reinstatements were ordered.	Percentage of wins for union depends on firing, with unions doing worse unless those reinstated return to job before election:	
	All elections in region	62%
	with 8(a)(3) firings	48%
	Election held before 8(a)(3) case is settled/person discriminated against refuses to return to job	41%
	Election held after person discriminated against returns to job	67%

Table 3.3 (Continued)

Study	Finding
10. Getman, Goldberg, and Herman; analysis of 1,293 workers in 31 elections in 1972–73.	Percentage of workers pro-union reduced by 10% during campaign regardless of campaign tactic. Percentage of workers voting union reduced by sizeable but statistically insignificant amount by management campaign tactics.
11. Dickens study of 966 workers in 31 elections in 1972–73.	Percentage of workers voting union reduced by employer activities: legal campaign −10% illegal campaign −4% employer threatening −15% acts against prounion workers Percentage of elections unions would win in simulation model: no campaign or light campaign against 53–67% intense campaign 22–34% campaign with violations 4–10%
12. Catler, study of 817 NLRB elections reported on AFL-CIO organizing reports	company campaigning activities, unfair labor practices, and delay reduce union success, with proportion of union wins lowered by 10 points by unfair labor practice.

Sources: 1. National Industrial Conference Board, *White Collar Unionization* (New York: NICB, 1970).

2. Statement of William Kirchner, AFL-CIO Director of Organization on a bill to amend the National Labor Relations Act in order to increase effectiveness of the remedies: Hearings on H.R.11725 before the special subcommittee on Labor of the House Committee on Education and Labor, 90th Cong., 1st sess., 1967 12, 15.

3. Richard Prosten, "The Largest Season Union Organizing in the Last Decade," Pro-

Table 3.3 (Continued)
ceedings of the 31st Annual Meeting of the Industrial Relations Research Association, Madison, Wisconsin, 1978: 240–49.
4. John Lawler, "Labor-Management Consultants in Union Organizing Campaigns" (Paper presented at the Thirty-fourth Annual Meeting of the Industrial Relations Research Association, Washington, D.C., 1981).
5. John Drotning, "NLRB Remedies for Election Misconduct: An Analysis of Election Outcomes and Their Determinants," *Journal of Business* 40(2) April 1967: 137–48.
6. Myron Roomkin and Richard Block, "Case Processing Time and Outcome of Elections: Some Empirical Evidence," *University of Illinois Law Review* V(1) (1981): 75–97. Calculated from tables 2 and 4 of their study.
7. R. Seeber and W. Cooke, "The Decline in Union Success in NLRB Representation Elections," *Industrial Relations* 22 (1), Winter 1983.
8. U.S. General Accounting Office, *Concerns Regarding Impact of Employee Charges Against Employers for Unfair Labor Practices* (Washington, D.C.: GAO–HRD 82–80 June 21, 1982).
9. Leslie Aspin, *A Study of Reinstatement Under the National Labor Relations Act* (Ph.D. diss., Massachusetts Institute of Technology, 1966).
10. Jules Getman, Stephen Goldberg, and Jeanne Herman, *Union Representation Elections: Law and Reality* (New York: Russell Sage Foundation, 1976).
11. William F. Dickens, *Union Representation Elections: Campaign and Vote* (Ph.D. diss., Massachusetts Institute of Technology, 1980).
12. Susan Catler, "Labor Union Representation Elections: What Determines Who Wins?" (B.A. thesis, Harvard University, 1978).

until the NLRB in Washington stipulates who can or cannot vote (studies 3, 7).

The studies of illegal company opposition show that employer discrimination against union activists, particularly firing, also has a great impact on the success rate of unions, though the magnitude of the impact varies. Two studies estimate a drop in union success in the area of 7 to 10 points (studies 8, 12), while two others estimate declines in union success by 14 to 24 points (studies 9, 11). Only in the rare case where a fired worker is ordered reinstated by the NLRB and actually returns to his job *before* the election does breaking the law backfire (study 9). Because of long delays before workers are ordered reinstated and because of worker fears that management will be out to get them if they go back to the job, however, relatively few return to the job before the election.

The evidence that company campaign activities affect election results is substantial and, on the face of it, compelling. Both labor and management practitioners agree that what the company does is important, and companies back this belief by spending time and money on NLRB election campaigns. Given all this, one might expect the conclusion that company opposition affects unionization significantly to go unchallenged.

It has not. In 1976 Julius Getman (Yale Law School), Steven Goldberg (Northwestern Law School), and Jeanne Herman (Northwestern University) published a book that argued the opposite: that even deceptive and illegal campaign tactics do not matter (study 10). They based this conclusion on analysis of the votes of over a thousand workers in thirty-three elections, which indicated that although company opposition reduced the probability that workers would vote union, it did not do so by what they viewed as statistically significant amounts. On the basis of their findings they recommended sweeping changes in NLRB regulation of election campaigning. In an intellectual climate favorable to deregulation this study won considerable attention and, for a period of time, may have influenced NLRB policies.[12] More recent analyses of their findings indicate, however, that they reached faulty conclusions from the data. First, they erred by placing too great a stress on statistical significance as opposed to estimated effects: statistics that show company opposition *reduces* voting for a union by "insignificant" amounts does not mean that opposition does not matter, but rather that it is poorly measured or weak. Second, reanalysis of their data by William Dickens of Berkeley found that some forms of company opposition do indeed have statistically significant effects and that, because many NLRB elections are decided by relatively small margins, even modest "insignificant" effects on individual voters can accumulate to have powerful significant effects on the proportion of elections won by unions (study 11). Viewed from this perspective the Getman, Goldberg, and Herman data are consistent with, rather than inconsistent with, the other work listed in the table.

Granted that company opposition matters, how much of the decline in union electoral success can be attributed to rising management opposition?

From a quarter to a half, according to our analysis of the impact of one major indicator of illegal opposition—unfair labor practices committed by employers—on the proportion of nonagricultural workers choosing representation in NLRB elections (table 3.4). Our estimates are based on three distinct studies of the relation between unfair practices and union success in elections: an analysis of success rates across states; an analysis of success rates over time; and an analysis of success rates within states over time. All of our calculations control for other potential

Table 3.4
Estimates of the effect of management unfair labor practices on percentage of
nonagricultural work force newly organized in NLRB elections

Analysis and data set	Estimated impact of 10% increase in unfair practices per election on proportion of workers newly organized in NLRB elections	Estimated proportion of decline in nonagricultural work force organized in NLRB elections due to increased management unfair labor practices
Comparison of union success across states, 1950–78	−2.5%	28%
Comparison of union success within states over time, 1950–78	−3.4%	38%
Comparison of union success over time, 1950–89	−6.0%	49%

Source: R. B. Freeman, "The Simple Economics of Declining Union Density," (NBER
Working Paper, 1983). For corroborating estimates of the effect of unfair labor practices
on new unionization using a different model see David Ellwood and Glenn Fine, "Effects
of Right-to-Work Laws on Union Organizing," (NBER Working Paper, 1983). We thank
Ellwood and Fine for providing us with their data set. In the first two categories, the
measure of management unfair practices is all CA cases, as reported in National Labor
Relations Board, *Annual Reports*, where CA cases relate to charges that employers violated
section 8(a)(3) of the act, divided by nonagricultural work force. In the third category,
the measures of management unfair practices are 8(a)(3) cases, those involving employer
penalization of worker for union activity, divided by workers in elections.

determinants of union electoral success, such as region, proportion of
workers who are blue-collar, and so on.

I have focused on unfair management practices not because I believe
they are management's only effective antiunion weapon—the studies
in table 3.3 show legal opposition also has a substantial impact on
union success—but rather because information on those practices, but
not on legal opposition, exists over time and across states. As legal and
illegal opposition have presumably grown together, we interpret the
analysis as showing the effect of "total" management opposition on
union success, not of illegal opposition only.

So interpreted, the analyses show that employer opposition has a
substantial and highly statistically significant depressant effect on union

success rates (the first column of table 3.4), which goes a long way toward explaining the decline in union organization of new workers in NLRB elections. For every 10% change in unfair labor practices per election, our estimates suggest that unionization of new workers falls from about 3% to 6%. From 1950 to 1980, when unfair labor practices per election increased sixfold, we further estimate that the rise in management opposition explains from over a quarter to nearly half of the decline in union success in organizing through NLRB elections. Put differently, had employer opposition to unionism remained at 1950 levels, our calculations suggest that unions would have organized about twice the proportion of the unorganized in 1980 as they in fact did.

The point is not that unfair practices per se have hurt unions in NLRB elections, though they obviously have, but that opposition, broadly defined, is a major cause of the slow strangulation of private-sector unionism. Analysis with other indicators of opposition (workers fired for back pay, the decline in consent elections) show comparable results.[13]

The Role of Public Policy

In 1977 the AFL-CIO proposed a major piece of labor legislation, the Labor Law Reform Bill of 1977, designed to penalize more severely employers who commit unfair labor practices and thus ease the problem of organizing. Underlying this bill was a belief that if public policy toward unionization were different, so too would be union success in NLRB elections. What evidence is there, if any, that legal changes affect union organization?

There are, I believe, three pieces of evidence to suggest that the specific institutional mechanisms by which a country regulates unionization, and in particular allows management to fight unionization, are critical factors in unionization.

1. Canada. The principal difference between unionization in the United States and in Canada is that U.S. laws allow management to conduct lengthy well-funded election campaigns against unions. Canadian labor law does not permit such activity. Indeed, in most provinces a union is certified without any secret-ballot campaign at all: if around 60% of workers sign authorization cards, the union is certified. Result: growing unionization in Canada.

2. Right-to-work. Under the Taft-Hartley Act, states are allowed to pass so-called right-to-work laws that outlaw union shops (workplaces

where workers must join a union, or at least pay dues, within thirty days to keep their jobs). In these states unions face serious "free-rider" problems that weaken them financially and make organizing more difficult. The free-rider problem is that some workers will enjoy all the benefits of unionism but not pay dues for those benefits. In right-to-work states upward of 20% of workers covered by collective bargaining are not union members, compared to 10% elsewhere in the country. A careful analysis of unionization across states and over time by David Ellwood and Glenn Fine of Harvard University finds that new organizing in a state is reduced by about one-third by passage of a right-to-work law.[14]

3. Public sector unionization. The great growth of public-sector unionization was *preceded* by new public-sector labor laws that often required municipalities to bargain with workers who had chosen to unionize. Before these laws, municipalities could simply refuse to bargain with public-sector unions; since strikes were generally illegal, workers had no easy way of "forcing" management to recognize them. Analyses of the relationship between the presence of law favorable to bargaining and unionization across states and the relationship between the timing of union growth and passage of laws within states shows that public-sector unionization was greatly enhanced by changes in the law.[15]

From these diverse alternative legal environments—Canada, right-to-work versus non-right-to-work states, U.S. public sector—I conclude that the labor law of the country does indeed influence the success of unions in representing workers. Under a different legal environment U.S. employers would behave differently, and unions might fare better in organizing the work force.

Conclusion

The declining rate of success of unions in NLRB representation elections is a critical factor in the fall in union density in past decades. Studies of the causes of the decline suggest that perhaps 40% is due to increased management opposition; perhaps 20% is due to reduced union organizing effort per nonunion worker; the remaining 40% is due in part to structural changes in the economy and in part to unknown forces. As the calculations yielding these figures take the change in management opposition and the change in union organizing effort as exogenous, the figures should not be viewed as showing the "ultimate" forces at work. To some extent at least, both management opposition and union organizing effort are responses to a changing economic and legal environment. What the calculations and studies underlying them do show is that success or failure in NLRB elections, and thus the future of unionization in the United States, can be traced back to specific activities by labor and management rather than to amorphous general social developments.

Notes

1. For a detailed discussion of the components of the decomposition equation see R. B. Freeman, "The Simple Economics of Changing Union Density," (National Bureau of Economic Research, forthcoming).

2. Unionization figures are from the U.S. Department of Labor, Bureau of Labor Statistics, *Handbook of Labor Statistics*, 1978, updated.

3. For derivation and discussion of this formula see R. B. Freeman, "The Simple Economics of Declining Union Density" (NBER Working Paper, 1983).

4. I have made several estimates of attrition using variants of the following formula: attrition rate = (change in union membership minus gains through NLRB elections)/union membership in initial period. All of our estimates range about a value of 3%. See R. B. Freeman, "The Simple Economics of Declining Union Density" (NBER Working Paper, 1983)).

5. This is obtained by setting the change in membership equal to zero in the difference equation: union share (t) = $(-$attrition rate) union share $(t - 1)$ + new gains in membership from NLRB elections divided by the work force and solving for the stable union share. In this formula t = years.

6. To estimate the potential impact of structural changes on election outcomes, I performed a two-part analysis. First, I estimated the impact of personal, job, and geographic factors on the probability an individual would vote for the union in an election using the data from the 1977 Quality of Employment Survey. Second, I multiplied the estimated impact of being in a particular category by changes in the proportion of workers in that category over time to obtain a contribution of that structural shift to the percentage of workers voting for the union. The logic of the procedure is simple. If, for example, white-collar workers are, say, 10 percentage points less likely to vote for the union than other workers and if the white-collar share of the work force (and, therefore, of workers in union representation elections) rises by 5 percentage points, we would attribute .005 point [= .10 (.05)] of the observed changes in the proportion voting for the union. Formally, if B_i is the estimated impact of the ith factor on unionization, we attribute B_iX_i of the change to the change X_i. Note that our analysis uses a linear probability model. More complex functional forms, such as the logistic, will yield comparable results.

7. My calculation of the 0.7 elasticity is based on Paula Voos, "Labor Union Organizing Programs, 1954–1977" (Ph.D. diss., Harvard University, 1982), 20, table 3–2. The dollars spent for nonunion workers are from Voos, table 1–3, pp. 87–88. To obtain the 21% estimate we multiply the 30% decline by the 0.7 estimated impact per percentage change in expenditures to obtain these figures.

8. National Labor Relations Board, Annual Report, vols. 16 and 44 (Washington, D.C.: Government Printing Office, 1954, 1980).

9. The differential success of unions in elections contested by several unions can be interpreted differently. It is possible that two or more unions contest an election only when workers are extremely eager to organize. Then the decline in the proportion of elections contested by unions represents a decline in worker interest, not organizing activity. As we have used the figures simply to check the plausibility of Voos's estimates, we do not pursue the alternative interpretation here.

10. The *AFL-CIO News* estimates about 1,500 practitioners (*AFL-CIO News*, January 15, 1983, 28(2), p. 1).

11. See Paul Weiler, "Reform of the Representation Process in American labor Law" (Harvard Law School, April 20, 1982, Mimeographed), 31–34 for a detailed discussion of illegal management activities.

12. In one decision in which it decided to weaken regulation of campaigns, the board cited the Getman, Goldberg, and Herman study (see table 3.3). *Shopping Mart Food Market, Inc.* 228 NLRB 1311 (1977).

13. In the Seeber and Cooke study (see table 3.3) virtually all of the decline in union success in NLRB elections is explained by means of a very different indicator, the proportion of elections that are "consent" elections.

14. David Ellwood and Glenn Fine, "Effects of Right-to-Work Laws on Union Organizing" (NBER Working Paper No. 1116, May 1983). See Richard Freeman and James Medoff, "New Estimates of Private Sector Unionism in the United States," *Industrial and Labor Relations Review* 32 (January 1979), table 4, for the number of workers covered by collective bargaining who are not union members.

15. Harrison Lauer, "The Effect of Police Unions" (B.A. thesis, Harvard University, 1981).

Discussion, Part I

Charles McDonald: Nobody in the labor movement would argue with the basic conclusion of Freeman and Farber that management opposition makes a difference in union organizing success. In recent years management opposition has seemed to leap ahead of the labor movement. It has become both more pervasive and more sophisticated. There is hardly a union election today in which we do not face a vigorous management campaign. Therefore, the labor movement now needs to catch up with the developments in management practices over the last few years.

Although I agree with the basic conclusion that one has to look at factors other than structural shifts in industry and the labor force to explain the decline in the percentage of the work force organized, I do think that structural shifts have had some effects. In going from a manufacturing-based economy, where most workers were familiar with unions, to a service economy, where this familiarity is often absent, unions have to do much more up-front education to interest workers in organizing. Therefore, we should be expending greater resources to deal with these up-front costs.

One of the things that was not mentioned is the difficulty that unions have in achieving first contracts in those cases where they do win elections. We have done a study at the AFL-CIO and found that we only get first contracts in approximately 63% of the cases where we win elections. Indeed, we have reason to believe that this number has gone down some in recent years as the recession has gotten deeper. Therefore, we need to organize almost twice as many workers as Freeman's estimates suggest just to stay even. Doubling his calculations suggests that we have to organize approximately 1.2% of the labor force, or over a million workers a year, just to stay even.

While employer behavior and the shifts in the economy have important impacts, we also recognize that our organizing strategies have not always been well targeted. Up until 1974 (before the Health Care Amendments to the National Labor Relations Act), only 8% of our elections took place in the service sector. Since 1974, service-sector elections have increased to approximately 22%, but this is still well below where it should be, given the movement of jobs toward this sector of the economy. We believe we should be holding 70 to 80% of our elections in the service sector.

What many people fail to recognize, however, is that few unions have a national organizing strategy; instead, most organizing efforts are initiated and carried out at the local level. This helps explain why we have fewer organizing efforts than we perhaps should have in the South, since more of our local officers and organizers are located in the North where the bulk of our current members are.

It is often assumed that all unions have a natural interest in organizing and assign it the highest priority. However, members may resist allocating scarce union dollars and staff resources to organizing new members. They have a hard time understanding why resources that could be allocated to improving services to them should be spent on recruiting new people. This can lead to inadequate resources for organizing until the situation deteriorates badly.

Another simple factor for NLRB and membership decline is that we are not holding as many elections as we should. In 1977, there were approximately 8,900 representational elections. When the data are finally tabulated for 1982, it looks like we will have held only 55% of the 1977 number.

Let me now turn to some comments on experiences our various unions have had recently in analyzing the prospects for organizing in the high technology industries. A survey of a set of high technology workers did not show much variation in worker attitudes or preferences for organizing from the results of the 1977 Quality of Employment Survey referred to by both Farber and Freeman. The stated propensity to join a union was slightly lower than the percentages reported in the 1977 survey, but there were many similar results. For example, there was a particularly strong correlation between skill level and interest in organizing. Interest in organizing goes down considerably as one moves up the skill level from entry-level blue-collar workers up to the professional ranks. There is also a very strong correlation between workers' view that group clout or pressure is important for getting things done and their willingness to organize. As in the earlier survey, workers who are dissatisfied with such things as opportunities for advancement and those who believe that they are not getting a fair share of the profits from these industries are more willing to organize.

While professional and technical employees in this survey expressed a low propensity to organize, this does not always appear to be the case. For example, at Western Electric, the Communications Workers of America are now engaged in an effective organizing campaign targeted on the specific concerns of professional and technical employees. Therefore, it is not impossible to reach these people if one can identify their specific concerns. It is just that there is little predisposition toward unions among these workers. We have other evidence to suggest that attitudes can change considerably during the course of a campaign. Thus, these reported preferences are not necessarily the last word in how workers will, in fact, vote once exposed to the arguments of both sides.

Rudy Oswald: There seems to be an attitude in society today, in part coming from universities, that suggests employer opposition to unionization is acceptable. This often makes it difficult not only to organize but also to pass very innocuous things like the Labor Law Reform bill.

Michael Piore: While I agree that management attitudes have hardened in recent years, I don't think this can be blamed on what the labor relations faculties in universities have been teaching. In fact, the vast majority teaching labor relations in the last twenty years have had the same set of values and perspectives on the role of collective bargaining and the rights of the labor movement as those of us here today. But it is true that this trend toward a more conservative management is a reflection of a deeper-seated, conservative market orientation that has been building up within business schools over the last decade. Having little concern for labor as an institution in society is more of a reflection of this growing tendency among business students, business faculty, and teaching. Given this growth in market orientation, faculty members in management or business schools responsible for labor relations have been under increasing pressure from their colleagues and from students to take a harder line toward labor and to change the way courses are being taught to reflect more of a personnel or human resource management orientation and to abandon the labor relations values of the past. This is something that will influence the managers of the future who are being educated at the moment, but I don't think the labor movement can blame the labor relations teachers for their current problems.

Robert McKersie: The statistics on representation elections that have been reported here suggest that the allegiance of American society to the election process as it applies to union recognition may have to be rethought. We seem to have a belief that the election and the campaign process is part of our American way of life. After all, that is the way the political process works. Out of an election should come a fair exchange of views so that people can make independent, educated judgments. But, as the statistics show, along with the election process can also come many "dirty tricks."

Richard Freeman: We have to probe a little deeper to ask why management attitudes seem to have worsened in recent years. One thing that seems to have changed over the course of the 1970s is that the union-nonunion cost differential has gone up, and that may underlie part of the increased managerial opposition.

Michael Bennett: If we go to the source of the problem, the philosophy of management, whether that comes from the instruction management gets in universities or from something else, we have to ask how we can begin to change management's point of view. If what Piore is saying is true, then we have to think along with academics about what is being taught today and how this will influence our experiences in the 1990s. But beyond that obvious point, we have to look at our own internal efforts. We have to recognize that when resources within our unions get scarce, the first thing that gets cut is the organizing department. Perhaps that has to change. Finally, we obviously have a big political problem with the National Labor Relations Board both now and in recent years. Nothing significant is going to change until we have increased political clout to change the behavior of the board and the policies it administers.

Jack Golodner: I want to touch briefly on the attitudes that are fostered by our educational system. It seems that schools of management have forgotten that we are a nation of laws and that they have a responsibility to teach students, whether current or future professionals, to respect the intent of our laws, which is to foster collective bargaining. The issue of worker representation involves more than just a game of winning or losing. If management insists on a game of battle to the end—winner take all—they will have to recognize that they are placing at risk the basic foundation of our democracy. We do not want to return to the law of the jungle, but that is where they seem to be going. The natural reaction of unions placed in this kind of environment is to expend more resources on politics. If employers won't work within the law, then they should not be surprised that unions will work to strengthen or change the law. All of this serves to encourage a kind of adversarial system that so many people in society—management and politicians included—want to eliminate.

I want to make another point in response to Freeman's finding that fewer dollars are being expended on union organizing efforts now than in the past. Maybe it is not a very good investment to expend more dollars on organizing at a time when organizing efforts appear to bear little fruit because of the way our laws are stacked against the organizer. Instead, dollars are beng spent on lobbying efforts to strengthen the law. This does not mean there is less interest in organizing; it only means that unions have found it necessary to address the legal situation as a prerequisite to more organizing.

Lynn Williams: We seem to have a Catch-22 here. We need better laws but with our declining political clout we can't get them. The reform has to come from within. We need organizational clout to get political power and vice versa. Clearly, we hear that things are getting worse, but my question is, from whence comes the clout for change? Clearly, it comes from a strong membership base to begin with.

Charles McDonald: There are some success stories out there. I think that from all of my experience in meeting with union organizers from all over the country, I am convinced that quality organizers make a big difference. We have some organizers who have 75 to 80% win records. These tend to be organizers who reflect the characteristics of the workers they are trying to organize. I think that there is a natural burnout of union organizers after two or three years in the field. Organizing is a very intensive, time-consuming, emotionally and physically draining process. We should recognize that we have to provide normal career progressions for people so that they are not out in the field with organizing responsibilities beyond the time when they have the energy and the creativity to do an effective job. One should be able to move from a field organizing role to a supervisor role in some orderly way. This would give us a group of fresh organizers coming in a more natural way and provide other career opportunities for people who have burned out.

We also have to sharpen the way we organize. There is no reason for us to maintain the practice of having a separation between the person who organizes and the person who negotiates the first contract. Too often we can't achieve a contract after we win elections because somebody new comes in. This person doesn't have an understanding of the background and the history of the organizing effort and the concerns of the workers for whom the contract is being negotiated. Our organizing strategies and tactics have to catch up with increased management sophistication.

Nancy Mills: I was struck by a finding by Farber of the correlation between nonwhite workers and the propensity to organize. Also, that women are more likely to organize than men is a factor we can build into our strategies. There are many bargaining units where minorities and/or women are predominant. The key to organizing these groups is to form political alliances with groups that are concerned with the social and political status of women and minorities. This is just another way to get greater political support as well. It is no accident that employers respect the Equal Employment Opportunity statutes; around 50% of our society happens to be women. Employers understand the potential political implications of this number. If we can unite these movements, we can gain greater strength.

Donald Ephlin: I agree that organizing is one of the toughest jobs in the labor movement. And I don't disagree with what seems to be a finding by Farber that management organizes workers for unions by failing to provide satisfying jobs. But we have to understand that unless we can offer a solution to workers' problems, they will not turn to us. Furthermore, the problems that workers have today have changed, and we as a labor movement have not. If one of my UAW workers in the Framingham plant leaves to take a job in a high tech firm, he doesn't want to organize because to him the union means work standards and all of the other rules that go with it, and he doesn't see a need for this, at least not for a while. We have to respond to his needs as he sees them today if we want to organize effectively.

There is another political aspect to the problem, however. We have put an organizing effort into the professional and technical workers at Rockwell International. To defeat us, that company spent over a million dollars of what is taxpayers' money—they are defense contractors. The government allowed them to pass these expenses through as "normal personnel policy" expenses. We began to make some headway on this problem with the Labor Department under the Carter administration but that all went by the board with the Reagan administration.

Finally, with respect to the way we organize, we have all had the experience of not being able to negotiate first contracts because organizers have gone out and organized units that they in fact knew could never be successful in negotiation. So the key is to have a coordinated strategy that thinks through not only the targeting of organizing efforts but the ability to negotiate with that employer.

Jack Joyce: I have just a few anecdotal observations about women coming into construction unions. Those coming in appear to me to be more militant than most of our male members and, what's more important, willing to do the nuts-and-bolts work needed to help organize and run the union. Second, I'd like to echo Lynn Williams's comment about organizing. Clearly, it is critical to increase our political clout. We can do more to increase the political effectiveness of our organizations. Right now there are probably only about ten or twelve unions within the AFL-CIO that are politically effective.

Finally, we have to deal with the mind-set that exists about the role of labor in society. If we can't get management, or those teaching management, to recognize that it's a choice of public vs. private regulation, that is, a choice between collective bargaining or public laws regulating the workplace and not a choice between unions and some visionary free and unfettered private enterprise management system, then we are not doing our job. History is not on the side of management in its search for a free and uncontested control of workers in the workplace. We agree that government must be neutral in the regulation of election campaigns, but we do have a basic public policy that says government does not have to be neutral in its preference for collective bargaining. That is the basic law of the land, and we have to find a way of making it a meaningful law in practice.

II

Employer Strategies for Union Avoidance

4

The Legal Setting for the Emergence of the Union Avoidance Strategy

Janice A. Klein and
E. David Wanger

Before the passage of the National Labor Relations Act (NLRA), most management actively opposed union organizing drives. Shortly thereafter, recognizing that unionization was most likely inevitable, many large corporations encouraged "friendly" unions to organize their facilities. However, something in the 1950s led corporate executives to reevaluate their strategy and once again aggressively oppose unionization. Economists and many industrial relations scholars attribute this change to market competition and the need for flexibility. Others would cite the increased professionalism of management, especially the industrial relations and human resource management function (Kochan and Cappelli 1982). However, something had to trigger this change in management strategy and say to executives that a nonunion facility was once again a viable alternative. Our contention is that the political environment set the stage and the NLRB provided the tools.

The political mood of the country in the early 1950s was changing. The New Deal had moved the pendulum in favor of organized labor, and the 1952 presidential election reflected the public's desire for a change. With the return of a Republican administration, management was given some confidence that the time was right to swing the pendulum back in their direction.

During the late 1940s, a few managers had begun to test the new provisions of the Taft-Hartley Act. Meanwhile, others watched attentively to see just how much latitude the new procedures provided them relative to presenting their views toward unions. Since the judicial process moves rather slowly, it was not until the early 1950s that these issues were really tested at a high enough level to give managers confidence that more sophisticated union avoidance strategies and techniques were worth the risk. Fortunately for management, these cases were ruled on by a promanagement National Labor Relations Board.

The political bias of the NLRB is not a new finding. (See Cooke and Gautschi 1982 for a recent review of both historical and empirical research finding this bias.) However, we believe that the NLRB rulings in the 1950s were key to reinforcing management's bias toward remaining nonunion and encouraging it to embark upon a double strategy, that is, to live with unions where they exist but expand into greenfield sites and oppose any organization attempts in these new facilities (Kochan and McKersie 1983). We will trace that historical development and briefly review several of the pertinent rulings.

The Rise of the Nonunion Strategy

Remaining nonunion has always been a management preference, but aggressive strategies to meet that objective have wavered over the years. Before the New Deal, management went all out to combat unionism; public policy, and hence government action, did little to suppress employer actions. But, as a 1954 *Business Week* Special Report noted, the election of Franklin Roosevelt as president led to a "failure of nerve" on the part of management.

On the labor front, business seemed to be suffering a paralysis of will as well. Its resistance to the new unionism was sporadic, thoughtless, and panicky. It shifted violently from aggressiveness to abject resignation (*Business Week*, September 4, 1954, p. 83).

But a change in the political climate in the 1940s and the passage of the Taft-Hartley Act which tightened the reins on union organizing efforts helped to lead to a "recovery of nerve" by management. Then with the election of President Eisenhower in 1952, "management felt an added surge of confidence in its ability to put across its point of view on the labor front" (*Business Week*, September 4, 1954, p. 83).

Recent interviews at several large corporations point to this period as pivotal in the development of management strategy toward unions. As the director of industrial relations at one large corporation stated,

Up until the early 1950s, we often encouraged cooperative unions to organize within our plants in an effort to avoid having to negotiate with one of the larger international unions. But in the 1950s, we got smarter in our personnel practices and the NLRB handed down a number of rulings which finally allowed us to tell our side of the story during organizing campaigns.

Hence, although several large firms had long provided comprehensive personnel policies in an effort to remain nonunion (Foulkes 1980), the

1950s appear to be the turning point for many of the traditionally unionized firms to branch out into greenfield sites with expressed strategies to keep those plants unorganized.

A review of the ages of union versus nonunion plants within several companies indicates that most of the union plants were built before the mid-1950s, while those plants built since have remained predominantly nonunion. This parallels the Kochan and Cappelli (1982) statement that since the 1960s, there has been a rise in the use of psychology-based, individual-oriented personnel policies as a management tool to avoid unions.

The Declining Rate of Union Growth

It is doubtful that it is just a mere coincidence that the mid-1950s were also the peak years for union membership. Foulkes (1980) noted that,

While union membership as a percentage of employees in nonagricultural establishments increased from 12% in 1930 to 35% in 1945, between 1955 and 1978 it declined from approximately one-third to 24%. If employee association membership is included, the figure is about 27% (p. 129).

Depending upon the data source, union membership peaked in either 1953 or 1954.[1] Since that time there has been a steady decline. (See the chapters by Farber and Freeman in this volume for further elaboration of these trends.)

A 1957 *Business Week* (July 13, 1957) article reporting that "Union Recruiting Dips to New Low" attributed the falloff in organizing successes to several causes: nature of the work force and the changing times, that is, the increase in white-collar employment; the marginal nature of organizing efforts since many large employers were already organized; corruption and racketeering; and the passage of the Taft-Hartley Act. Relative to the last, the article noted,

The greater degree of free speech for management provided by the Taft-Hartley Act gives employers more weapons to fight union organization. This has hurt the unions' organizational efforts in the South (p. 146).

Although some industrial relations scholars are reluctant to attribute much significance to the Taft-Hartley Act in the decline in union growth, Spielman (1962) concluded that the law was a major barrier to the growth of union membership in the United States as compared to Canada, whose economic conditions were similar.

Our contention is that the Taft-Hartley Act provided the opening of the door for management to embark upon a new strategy. But the law, in and of itself, was not necessarily the driving factor. The law provided the basis for decisions that ultimately allowed many of the new weapons used by management. It was employer resistance in the form of these new weapons which has contributed to union decline (Seeber and Cooke 1983). Before reviewing the NLRB decisions, it is first useful to look at one additional actor in this drama, the popular press. Although there are numerous informal and professional networks within the business fraternity, a primary conveyor of new ideas or strategies is the popular journals read by managers.

What the Popular Press Was Saying to Managers

A brief review of headlines from magazines or journals often read by executives quickly points to a prime interest of managers during the 1950s.

"How Free is 'Free Speech?' Pretty free, NLRB rules in two significant Taft-Hartley cases." (*Business Week*, April 8, 1950)

"Freer Speech for Employees: NLRB relaxes its rules on what an employer can say to workers before an election. Other policy shifts are in the making." (*Business Week*, December 5, 1953)

"Legitimate Ways to Resist a Union Drive" (*Personnel*, January–February 1958)

"Free Speech and the Taft-Hartley Act: When is management free to speak what it thinks and when not, under our labor relations laws? Management is freer than you might think, under the Taft-Hartley Act." (*Personnel Administration*, July–August 1959)

The journals appear to be helping managers set out their new rights under the Taft-Hartley Act.

It is clear from the press's point of view that "A New Era in Labor Management Relations" (*Mill & Factory*, March 1954) had been born with President Eisenhower in the White House. The article began as follows:

It seems that we are at last entering a more sensible era of labor management relations.

• First, the government is adopting a "hands off" attitude in labor disputes

• Second, the Taft-Hartley is being administered more in line with its intent (p. 77).

Of course, this new intent is in the eye of the beholder, but there appears little doubt that the new administration was taking a different look at the balance between labor and management. *Fortune* magazine was quick to deliver the new message to its readers.

The new labor board tends to guard employers' rights more carefully and, in Farmer's [Chairman of the NLRB] words, to follow a "rule of realism." Thus, Farmer suggests that automatic condemnation of every employer's statement to an employee about unionism is unrealistic. (January 1954)

Though the Eighty-third Congress left the text of the Taft-Hartley [Act] unchanged, the effective meaning of the law has been altered considerably in recent months. For the first time in the nineteen-year history of the National Labor Relations Board, a majority of its members are Republican appointees. And though all three of these appointees—Chairman Guy Farmer, Philip Ray Rodgers, and Albert Beeson—have staunchly insisted that they are there to interpret the act, not to represent management, management is unquestionably getting a better break at NLRB than it has had in many years. (October 1954)

The intent of this brief review has been to point out how management thinking, as reported by the popular press, was changing. It would appear that the groundwork was being laid for the new strategies that have since reshaped industrial relations in this country. To complete the picture, the following section will highlight several of the key NLRB decisions that paved the way for the rise of many of today's union avoidance techniques. In addition to reviewing issues of free speech, we will look at changes in the determination of the appropriate unit for bargaining. The changing focus of the board toward these issues also thwarted unions in their efforts and aided companies in their quest to remain nonunion.

Legislative and Decisional Analysis

To provide the political/legal context for the chronological trends cited, we will examine several provisions of national labor relations legislation dealing with employee organizing activities as interpreted and applied by the National Labor Relations Board. Changes in the national labor statute and in the prevailing political forces during the decades of the 1940s and 1950s produced changes in the board's interpretation and enforcement of the National Labor Relations Act.

Electioneering and Free Speech

Employees vote after they are provided with information enabling them to make an informed judgment, and the latitude given to employers in their efforts to influence employees' votes is viewed as a crucial element in the outcome of an election. Although the Getman et al. (1976) study did not support this contention, the finding is not necessarily consistent with beliefs of practitioners or other researchers. (See the chapter by Freeman in this volume for a summary of relevant studies.) The issue of employer free speech is paramount to the basic techniques used by management in its union avoidance strategies.

In its 1935 text, the National Labor Relations Act contained no explicit provision regarding freedom of expression.[2] However, the following analysis illustrates NLRB and judicial interpretations of the extent to which an employer could attempt to influence the outcome of a representation election. Within the context of a 1939 union organizing campaign, the following statements were made by employer representatives to various employees:

"You know, once before they tried to unionize this place. It was a year back and it didn't work."

(warning) "Well, don't you sign (an application for membership in the union). They are just a bunch of racketeers. They are trying to collect dues, charge you $2.00 a month and it won't get you nowhere in the end. They won't secure you a job."

A statement indicating that the employer was operating on a very small margin of profit, and that if the plant was organized the employer would be able to accept only the most profitable orders and hence would be unable to operate for more than six months a year.

"It really don't pay for you to join a union. You won't gain anything by it and you will have everything to lose."

The following exchange: (employer representative) "I heard that you are the leader (referring to the Union)." (employee) denied that but admitted to being a shop committee member. (employer representative) "What's the matter? Haven't you been treated well? You got a raise. Then why are you turning against us by joining a union?" (*The Federbush Co., Inc.*, 24 NLRB 829, 832–833 [1940])

On that record, the board concluded that the employer, "by making anti-union statements to its employees, by disparaging the leaders of the Union and their motives, by threatening to close the plant part of the year if employees organized (and by other, related conduct), had interfered with, restrained, and coerced its employees in the exercise of the rights guaranteed in Section 7 of the Act" (*supra* [*The Federbush Co., Inc.*, 833]).

Notwithstanding the Supreme Court's admonishing the board in 1941 to avoid findings of statutory violations based solely on employer oral or written speech to employees regarding union organizing efforts (*National Labor Relations Board v. Virginia Electric and Power Co.*, 314 U.S. 469, 479–480 [1941]), the board continued its prior policy of carefully scrutinizing employer speech.

Within the context of a 1944 union organizing campaign an employer engaged in the following conduct:

informing employees that a wage increase might be abandoned because they had joined the Union and the employer might get into trouble by granting the increase "in the face of the Union"

telling employees that although the employer had no objection to its employees joining the union, a customer of the employer refused to have its work done in a union plant so that if the employees unionized, the customer might withdraw its business and, if that occurred, the employer would probably have to close because that customer represented about 95 percent of the employer's work

inquiring of an employee as to how long the employees had been members of the union and how many employees had joined the union. (*A. J. Showalter Co.*, 64 NLRB 573, 575–578 [1945])

On the basis of the entire case record, the board concluded that the employer's statement regarding the loss of a customer constituted a warning that job security depended upon withdrawal from the union and, as such, was coercive and not protected by the constitutional guarantee of free speech.

It is now well settled that an employer's fear of economic reprisal, or loss of business, resulting from the unionization of his employees, does not justify the commission of unfair labor practice.

The board also concluded that the employer's statements regarding the wage increase suggested that the union might be an obstacle to the granting of the increase. Such employer conduct, together with the interrogation of an employee regarding the union, were held to be violations of Section 8(a)(1) of the Act [*A. J. Showalter Co.*, 578–580].

In the 1947 Taft-Hartley amendments to the act, Section 8(c) was added as follows:

The expressing of any views, argument, or opinion, or the dissemination thereof, whether in written, printed, graphic, or visual form, shall not constitute or be evidence of an unfair labor practice under any of the provisions of this Act, if such expression contains no threat of reprisal or force or promise of benefit.

After enactment of this section the board assumed, in the 1950s, a forgiving posture in evaluating employer speech within the context of employee organizing campaigns. The following employer statements were found by the board to be "privileged electioneering" constituting "prophecy that labor trouble might bring financial difficulties which would in turn prevent the Employer from continuing to operate":

the Union might strike to force the employer to capitulate to its demands
the "Company has no intention of yielding to any such pressure"
everybody "knows that strikes mean trouble, misery, lost work and lost pay"
the Company "is not required to grant (the Union's) request, but is only required by law to bargain in good faith"
if everybody's wages were raised "with the result that the cost of producing hose would be so high that we could not obtain any orders, the mill would then be forced to close"
"I am not saying that if the Union came in here that this thing would necessarily happen. I certainly hope it wouldn't." (*Silverknit Hosiery Mills, Inc.*, 99 NLRB 422, 424 [1952])

In a 1954 decision, the board viewed as "merely an expression of the Employer's legal position" a statement made to employees in the context of a pending board election that the employer believed the board's unit determination was wrong, that the only means through which the employer could obtain redress, if the union won, would be by a refusal to bargain (a correct statement of the law), and that a year or two might be required before the courts could review a board order to bargain (*Esquire, Inc.*, 107 NLRB 1238, 1239 [1954]). In a 1955 decision, an employer representative stated that the alien employees might be deported by the Justice Department if they joined the "Communist" union, and that the union, if it won the election, would control hiring and would replace the present employees with persons having greater union seniority and with allegedly undesirable persons. In concluding that such employer statements were privileged under Section 8(c) and did not constitute unprotected threats of reprisal the board noted:

We can find no threats of reprisal in these statements. (The Employer) merely opined concerning the possible actions of third parties, completely detached from (the Employer), should the employees continue their adherence to the Union. The statements contained no threat that (the Employer) would take any steps to induce the happening of predicted events. (*Southwestern Co.*, 111 NLRB 805, 806 [1955])

These decisions of the board were not mandated by the language of Section 8(c). By its terms, Section 8(c) provided that speech could not constitute and could not be evidence of unfair labor practices. However, the board's 1950 approach applied the Section 8(c) protection to employer speech in both unfair labor practice proceedings and in preelection conduct representational cases not involving allegations of unfair labor practices. [Cf. *Silverknit Hosiery Mills, Inc., Esquire, Inc.*]

By its extended application of the protections offered to speech by Section 8(c) in the 1950s, the board gave employers access to additional tools to defeat employee organizing efforts. This approach deemphasized the effort of the board in the 1940s to establish for employees a preelection atmosphere free from potentially coercive elements. In the 1950s, the board appeared to ignore the employer-employee context in which employer speech was delivered and thereby avoided finding such speech to be threatening or coercive. The board's approach to permissible employer electioneering during this decade reflected the exercise of discretion grounded as much in inclinations fostered by political philosophy as in the language of the statute.[3] This was also the case in decisions concerning bargaining unit determinations.

Bargaining Unit Determinations

The determination of the union appropriate for purposes of collective bargaining is also central to the ultimate success of a labor organization's efforts to achieve a majority vote of employees during an organizing drive. Section 9(b) of the 1935 statute empowered the board to decide, "in order to assure to employees the fullest freedom in exercising the rights guaranteed by [the statute], the unit appropriate for the purposes of collective bargaining. . . ." In the Taft-Hartley amendments to the National Labor Relations Act, the following was added:

In determining whether a unit is appropriate for the purposes specified in subsection (b) the extent to which the employees have organized shall not be controlling. (Section 9(c)(5))

What was the impact of this legislative change upon bargaining unit determinations? How did board decisions affect the constituency in which a labor organization would have to garner majority support in order to become the bargaining representative? In its pre-Taft-Hartley precedent, the board, in exercising its Section 9(b) unit determination prerogative, appeared to actively encourage success of a labor organization's election efforts by relying upon the extent to which the organization had marshaled employee support prior to the election. Thus, in 1943, when a labor organization petitioned the board for a unit of one department (tailors doing clothing alterations) of a retail store having the traditional number of multiple departments, the board determined as follows:

Assuming, without deciding, that a store-wide, industrial unit will best effectuate the purposes of the Act, we note that no labor organization claims to represent the employees in such a unit. We believe that collective bargaining should be made an immediate possibility for the employees in the busheling rooms [the tailors], without requiring them to await the uncertain date when the employees may be organized in a larger unit. We find accordingly that the employees in the busheling rooms constitute an appropriate unit. However, our finding in this respect does not preclude a later determination at another stage of self-organization that a larger unit is appropriate. (*May Department Stores Co.*, 59 NLRB 669, 672 [1943])

That board approach of facilitating employee organizing activities was also reflected within the context of retail store chains. Thus, where one employer operated stores in the state of New Hampshire, and a labor organization petitioned the board for a unit of the stores in only one city, Manchester, within the state chain, the board, after noting that "the extent of the Union's present organizational activities is limited to Manchester," determined that the single-city unit sought by the labor organization was appropriate on the basis of the following rationale:

Whenever possible, it is obviously desirable that, in a determination of the appropriate unit, we render collective bargaining of the Company's employees an immediate possibility. There is no evidence that a majority of the other employees in the State of New Hampshire belong to any union whatsoever, nor has any other labor organization petitioned the Board for a certification as representative of the Company's employees on a State-wide basis. Consequently, even if the employees in the city of Manchester do not constitute the most effective collective bargaining unit, nevertheless, in the existing circumstances, unless they are recognized as a separate unit, there will be no collective bargaining agent whatsoever for these workers.

At the present time, and in view of the existing state of labor organization among the employees in the State of New Hampshire, in order to assure to the employees in the city of Manchester the full benefit of their right to self-organization and collective bargaining, we find that all employees of the Company employed in its Manchester, New Hampshire stores. . . , constitute a unit appropriate for the purpose of collective bargaining, within the meaning of Section 9(b) of the Act. (*First National Stores, Inc.*, 55 NLRB 1346, 1348 [1944]).

In its pre-Taft-Hartley unit determination posture, the board emphasis upon fostering the establishment of collective bargaining relationships by deciding upon units coextensive with the petitioning labor organization's degree of support within employee groupings avoided consideration of such employer-related unit determination interests as the administrative structure of the business enterprise and the deployment of personnel functions existing before a union's organizing efforts.

After the Taft-Hartley inclusion of Section 9(c)(5), the board's unit determination approach changed to a degree not mandated by the legislative amendment. Notwithstanding the unit wishes of a petitioning labor organization based upon the extent to which it had acquired employee support for designation as bargaining representative, the board analysis of unit determination issues focused upon employer-related interests. Thus, where an employer owned and operated a corporate division of eighteen stores in a 230-mile stretch of southern California and a labor organization petitioned for two separate units, one store in Bakersfield and two in San Diego, the board found the following factors relevant in determining that the only appropriate unit was that encompassing all retail sales employees of all the employer's stores in its southern California division:

• all stores were identical in architectural design and internal arrangements;

• all stores sold the same kind of merchandise;

• all stores were centrally administered through a regional office;

• many aspects of the stores' operations were uniform . . . including pricing and interstore transfer of merchandise; and

• advertising, training, and personnel policies were centrally formulated and administered with uniform wages and hours and a division-wide seniority system.

Emphasizing the high degree of operational centralization, explicitly discounting the geographic separation and, without reference to any consideration of the extent of the petitioning local organization's employee support, the board found appropriate the largest possible unit. (*Robert Hall Clothes, Inc.*, 118 NLRB 1096 [1957]. See also *Father and Son Shoe Stores, Inc.*, 117 NLRB 1479 [1957])

The board policy, reflecting its post-Taft-Hartley shift of emphasis, was stated in the following terms:

The Board has held in cases involving chains of retail stores, that, absent unusual circumstances, the appropriate bargaining unit should embrace employees of all stores located within an employer's administrative division or geographical area. (*Robert Hall Clothes, Inc.*, 1098)

The extent of employee support for a labor organization within groupings smaller than the employer's administrative division or geographical area was not considered as either an "unusual circumstance" or a factor of relevance to be balanced against employer interests suggesting broader unit determinations. Although the 1947 enactment of Section 9(c)(5) reflected legislative intent to overrule board unit determinations supported only by extent of organization, that amendment was not intended to preclude the board's consideration of extent of organization as one factor in such determinations. (Cf. Decision of United States Supreme Court in *National Labor Relations Board v. Metropolitan Life Insurance Company*, 330 U.S. 438, 441–442 [1965]) The board's apparent tendencies in the 1950s to ignore the relevance of extent of organization in unit determination proceedings reflected more of a shift in political philosophy than a legislatively mandated posture.[4]

Conclusion

Our analysis has shown that political and legislative issues created an atmosphere and environment that not only allowed but encouraged corporate executives to again actively oppose the unionization of their workers. It would appear that this new management strategy has proved successful. Since the mid-1950s, union membership as a percentage of the nonagricultural work force steadily declined. This is not to imply that management actions were in any way the sole cause for this decline, but they cannot be ignored. There is little question that increased sophistication on the part of management has made union organization more difficult.

The present-day relevance of this historical analysis constitutes a clear message to those with interests in the progress of employee organizing efforts: political power is the touchstone. The political pendulum swung toward management, which altered its practices in response. If unions are to regain their strength they must once again become influential in key appointments to the NLRB and in shaping any new legislation. But they cannot rely solely on the legislative or judicial arms of the government to remedy their plight. If they are successful in regaining political clout, they must put together an integrated approach to combat the sophisticated union avoidance strategies used by corporate executives.

Notes

1. The Bureau of Labor Statistics calculated the peak year to be 1954, while the National Bureau of Economic Research reported it to be 1953 (Blum 1968).

2. Section 8(a)(1) of the 1935 act, left intact in the 1947 amendment, made it an unfair labor practice for an employer "to interfere with, restrain, or coerce employees in the exercise of the rights guaranteed in Section 7." Section 7 provided employees with "the right to self-organization, to form, join, or assist labor organizations, to bargain collectively through representatives of their own choosing. . . ."

3. In the early 1960s, applying the National Labor Relations Act as it had existed since the 1947 amendments, the board abandoned its 1950s latitude of speech posture and announced a new policy: "We shall look to the economic realities of the employer-employee relationship and shall set aside an election where we find that the employer's conduct has resulted in substantial interference with the election, regardless of the form in which the statement was made." (*Dal-Tex Optical Company, Inc.*, 137 NLRB 1782, 1787 [1962]). In *Dal-Tex Optical*, the board reversed its prior application of the Section 8(c) protections to preelection employer-conduct cases not involving unfair labor practices, thereby reversing such 1950 cases as *Esquire, Inc.* Applying its economic reality test and emphasizing the statutory goal of providing employees with an unencumbered atmosphere in which to decide upon organizing, the board began to carefully scrutinize and to hold as impermissible employer electioneering statments which would have been adjudged as mere expressions of opinion or legal position in the 1950s. (Cf. *Dal-Tex Optical Co., Inc.*, at 1785–1787).

4. Although beyond the chronological scope of this analysis, the board's unit determination approach in the early 1960s supports the view that national political trends may be a compelling basis for board legal judgments. Between 1957, the year of the *Robert Hall Clothes, Inc.* case and 1962, there were no relevant legislative amendments relating to the board's unit determination prerogatives. Nevertheless, with the change in the national administration and, thus, new appointments to the board, a case came before the board where, within the context of a chain of nine retail stores in New York and New Jersey, an administrative division of the employer, a labor organization petitioned for a one-store unit. The board, upon finding factors supporting the propriety of both a divisionwide unit and a one-store unit, the latter including the fact that no labor organization sought a unit broader than the one store, determined that the petition for the one-store unit was appropriate. (*Sav-On-Drugs, Inc.*, 137 NLRB 1032 [1962]) The following quotation from that decision is pertinent:

Reviewing our experience under that policy we believe that too frequently it has operated to impede the exercise by employees in retail chain operations of their rights to self-organization guaranteed in Section 7 of the Act. In our opinion that policy has overemphasized the administrative grouping of merchandising outlets at the expense of factors such as geographic separation of the several outlets and the local managerial autonomy of the separate outlets; and it has ignored completely as a factor the extent to which the claiming labor organization had sought to organize the employees of the retail chain. We have decided to modify this policy and to apply to retail chain operations the same unit policy which we apply to multiplant enterprises in general. Therefore, one of two or more retail establishments making up an employer's retail chain is appropriate will be determined in the light of all the circumstances of the case. (*Sav-On-Drugs, Inc.* 1033)

References

Blum, Albert A. "Why Unions Grow." *Labor History* 9 (Winter 1968).

Cooke, William N., and Frederick H. Gautschi III. "Political Bias in NLRB Unfair Labor Practice Decisions." *Industrial and Labor Relations Review* 35 (July 1982).

Foulkes, Fred K. "Large Nonunionized Employers." In *U.S. Industrial Relations 1950–1980: A Critical Assessment*, edited by Jack Steiber, Robert B. McKersie, and D. Quinn Mills. Madison, Wis.: Industrial Relations Research Association, 1981.

Foulkes, Fred. K. *Personnel Policies in Large Non-Union Companies*. Englewood Cliffs, N.J.: Prentice-Hall, 1980.

Getman, Julius G., Stephen B. Goldberg, and Jeanne B. Herman. *Union Representation Elections: Law and Reality*. New York: Russell Sage Foundation, 1976.

Kochan, Thomas A., and Peter Cappelli. "The Transformation of the Industrial Relations and Personnel Function." In *Internal Labor Markets*, edited by Paul Osterman. Cambridge: MIT Press, 1984.

Kochan, Thomas A., and Robert B. McKersie. "Collective Bargaining: Pressures for Change." *Sloan Management Review* 24 (Summer 1983).

Seeber, Ronald L., and William N. Cooke. "The Decline in Union Success in NLRB Representation Elections." *Industrial Relations* 22 (1), 1983.

Spielman, Lester. "The Taft-Hartley Law: Its Effect on the Growth of the Labor Movement." *Labor Law Journal* 13 (April 1962).

5   The Growth and Nature of the Nonunion Sector within a Firm

Anil Verma and
Thomas A. Kochan

The growth of the nonunion sector of the American economy has been one of the most significant developments in U.S. industrial relations since the 1960s. The corresponding decline of the union sector has attracted widespread attention from managers, union leaders, academics, and workers. Each of these groups has widely varying perspectives on this development. Yet the need to understand and explain the nonunion growth is shared by everyone, albeit for different reasons.

Several explanations have been offered to explain the decline of the union sector, many of which are discussed in other chapters. It has been pointed out that most of the growth in the economy since 1960 has been in industries that have high proportions of technical, professional, and white-collar workers who are less prone to unionization than blue-collar workers. The high growth rates of these firms have allowed them to be innovative in responding to the needs not only of these professional and technical workers but to their blue-collar workers as well. Other explanations point to the stagnation and economic decline in industries where unions have traditionally been strong. The shift in the composition of the labor force toward younger, skilled and female workers is another factor cited in this regard. All these explanations involve aggregate changes in the economy or other parts of the external environment.

While, as Henry Farber points out, these trends have contributed to the overall effect, they do not adequately explain declines in unionization among blue-collar workers *within* manufacturing firms. The Freeman and the Klein and Wanger chapters in turn focus on the effects of declining union successes in representation election processes in the face of aggressive managerial opposition. Yet part of the explanation is so far unaccounted for, namely the role of managerial strategies and policies that reduce the incentives of employees to organize before an election process is even started. Thus, a micro- or organizational-level analysis, supplemented by a historical tracing of the development of management strategies, is needed not only to supplement the analysis of sectoral and occupational shifts but to capture the independent role played by management policies and strategies.

This chapter provides a case study of one large manufacturing conglomerate currently half union and half nonunion. While it is clearly a case study of a single firm, data collected elsewhere lead us to believe that it serves as a prototype for many large diversified conglomerates that have expanded through acquisitions and new plant openings over the past twenty years. In the first section, a historical sketch of the company provides background and describes the evolution of the company's current nonunion strategy. The second section contains an analysis of labor costs across the union and nonunion plants. The third section profiles the union and nonunion plant-level industrial relations systems of the firm. All of this shows that the company's current strategy does not represent any shift in management philosophy, but rather capitalizes on new human resource management policies that both make good business and employee relations sense and are effective in reducing the incentives for employees to unionize. The last section discusses some implications of these findings for the labor movement.

A Historical Profile

The roots of the corporation go back to 1901 when a small company began to manufacture screws with twenty-nine employees and a capital of $2,500. It began to acquire the shape of a modern corporation in 1926 when it was renamed in honor of its president. Today this firm has grown to over 94,000 employees in 300 locations in fourteen countries. Sales in 1982 reached $6 billion, placing the corporation among the top 150 manufacturing companies in the world. The company manufactures a wide range of industrial products, the main lines of business being automotive parts, high technology electronics, and other industrial products such as compressors, valves, and pumps.

The company's history can be organized into three periods. The first, which may be called the early years, spans the period from 1901 when the company was founded to 1933 when one of the most eminent presidents of the company retired. The second, from 1933 to 1958, saw the company grow into a mid-sized corporation. The third, from 1958 to the present, began with the company merging with another manufacturer. Each of these periods also captures a number of significant developments in industrial relations.

The Early Years: 1901–1933

From 1901 until 1915 the company was primarily engaged in the manufacture of automotive parts. All manufacturing was located in one unorganized plant. In 1915, the founder became the president of this fledgling organization and began expanding into aviation parts, a market that developed during World War I. During this time, the company remained highly centralized. When the founder retired in 1933, the company had five plants (four in the United States and one in Canada), all of which were unorganized.

This first period in the company's history appears to have laid the foundation for the nonunion, proemployee philosophy that was developed to the full during the second. No data are available on union attempts to organize any of these plants nor on management strategies to deal with it. But oral historians within the company suggest that employees were treated like members of the corporate family. Plant relations were informal and managers knew most workers by their first names. There was also a heavy emphasis on social activities such as picnics, Christmas dinners, and the like.

Consolidation: 1933–1958

In 1933 a new president took over leadership of the company, after which the company grew manyfold in size. He developed and pursued a nonunion, proemployee philosophy so relentlessly that its effects can still be seen in the company. When in 1941 a new plant was opened to expand the aircraft parts manufacturing capacity, business operations grew significantly. Revenues of the company grew rapidly during World War II and thereafter. Sales reached a wartime peak of $33 million in 1944. The postwar sales level of $64 million (in 1946) grew to $300 million by 1953.

Industrial Relations

The industrial relations philosophy was shaped single-handedly by the company president who, by the 1940s, had become a leading figure in the corporate world. In his view, unions were both unnecessary and undesirable in the workplace. He believed in strong direct contacts between employer and employees and felt that a third party such as a union was an outsider which had no role to play within the plant. There was no problem, he preached, that "men and management" could not solve together. The presence of a union, therefore, could only do harm by driving a wedge between "men and management." He was also a fierce anticommunist and pro–free enterprise spokesman who harbored strong suspicions about the labor movement being mixed up with the Communists. When referring to workers, he insisted on calling them "my employees" rather than "members of the union" even after some unions had been certified in the company. Like many other business leaders of his time, notably Thomas Spates of General Foods, he believed that if management did a professional job of managing the personnel function, workers would have no reason to join unions. As Harris (1982) points out, in this view,

Unionization was neither inevitable nor in some ways desirable, but an indication of managerial failure. It was unnatural, illegitimate, un-American, and to be resisted, within the law, by the more intensive practice of the sophisticated antiunionism of the 1920s progressives.

In the company, at least one initiative by the employees themselves and another by an international union had failed to get a union certified between 1933 and 1941. In 1941 the new plant attracted the organizing efforts of a major international union. The company fought these elections with extensive communication campaigns and improved working conditions. The union lost all its bids despite having spent large sums of money (by some accounts, a million dollars between 1941 and 1946). At first, only a weak internal (independent) union was evident. During the period 1941 to 1947, the plant saw ten elections and twenty attempts to organize the plant. Even though the chief executive remained opposed to the idea of any union at all, other members of his management team, particularly plant management, realized that the plant was going to organize eventually. Several managers began to promote the idea that an independent union would be a lesser evil than an international union. In the mid-1940s an independent union was formed, with some help from management, certified in 1947, and the union sector within the company was born. Another plant was organized by an international union a few years later. The example of setting up an independent union was then quickly emulated by three other plants where organizing efforts were strong. Thus in 1957, on the eve of a major expansion, the company with eight plants in all was about 80% unionized. All employees, except those in one plant, were organized by independent unions whose influence on the employer-employee relationship was overshadowed by the kind of informal contacts that the president had fostered during his twenty years in office. Independent unions were seen as the company's "own boys" and, therefore, despite philosophical opposition to unions, the company promoted cooperative working relationships with the independent unions. All this time, programs to maintain strong company-employee ties were vigorously implemented, symbolizing management's refusal to allow the formal relationship with the union to supplant its direct rapport with employees.

Growth: 1958–1983

In 1958 the company merged with another firm that had grown rapidly in the postwar years through the application of new technologies to sophisticated products used in space exploration and electronics. This merger not only increased the size of the company but started it on its way to becoming a diversified conglomerate, a character that guided its growth from 1958 on. The growth came from two sources: one was acquisitions, concentrated in the decade immediately after the merger; the second was opening new plants.

After the 1958 merger, the company acquired forty-two plants— almost half of the plants in the company today. The largest acquisition thrust came in the ten years after the merger. Nearly thirty plants were acquired in the 1960s, the majority being electronics and industrial products manufacturing. The pace of acquisition slowed to ten plants in the 1970s and fell to zero in the early 1980s.

During the 1950s and 1960s no company strategy on the union status of the plant or the company being acquired is evident from these numbers. In the decade after the merger, thirty plants were acquired, of which fifteen were unionized and an equal number were nonunion. However, between 1970 and 1980 ten plants were acquired, none of which are unionized. These numbers suggest that if the company does have a strategy to factor in the union status of a plant to be acquired, it did not evolve until the late sixties or seventies. Perhaps as a result of such a strategy, of the forty-two plants acquired, twenty-six or nearly 60% are unorganized. When asked directly about the role a plant's union status may play in the acquisition decision, a vice-president of the company said:

In reviewing a candidate for acquisition, we look much more at the employee relations component now than we did in the 1960s. For example, we assess the quality and "style" of management in the plant and review the cost of integrating the plant's benefits and wages with our own compensation. The union status itself plays no role in the decision but if it adversely impacts costs, it will be a consideration. The same is true of the decision to divest. We have a plant in the Midwest that is organized where we haven't got the concessions we wanted and I am sure we would be happy to find a buyer for it.

The acquisitions brought a new challenge to the industrial relations managers in the company. All the organized plants that were acquired except one were also organized by international unions. The company and its managers up until the 1950s were not experienced in dealing with international unions. Corporate management found extremely antagonistic labor-management relations in two acquired companies with international unions. Part of the initial task was to export the corporate philosophy of treating workers as employees of the company rather than as members of the union; this translated into greater accommodation with the unions even though they were international unions. No systematic assessment of labor-management relations in the acquired plants has been conducted, but it is generally believed that since acquisition, the labor-management climate has improved. The general willingness to accommodate and work with unions, both international and independent, is a dominant philosophy in the company today; its evolution can be traced, ironically, to the earlier president's vehement opposition to unions in favor of direct and personal contacts with employees.

It should be noted that all organized plants bargain separately and no single union represents a significant proportion of the organized work force of the firm. Thus, within the firm collective bargaining remains highly decentralized.

New plants opened by the company account for nearly half of the growth since 1950. In all, twenty-nine new plants were opened in the thirty-year period beginning in 1951. The major thrust came in the 1970s when seventeen new plants were established. While the emphasis in the sixties was on acquisitions, it shifted to internal growth in the seventies. In industrial relations, the late sixties and seventies also signaled the development of the nonunion or union-free strategy within the company. Of the seventeen plants opened between 1970 and 1982, all except one have remained unorganized. As we have seen, this was not a completely new idea in the company; management's philosophical opposition to unions was long-standing. What was new in this period was a unique strategy for implementing this philosophy. In fact, this firm, along with several others, was shaping a kind of industrial relations so unique and innovative that its impact would fundamentally alter the practice and understanding of industrial relations in the United States.

The company's history of how the modern nonunion alternative developed is a bit fuzzy, complex, and therefore difficult to sort out. Several related developments can be reconstructed, however. One way to understand change is to look at the forces pushing and pulling for change. The philosophical foundation laid down in the company clearly was one of the factors pushing for a nonunion option. The second factor was the company's desire to contain rising costs of labor in the union plants. (Later we will present some detailed analysis of labor costs within the company.) Another factor adding to the concern over rising labor costs was the stiff competition from imports, a relatively new development that was absent during the 1950s. Among the factors that may have been pulling in the nonunion direction was the development of expertise on how to maintain the nonunion status of a new plant.

In the early 1960s a number of key executives in both human resource and line departments became interested in the growing innovations in human resource management. Many of these innovations grew out of developments in the behavioral sciences. The person who became the vice-president of human resources in 1965 played a key role in decisions to experiment with new ways to manage the work force. He came from the electronics and high technology part of the company and was a keen innovator. Between 1961 and 1966, the company introduced organization development (OD) as a key concept in managing people. In the beginning, OD, with its emphasis on eliminating interpersonal conflict, was confined to management ranks. After 1965 the new vice-president began exploring ways to extend some of the OD concepts to the workers on the shop floor. In the late 1960s several external consultants were hired to work on a wide variety of employee productivity projects. In 1971 one of a long series of efforts undertook to restructure work along the lines of experiments in Scandinavia. Almost all of the successful efforts took place in the new nonunion plants; some early experiments were started in union plants but most were abandoned because of opposition or lack of support from the unions. By 1974 a well-articulated plan for restructuring work in *new* (and thus nonunion) plants had evolved.

Table 5.1
Plant age and employment by union status

	Age of plant	Average employment			
		1979	1980	1981	1982
Nonunion	18.40	246.8	246.4	258.0	213.7
Union	47.23	548.6	512.8	470.1	390.7
All plants	28.58	366.0	351.6	335.6	276.2

While the details of these plans vary somewhat across plants, all were expected to incorporate the following basic principles:

Organizing the work force into relatively autonomous work teams;

Rationalized wage systems based on pay-for-knowledge;

Some form of productivity "bonus."

Between 1960 and 1980, almost all the new plants opened by the company were so structured. Only one of those plants structured this way has so far been unionized. But if the work restructuring program had a union-avoidance potential, it was not well understood by management initially. As time passed, more and more operating managers were exposed to these concepts and the ability of such programs to motivate employees and improve communications in the plant was quickly recognized. It then became a vehicle for management to pursue its union-free objectives. By the mid-1970s, after a decade of experimentation with such methods, the company had clearly integrated its formerly separate strategies of increasing productivity and remaining union-free.

Largely as a result of the development of such a strategy, the company is now almost 50% nonunion. Data on employment and number of plants from 1979 to 1982 are presented in tables 5.1 and 5.2.

Table 5.1 shows the average age and employment in each of the four years. As expected, the average union plant is much older (forty-seven years in 1982) compared to the average nonunion plant (eighteen years). It may be worth noting that the average age of nonunion plants is likely to decrease in the next few years as more new nonunion plants are opened. The difference in the average age of the two sectors was twenty-seven years in 1980 and twenty-nine years in 1982.

Average employment in all the plants decreased over this period. The average plant size declined by 24% from 366 in 1979 to 276 in

1982. The decline in the union sector was 29% compared to 13% in the nonunion sector. In the union plants, the decline is attributable to layoffs occurring in the same number of plants whereas the change in the nonunion sector is due to more plants being opened as well as a decline due to the recession. Table 5.2 shows employment levels in the two sectors. The union sector has consistently lost employment, going from 16,458 in 1979 to 11,722 in 1982, a decline of 29%. As a percentage of total employment, its share went down from 59% in 1979 to 50% in 1982. Employment in the nonunion sector, by contrast, grew from 1979 to 1981. In 1982, it declined due to layoffs but at 11,753 it was higher than its 1979 level and for the first time since the early 1950s exceeded the union sector employment.

Analysis of Labor Costs

The growth of a nonunion sector within the company has several important implications for the company's economic performance. One of the most critical outcomes is the makeup of labor costs within the company. Most previous surveys have indicated that unionized firms pay 10% to 20% higher wages compared to nonunion firms (Ashenfelter 1976; Oaxaca 1975; Lewis 1963). However, in a survey of nonunion firms, Foulkes (1980) found that many successful large nonunion companies pay salaries that are frequently equal to or better than those available in the union sector. It is necessary, therefore, to determine the exact nature of relative wages in the two sectors of the firm. A survey was accordingly made of eighty-five plants located in the United States. Table 5.3 shows the distribution of these plants by region and industry. Six different measures of wage rates and benefits costs were used across the union and nonunion sectors: (1) Low Rate, defined as the wage rate for the lowest-paid occupation in the plant, (2) High Rate, defined as the wage rate for the highest-paid occupation in the plant, (3) Average Rate, defined as the average of all wage rates paid in the plant weighted by the number of employees at each wage rate, (4) Total Benefit Costs, defined as the costs of health benefits, pension benefits, company-sponsored benefits, legally required benefits and pay for time not worked such as vacations, holidays, absence for other reasons, and rest periods, (5) Total Labor Cost, defined as the sum of the average rate and total benefit costs. The analysis was performed in two stages. (Results are shown in table 5.4.) First, each component of labor costs was averaged separately for the union and nonunion

Table 5.2
Production and maintenance workers by union status

	1979		1980		1981		1982	
	No. of plants	Employment	No. of plants	Employment	No. of plants	Employment	No. of plants	Employment
Nonunion	46	11,355	46	11,335	52	13,416	55	11,753
Union	30	16,458	30	15,385	30	14,103	30	11,722
All plants	76	27,813	76	26,720	82	27,519	85	23,475
Union Share								
Employment		59%		57%		51%		50%
No. of plants		39%		39%		36%		35%

Table 5.3
Number of plants in 1982 by region and industry

	Nonunion	Union	Total
Midwest	16	15	31
Northeast	7	11	18
Northwest	1*	0	1*
Southeast	14	2	16
Southwest	17	2	19
Total	55	30	85
Electronics	23	6	29
Transport	10	8	18
Metal Fabrication	22	16	38
Total	55	30	85

*Merged with Southwest in the analysis.

sectors to assess the overall differential. Then the gross labor-cost differential was adjusted by comparing plants of comparable age, size, and similar geographical regions and industries. This was accomplished through multiple regression analysis.

Wage Rates

In 1982 the average low rate was \$8.51/hour in union plants compared to \$5.55/hour in nonunion plants (see table 5.4). This makes the union wage 1.53 times the nonunion wage, a rather large differential. Historically, this gap was higher in 1979 when the ratio stood at 1.59. Thus while the narrowing of union/nonunion wages is apparent, the process is rather slow and the gap is still large and significant. To test the independent effect of unionism on this wage rate, an ordinary least squares analysis was used to regress the low rate on union status, with controls added for plant size, age, region, and industry (see appendix A). These results show that after controlling for the effects of these other variables, the net effects of the union on the low rate are estimated to be 27.8% in 1979 and 23.7% in 1982.

As table 5.4 shows, there is no substantial differential in union and nonunion wages at the higher skill levels. In 1979, the union plant rate was marginally higher (9%) but this gap narrowed and was reversed in 1981 and 1982. In 1982 the nonunion high rate was about 2% higher

Table 5.4
Labor costs by union status (dollars per hour)

	1979	1980	1981	1982	% Increase 1979–82
Low Rate	5.72	6.33	6.64	7.03	23
Nonunion	4.24	4.81	5.28	5.55	31
Union	6.75	7.45	7.94	8.51	26
Ratio: Union/Nonunion	1.59	1.55	1.50	1.53	
High Rate	8.79	9.67	10.65	11.37	29
Nonunion	8.36	9.40	10.72	11.48	37
Union	9.09	9.87	10.58	11.25	24
Ratio: Union/Nonunion	1.09	1.05	0.97	0.98	
Average Rate	6.91	7.65	8.41	9.00	30
Nonunion	5.92	6.72	7.59	8.12	37
Union	7.60	8.34	9.20	9.89	30
Ratio: Union/Nonunion	1.28	1.24	1.21	1.22	
Benefits (Total)	2.79	2.99	3.46	4.12	49
Nonunion	2.09	2.29	2.72	3.25	56
Union	3.28	3.52	4.16	4.99	53
Ratio: Union/Nonunion	1.57	1.54	1.53	1.53	
Total Labor Cost (Av. Rate + Benefits)	9.70	10.63	11.87	13.12	35
Nonunion	8.02	9.01	10.31	11.37	42
Union	10.87	11.85	13.35	14.88	37
Ratio: Union/Nonunion	1.35	1.31	1.29	1.31	

than the union wage. The absence of any substantial wage differential at the high end of the wage distribution suggests that both union and nonunion plants operate in similar labor markets for skilled workers. The lack of any union effect is confirmed by the regression results (see appendix A).

In 1979 the gross differential in the average rate was 28% in favor of the union plants; by 1982 it had narrowed to 22%. Regression results (see appendix A) indicate that no significant union effects were present in 1979. In 1982 union plants appeared to have a positive 11.5% effect on the average rate.

Benefit Costs

In 1979 the total benefit costs in union plants were nearly 57% higher than in the nonunion plants. This differential has also, in keeping with other trends, narrowed a little to 53% in 1982. When plant size, age, region, and industry effects were controlled for (see appendix A), the union effect dropped to 23.9% in 1979 and 23.2% in 1982. The importance of benefit costs is underlined by their rapid escalation. A more detailed look at the various components of benefit costs is provided in appendix B. Health benefit costs show the greatest escalation (93% in nonunion and 98% in union plants) while pension benefit costs were the best contained (3% in nonunion and 17% in union plants). The only benefit component in which the union/nonunion differential decreased substantially was pay for time not worked, which rose 60% overall and 79% and 58% for the nonunion and union sectors, respectively. The union/nonunion ratio decreased from 1.59 in 1979 to 1.40 in 1982. The hours that go into the computation of pay for time not worked are shown in appendix C. Average hours of absence were best controlled, decreasing by 28% in this period. The union/nonunion differential also went from 30% in 1979 to 13% in 1982. The number of holidays increased very modestly (7% overall) and the ratio of union to nonunion benefits increased from 1.28 to 1.35. Vacations registered a larger increase—17% overall. The relative position of the union sector remained unchanged in 1982 compared to 1979. Daily rest and lunch periods showed no appreciable change.

Total Labor Cost

Table 5.4 shows a union premium which ranges from 35% in 1979 to 31% in 1982. In the regression analysis, union effects range from 10.5%

in 1979 to 14.7% in 1982 when region and industry effects are controlled for in addition to those of plant size and age. It is interesting to note that the union effect has increased during these four years although the overall differential has narrowed a little. This suggests that during this time more nonunion plants have been opened that pay wages better than the nonunion sector as a whole but not nearly as good as comparable union plants.

The results of the analysis of labor costs in this firm are consistent with the findings of many other studies at various levels of analysis, namely, that unions cause firms (plants) to pay a wage premium above the wage levels prevalent in comparable nonunion plants. The effect is greatest at the lower end of the wage distribution. Also, the union effect on benefit costs is greater than the union effect on wages. If union plants pay more to their workers, how is it that they are able to remain economically viable? There are a number of possible explanations.

Union and Nonunion Human Resource Management Systems

The idea that management may respond to unionization and the resulting hike in wages by improving work practices was first articulated by Slichter (1941) and later investigated by Slichter, Healy, and Livernash (1960) in their comprehensive study of management response to collective bargaining. Slichter (1941) suggested that, faced with unionization, management begins to search for more efficient practices. It rationalizes many ad hoc policies and streamlines planning and production methods. Slichter called this the "shock effect" of unionization on management. Clark (1980) investigated a number of plants in the cement industry and found that union plants were frequently more productive and that such increases in productivity derive in large part from a series of improvements in personnel and procedures. Although some evidence has been gathered to support the existence of a "shock effect," it is neither conclusive nor persuasive as an explanation for the historical behavior of this firm as reviewed earlier.

Another explanation of management response to unions is provided by those researchers who suggest that firms have created an alternative system of industrial relations or human resource management in which the union is absent. Such systems are designed to focus on effectively managing employees at the individual or small-group level in contrast to the "shock effect" view in which efficiency is obtained within a unionized context through the more effective management of systems and procedures at the organizational level. Foulkes (1980) provides a description of the nonunion industrial relations systems used in a select sample of large high-growth companies in the United States. The main point of such systems is to create an environment in which individual employees are satisfied and involved with their jobs. To provide greater satisfaction, innovative methods of compensation are used. More extensive communication and employee involvement programs provide for a work environment in which the employee can feel more involved. These two views, namely, the shock effect and the nonunion innovative response, are essentially competing explanations of the union-nonunion differences that may be expected.

To determine the nature of the union and nonunion differences in work practices within this company, a detailed survey of eight plants was undertaken. This survey includes plants that are nonunion but are not necessarily managed along the lines of innovative work structures. Of the eight plants, five are nonunion and three are unionized. Of the nonunion plants, two were opened in the mid-1970s and both are structured as described earlier. Of the other three nonunion plants, one was opened in the 1960s, the second in the 1950s and the third, dating back to the 1930s, was acquired by the company in the mid-1960s. These three plants are organized in a more traditional fashion. Of the union plants, one is represented by an international union and the other two are organized by independent unions. Products manufactured in all these plants are industrial products that go into automobile, aircraft, energy, and similar industries. Manufacturing processes such as machining, forging, casting, drawing, and heat-treatment of metal are predominant and describe the bulk of the production in these plants. The average employment in 1982 was 300 in the nonunion plants and 670 in the union plants. Consistent with the data reported in table 5.1 the smaller size of these nonunion plants reflects a companywide pattern.

Dimensions of Differential Work Practices

While the Foulkes (1980) survey of corporate policies varies in scope and level of analysis from ours, it does provide some meaningful insights into various dimensions along which differences in work practices may be expected. For instance, Foulkes stresses the innovative nature of compensation systems and the importance of communication and feedback programs in nonunion companies. A study of the construction industry by the Business Roundtable (1983) found important differences in the way work is assigned to workers in union and nonunion firms. Nonunion firms appear to have greater flexibility in hiring practices, job design and classification, and in work assignments. This study suggests that we also examine the personnel management and work assignment rules in the two sectors. Our survey therefore focuses on four dimensions along which the two sectors are expected to differ.

A. Compensation

The analysis of labor costs presented earlier showed that union plants pay higher wages and fringe benefits than nonunion plants. The data in table 5.5 on vacations, holidays, life insurance, sick pay, and health care coverage reinforce this general finding with more detailed data from the eight plants. The remaining items in table 5.5 take this result a step further by demonstrating that there are differences in the *structure* of union and nonunion compensation systems aside from differences in levels.

The most striking feature of nonunion compensation is a large percentage (63%) of production and maintenance workers who are paid on a salary rather than hourly basis. No bargaining-unit workers are on a salary system in the union plants. Another important difference is that two of the five nonunion plants use a "pay for knowledge" compensation system. No union plants report using this system.

While the incidence of cost-of-living allowance (COLA) is much higher in the union sector, the rate of COLA payments is nearly the same. The nonunion COLA adjustment at 2.25 cents/hour for every 1 point increase in the consumer price index (CPI) was slightly higher than the 2.07 cents/hour in the union plants. Also, 50% of the nonunion and 33% of the union plants reported some capping provision on COLA increases.

The two sectors also look very similar in their premium pay for second- and third-shift work. Plants are evenly split between the two modes of payment, namely, straight cents-per-hour and a percentage of the base wage rate. Overtime rates are higher in the union plants. Also, more employees are eligible for premium pay in union plants when work exceeds the normal workweek. About 20% of the nonunion plants and 33% of the union plants report some form of supplementary unemployment benefits.

Table 5.5
Compensation

	Work practice	Nonunion	Union
1.	Salaried payment for workers: (% employees)	63%	0%
2.	Pay-for-knowledge schemes	40%	0%
3.	COLA:	40%	100%
	Increase for every 1-point increase in CPI	2.25¢/hr.	2.07¢/hr.
4.	Premium pay for second shift:		
	plants paying by cents/hr.	60% @ 25¢/hr.	67% @ 22¢/hr.
	plants paying by % of the base rate	40% @ 7%	33% @ 8%
5.	Overtime rate of pay:		
	in excess of the designated workweek	1 1/2	1 2/3
	in excess of the designated workday	1 1/8	1 1/2
6.	Percentage of employees entitled to premium pay for weekend work in excess of the workweek	50%	67%
7.	Supplementary unemployment benefit (% plants reporting)	20%	33%
8.	Severance pay	20%	0%
9.	Percentage of employees on paid lunch time	57%	69%
10.	Vacation:		
	After 1 year of service (days)	9.4	10.3
	After 3 years of service (days)	12.2	16.7
	After 10 years of service (days)	18.6	26.3
	After 20 years of service (days)	22.0	31.3
11.	Holidays (number of days)	23.8	13.0
12.	Life insurance:		
	Insured amount	$ 9,000	$10,000
	% premium paid by the company	94%	100%
13.	Sick pay: amount and duration		
	Amount	$117/wk.	$150/wk.
	Duration	for 27 wks.	for 26 wks.
14.	Health care (% cost paid by the company)		
	Doctor's visit	84%	80%
	Prescription drugs	84%	93%
	Hospitalization	96%	100%
	Dental care	73%	100%
	Oral surgery	81%	100%
	Eyeglasses	33%	67%

In conclusion, it appears that union plants provide higher levels of benefits in most instances. In some cases, such as premium pay for shift work and the COLA payment formulae, the differences are not large. The most significant difference in the compensation systems is that nonunion plants have begun to pay many workers on the basis of monthly salaries and introduced pay-for-knowledge schemes.

B. Work Organization and Human Resource Allocation
The rules governing work organization and allocation of human resources influence the degree of flexibility management enjoys at the workplace in making such decisions. Here we examine several of the rules that affect the degree of flexibility.

The Structure of Work. Table 5.6 shows the number of job classifications and wage grades found in these plants. Union plants have many more job classifications (96) compared to nonunion plants (30). Some of this difference may reflect the more complex nature of products made in union plants. But given that the eight plants were chosen so that their products and processes were quite similar, the large number of classifications indicates that jobs in union plants are more narrowly defined. Nonunion plants employ fewer job classifications and distribute workers in fewer wage grades (9) than union plants (14 wage grades). The number of job classifications in maintenance departments is also lower (4.8) as opposed to union plants (11.3). Within these departments, nonunion plants employ 38% of workers in broadly defined, multiskill categories such as "General Maintenance" or "General Mechanic." Only 1% of such multiskill workers in the union are so classified. Thus the overall assessment indicates that nonunion plants have wage and job structures that lend themselves to greater flexibility in the management of production.

Subcontracting. Nonunion plants have fewer limits than union plants on subcontracting work to outside firms. For instance, as table 5.6 shows, managements in all union plants have contractual obligations to meet with the union over subcontracting work. In the event of a cutback in production, union plants are more constrained in general to subcontract work than the nonunion plants. These rules do not appear to be a major issue in the eight plants in this survey because none of these plants used subcontracting to any significant degree to manufacture parts that could be made by its own workers. Nonetheless, the ability to subcontract is a potential resource that can be and frequently is used by other plants to increase productive efficiency.

Table 5.6
Work organization and human resource allocation

Work practice	Nonunion	Union
1. Job and wage structure:		
No. of job classifications	30	96
No. of wage grades	9	14
No. of job classifications in maintenance	4.8	11.3
% of employed classified as "General Maintenance"	38%	1%
2. Subcontracting:		
Obligation to meet with the union/employees	0%	100%
Reduced to zero before layoffs occur	40%	0%
Reduced proportionately	0%	33%
Reduced to zero except for some work	0%	67%
3. Percent of plants with the provision:		
to change the workweek duration	60%	67%
with some limit on the changed workweek	33%	50%
4. Employees eligible to request a transfer	100%	67%
% of employees requesting transfers	5–10%	10–25%
Eligibility criteria for transfers:		
Minimum service in the company	20%	0%
Minimum service in the department	0%	0%
Performance on current job	80%	33%
Willingness of the department to release	40%	0%
Cost of training in the new job	20%	0%
Minimum time on the present job	40%	100%
5. Temporary transfers:		
Higher pay on a higher-level job	40%	100%
6. Overtime:		
Employees can refuse overtime	80%	100%
Equalization	40%	100%
7. Dominant role of seniority:		
Promotion decisions	80%	100%
Transfer decisions	80%	100%
Layoff decisions	80%	100%
Seniority relaxation for temporary transfers	80%	67%
8. Supervisor prohibited from doing subordinates' work	0%	100%
9. Job openings and promotions:		
Posting job openings	80%	100%
Promotion from within:		
Production and maintenance workers	70–90%	75–100%
Supervisors	70–90%	35–60%
Office workers	60–80%	0–25%
Salaried workers	15–35%	0–25%

Provisions to Alter the Workweek. More union plants (67%) have provisions to shorten or lengthen the workweek to meet the demand for its products than nonunion plants (60%), but almost half the union plants place a limit (upper/lower) on the change that is possible. In contrast, nonunion plants place no limits on changes in the workweek.

Transfers. In all nonunion plants and most union plants (except one) employees are eligible to request a transfer to another job. The incidence of such requests is slightly higher in unionized plants. The major restraint on such lateral transfers in union plants is the requirement that the employee must spend some time on the present job before becoming eligible to request a transfer. In the past, this period has been no more than a few weeks, resulting in many employee requests in some plants. In nonunion plants, there are many more restraints on such movement. These range from minimum time on the job to the cost of retraining to the willingness of the concerned department to release the employee.

In the case of temporary transfers required to fill absent or sick employees' jobs or to shift production priorities, both union and nonunion plants appear to have similar flexibility in reassigning workers. The important difference is that while all of the union plants pay higher wages when the worker is transferred to a higher-paying job, only 40% of the nonunion plants report following this practice. Thus half of the nonunion plants continue to pay the worker at the same rate as the one he or she was transferred from. This helps nonunion plants to economize on labor costs.

Overtime. In 80% of the nonunion and all of the union plants, employees can refuse to work overtime. This in itself is not as significant as the practice of overtime equalization, which is required in all the union but only 40% of the nonunion plants.

Role of Seniority. The dominant role of seniority provisions governing personnel movement decisions are commonly considered to be the heart of collective bargaining agreements. In all the union plants, the most senior employee is favored in promotion, transfer, and layoff decisions unless a junior employee is a significantly better performer. Eighty percent of the nonunion plants reported similar practices. Given the small number of plants in our sample, this does not appear to be a significant difference. Abraham and Medoff (1983) report similar results using a much larger sample. Similarly, seniority provisions are allowed to be nearly equally relaxed in the case of temporary transfers in both union and nonunion plants.

Supervisor Fill-in. In all union plants, supervisors are explicitly prohibited from filling in for absent workers. In contrast, none of the nonunion plants report this policy. In fact, having supervisors fill in for missing workers appears to be a frequent practice.

Communication and Employee Involvement

Communication

The incidence of formal joint committees appears to be nearly the same in both sectors (see table 5.7). One plant in each group also reports use of a formal complaint procedure for unorganized employees. On the informal side, nonunion plants appear to practice more of an open-door policy to discuss grievances. Sixty percent of the nonunion plants and 67% of the union plants have some variant of a suggestion scheme.

Nonunion plants appear to stress more formal feedback from employees. Most nonunion plants conduct attitude surveys whereas none of the union plants report this practice. "Sensing sessions" are another informal or semiformal technique to elicit employees' response to the workplace. In a typical sensing session, a manager or several managers meet with small groups of employees to talk about job-related concerns. Employees can provide feedback to management and ask questions to get more information on plant operations, policy, and such matters. While there is no major difference in their use of this technique (80% nonunion vs. 67% union), from case-study evidence we found that the method is more effectively used in nonunion plants. Nonunion plants are smaller and permit managers to communicate more quickly with most employees. In union plants, the method is used much more selectively and is spread over longer periods of time because of the larger number of employees involved.

All the nonunion plants and 67% of the union plants report holding large meetings with the employees at the plant or department levels. The frequency of such meetings, an average of 3.14 per year in nonunion plants, was much higher than 1.33 per year in union plants. Again, smaller numbers in nonunion plants further accentuate this difference in communication with employees.

Involvement

In general, nonunion plants appear to be ahead of union plants in their use of employee involvement programs. The incidence of such programs (80% in nonunion vs. 67% in union) is not very different, but the

Table 5.7
Communication and involvement

Work practice	Nonunion	Union
Communication		
Nonunion complaint procedure	20%	33%
Open-Door policy to discuss grievances	100%	67%
Joint committees:		
Health and safety	80%	100%
Productivity	40%	67%
QWL	75%	60%
Industrial relations	20%	33%
Job evaluation	20%	0%
Training	20%	0%
Suggestion schemes	60%	67%
Attitude survey:		
Production and maintenance	40%	9%
Salaried workers	60%	0%
Sensing sessions:		
Production and maintenance workers	80%	67%
Salaried workers	80%	67%
Meetings with employees	100%	67%
Frequency of such meetings (number per year)	3.14	1.33
Involvement		
QWL or similar program instituted	80%	67%
QWL intensity index	2.4	1.3
Number of employees involved in QWL	50%	47%
Employee role in decision making [Scale: 0 (no program) 1 (no role). . . . 4 (complete authority)]		
Work procedures	1.70	0.83
Production decisions	1.65	0.41
Quality decisions	1.30	0.67
Material control	1.40	0.50
Safety and housekeeping	2.20	1.00
Personnel decisions	1.74	0.38
Number of social activities in the last year	3.00	3.33
No. of formal employee counseling avograms	0.40	0.67
No. of employee benefit plans	5.0	3.3
Relocation:		
Employee rights to relocate	20%	0%
Compensation for relocation	20%	0%

quality of design and implementation of these programs are not at all the same. For instance, measured on an overall index of the intensity of the program, nonunion plants score 2.4 in contrast to union plants' 1.3. The index is a 4-point scale, where 1 indicates low intensity and little impact on the way work is performed on the shop floor and 4 indicates the highest intensity in which work is completely restructured along the innovative designs discussed earlier. The percentage of employees involved in these programs in union (47%) plants is similar to that in nonunion plants (60%).

The content of each program was also measured in terms of the role of the worker in a number of decisions affecting his or her immediate work area. No points were allotted if there was no program in place, 1 point was used to indicate that the program was in place but ascribed no role to the workers, and 4 points indicated that the worker or the work team had full responsibility for the decisions. The work area responsibilities were subgrouped into six major decision areas: work procedures, production decisions, quality decisions, material control, safety and housekeeping, and personnel decisions. The average scores in each of these six decision areas are higher for nonunion than for union plants. This more detailed measurement supports the difference observed in the overall intensity index.

Three other measures of the quality of work life were employed: number of social activities, number of formal counseling programs, and the number of employee benefit programs. While union plants report more social activities and more formal counseling programs, nonunion plants have a somewhat larger number of employee benefit programs. These differences, however, are not really significant.

The overall summary of this survey is that nonunion plants appear to be ahead of union plants in the use of flexible work systems and informal and extensive communication and employee involvement programs. With the exception of pay-for-knowledge and all-salary compensation systems, none of the practices that are designed to increase flexibility in the management of human resources are totally absent in the union plants. Thus while we find no evidence in this small sample to support the traditional shock effect hypothesis, neither do we find convincing evidence that flexible work systems and extensive employee communications and involvement programs are only possible in nonunion settings. It would appear to us, therefore, that many of the differences in union and nonunion plant-level work practices or industrial relations systems could be reduced without turning either system upside down.

Learning from This Case

The story of this firm can be used to understand some of the fundamental changes that have taken place in industrial relations in this country. The evidence, both historical and statistical, can be used to infer a number of guiding assumptions and strategies that the company has consciously or inadvertently pursued. These are summarized below in propositional form so that they may be more fully tested in other contexts.

Proposition 1: The development and expansion of the nonunion sector within the firm is not a new objective but rather an articulation of management's long-term philosophical opposition to unions.

Proposition 2: The nonunion strategy is driven by both a philosophical opposition to unions and by the differences in labor costs.

Proposition 3: The nonunion strategy is carried out by opening new plants in low-labor-cost regions and keeping their size small enough to allow for implementation of an alternate human resource management system.

Proposition 4: The alternate human resource management system is based on:

(a) wages and benefits being competitive in the local labor market rather than matching union or overall industry levels;

(b) a structure of compensation that emphasizes fewer job classifications and wage grades and in some cases uses pay-for-knowledge or all-salaried payment systems;

(c) work organization and human resource allocation rules that emphasize flexibility in assigning jobs to workers and in moving people across jobs and skills needed for efficient production; and

(d) extensive communication with employees and involvement through active participation in small task-related groups.

Implications for the Labor Movement

This case study describes the history of a firm, a prototype of the conglomerate that has grown and diversified over the 1960–1980 period. For this reason, it is representative of the change that has taken place in industrial relations generally in the last two decades. What we learn from this case is more than just the story of one company; it illustrates a number of phenomena that have far-reaching implications for the labor movement. Clearly the development of a nonunion option in this firm has been slow and gradual. In the beginning, the unions that represent employees in this firm, like their management counterparts, were not fully cognizant of the full impact of the various components of what is now the nonunion strategy. However, more information on management strategy would have been of little or no help because the decentralized structure of the firm would have made it difficult if not impossible for the various unions to forge a joint response to the management initiatives. For the unions to meet the challenge would require a new coordinated structure in which they can work together. In this case, several independent and approximately ten different international unions would need to participate.

Nonunion status has been maintained in these plants not so much by aggressive suppression of unionizing efforts but rather by use of innovative human resource management techniques that appear to have reduced the incentive to unionize. This is a challenge that is relatively new to the labor movement born and nurtured in the 1960s and calls for the union movement to reexamine the nature of its appeal to the workers in these nonunion plants who appear to have lost interest in a labor movement built on aggressive opposition to management. The case suggests that workers today have acquired a taste for a cooperative, productive and informal workplace. A workplace characterized by conflict, legalistic and impersonal work rules, and lack of concern for the economic health of the organization is no longer attractive even with the lure of higher wages.

Our survey indicates that some of the differences in union and nonunion practices are not as large as is commonly believed. Thus, bridging the gap in efficient work practices may be within the reach of the union plants. However, it requires a change in priorities and the tactics employed. By redefining its priorities and redirecting its efforts the labor movement can contribute much toward transforming the workplace.

References

Abraham, K. G., and J. L. Medoff. "Years of Service and Probability of Promotion." Massachusetts Institute of Technology, 1983. Manuscript.

Ashenfelter, Orley. "Union Relative Wage Effects: New Evidence and a Survey of Their Implications for Wage Inflation." Princeton University, 1976. Mimeographed.

Business Roundtable. *More Construction for the Money.* Summary Report of the Construction Industry Cost Effectiveness Project. New York, January 1983.

Clark, Kim B. "The Impact of Unionization on Productivity: A Case Study." *Industrial and Labor Relations Review* 33 (July 1980): 451–69.

Foulkes, Fred. *Personnel Policies in Large Non-Union Companies.* Englewood Cliffs, N.J.: Prentice-Hall, 1980.

Harris, Howell John. *The Right to Manage.* Madison: University of Wisconsin Press, 1982.

Lewis, H. Gregg. *Unionism and Relative Wages in the United States.* Chicago: University of Chicago Press, 1963.

Oaxaca, Ronald L. "Estimation of Union/Nonunion Wage Differentials within Occupational/Regional Subgroups." *Journal of Human Resources* 10 (Fall 1975): 529–36.

Slichter, Sumner H. *Union Policies and Industrial Management.* Washington, D.C.: The Brookings Institution, 1941.

Slichter, Sumner H., James J. Healy and E. R. Livernash. *The Impact of Collective Bargaining on Management.* Washington, D.C.: The Brookings Institution, 1960.

Appendix A   Union effects on labor costs

	Controlled for size, age, region, industry	
	1979	1982
High Rate[2]	0.052	0.008
Low Rate[2]	0.278***[1]	0.237***
Average Rate[2]	0.063	0.115**
Total Labor Cost[2]	0.105*	0.147**
Total Benefits Costs[2]	0.239**	0.232**
Percent Benefit Cost[3]	0.058*	0.045
Wage Spread[2]	−0.389**	−0.416**

Note: 1. *** Significant at the 1% level; ** Significant at the 5% level; * Significant at the 10% level.
2. Coefficients roughly approximate percentage effects since the dependent variables were transformed from dollars and cents to the log of the rate.
3. Since these measures are ratios (rather than rates in dollars and cents) no transformation was done. Coefficients in these cases may be interpreted as net change in these ratios. Interpreting the union effect—example: A coefficient of 0.320 on the low rate implies that compared to a nonunion plan, union rates were 32% higher for plants of comparable size and age. Coefficients that are not statistically significant (not starred) could be nearly zero and, therefore, indicate no discernible effect.

Appendix B Benefit costs by union status (in dollars per hour)

	1979	1980	1981	1982	% Increase 1979–82
1. Benefits (health)	0.50	0.59	0.71	0.92	84
Nonunion	0.31	0.38	0.49	0.60	93
Union	0.63	0.75	0.93	1.25	98
Ratio: Union/Nonunion	2.03	1.97	1.89	2.08	
2. Benefits (pension)	0.56	0.48	0.51	0.60	7
Nonunion	0.36	0.32	0.34	0.37	3
Union	0.70	0.60	0.66	0.82	17
Ratio: Union/Nonunion	1.94	1.87	1.94	2.21	
3. Total employee benefit plans	1.30	1.32	1.52	1.87	44
Nonunion	0.88	0.91	1.11	1.28	45
Union	1.59	1.63	1.91	2.45	54
Ratio: Union/Nonunion	1.81	1.79	1.72	1.91	
4. Benefits (legally required)	0.66	0.70	0.83	0.94	42
Nonunion	0.60	0.64	0.75	0.87	45
Union	0.70	0.75	0.91	1.00	43
Ratio: Union/Nonunion	1.16	1.17	1.21	1.15	
5. Pay for time not worked	0.82	0.96	1.11	1.31	60
Nonunion	0.61	0.74	0.87	1.09	79
Union	0.97	1.13	1.34	1.53	58
Ratio: Union/Nonunion	1.59	1.53	1.54	1.40	

Appendix C   Hours not worked by union status

	1979	1980	1981	1982	% Increase 1979–82
1. Average hours of absenteeism	102.4	91.5	84.6	74.0	−28
Nonunion	89.2	82.8	77.2	70.3	−21
Union	116.3	101.4	95.3	79.5	−32
Ratio: Union/Nonunion	1.30	1.22	1.23	1.13	
2. Average hours of holidays	95.8	96.9	100.1	102.1	7
Nonunion	81.8	86.4	85.2	86.7	6
Union	104.8	104.9	114.6	117.6	12
Ratio: Union/Nonunion	1.28	1.21	1.34	1.35	
3. Average hours of vacation	107.4	107.1	115.0	126.1	17
Nonunion	86.1	85.5	90.9	104.6	21
Union	120.7	122.9	137.8	147.1	22
Ratio: Union/Nonunion	1.40	1.44	1.52	1.41	
4. Daily rest and lunch periods	27.4	27.3	27.1	27.1	−1
Nonunion	25.5	25.7	25.3	24.7	−3
Union	28.7	28.4	28.5	29.1	1
Ratio: Union/Nonunion	1.12	1.10	1.13	1.18	

Discussion, Part II

Richard Prosten: I have two questions about the company described by Verma and Kochan. First, to what extent have the acquisitions made by this company been in the sectors of the economy that are traditionally not organized? Second, to what extent is this a case study of a special or unique firm, or to what extent is the pattern described in this paper representative of other firms that grew through acquisitions and plant openings in the last twenty years?

Anil Verma: The acquisitions cover a wide spectrum of industries including some metal-working sectors that are quite highly unionized and some other industries where unions are not as common.

Thomas Kochan: This pattern is a prototype for many decentralized firms that grew through acquisition and new plant expansions in recent years.

Leslie Nulty: Isn't it a necessary condition to dominate or be reasonably successful in its market for a firm to maintain this strategy? Companies like IBM, Kodak, and Texas Instruments haven't suffered, so they can distribute a portion of their economic surplus to their employees and satisfy both employees and stockholders.

Thomas Kochan: Yes, most of those companies successful in this strategy have been in growth industries. But several recessions in the last twenty years have affected many of these firms, and we have not seen any major union growth when coming out of a recession. These firms have maintained their nonunion plants through some tough times. The human resource management systems in place in these plants have proved to be quite stable for a long period of time.

Lee Price: We have seen this in the auto parts industries. Firms set up a sister plant that is nonunion and then, when a downturn comes, they cut back more in union plants. It is a slow attrition process.

Thomas Kochan: That's right, but that is an old strategy. Studies by Sumner Slichter in the 1940s documented that type of behavior during the Depression. Basically, employers will always cut back the most in their highest-cost plants during times of excess capacity.

Jack Golodner: Union plants are not necessarily less productive. Since they are usually older, they are most likely to have older and less efficient technology. Maybe the nonunion plants have better equipment.

Thomas Kochan: That is also true. But I have to say that one has to stretch one's imagination quite far to find some evidence that would suggest the union plants on net are more productive than the nonunion plants. We specifically looked for evidence of what Slichter described as the "shock effect." But there is nothing in the union plants that would suggest to us there are significant offsetting factors that make them more productive than the nonunion facilities. You have to put yourself in the position of corporate executives asking themselves whether to allocate scarce dollars to the union or nonunion facilities. Given the option, they are clearly going to be inclined to put more resources into ensuring that the nonunion plants remain productive while allowing the type of attrition process Lee Price mentioned to take place in the older union plants.

Donald Ephlin: Regarding the innovative practices in the nonunion plants, are they due to resistance to change in the union plants or are the companies only going to their nonunion plants with these experiments?

Anil Verma: That's a good question. There is sufficient indication that both have happened. The company did try a few experiments in union plants in the early 1970s but none succeeded. Then there was a period when the company put most of its efforts into innovations in nonunion plants. Recently, the company is beginning to ask not only for concessions in union plants but also for more meaningful changes in job structures and employee involvement programs.

Jack Joyce: This brings us back to an earlier discussion of the need to take wages out of competition. My question is whether it is possible to do this through collective bargaining in a company like the one described here, or does it require the union to get involved with the company at the corporate or strategic decision-making level?

Thomas Kochan: Unless unions can get involved at the strategic level of this firm, they will not be able to take wages out of competition. That is, if this is to be dealt with, the employer policies that create these differentials have to be dealt with at their source. I recognize that it will not be easy to engage this type of company at this level, nor will any discussions that take place at that level necessarily be highly cooperative in nature. There will have to be intensive negotiations once the door is opened. If we can analyze the cost differences across these plants and see differences in work practices that make the nonunion plants more flexible and perhaps more productive, the company can clearly see these same things, and any discussions about changing their strategies will have to deal with these real differences in costs and practices. Also, given the inability of unions to organize plants of this company plant by plant, there is at the moment little chance of taking wages out of competition through the traditional means of organizing them one by one and negotiating more standard wage packages.

Rudy Oswald: If the union can't organize this company on a plant-by-plant basis as it is set up, somehow you have to change the overall climate in the company.

Michael Bennett: If we carry that argument one step further, look at it in the broader sense, and apply it to American companies in general, then are you saying that it is not possible to organize the unorganized on a plant-by-plant basis?

Thomas Kochan: I would apply that statement to this company, but I would not generalize to companies that do not have these types of positive employee relations practices.

Rudy Oswald: That is a very important statement; it bears repeating because if you are right it has profound implications for labor movement strategy. So would you repeat what you just said so that we all understand it? Are you saying that unions cannot organize this type of company by traditional means through the election process on a plant-by-plant basis?

Thomas Kochan: I believe that is correct. Unions have had almost no sucess in getting to an election or in winning an election in plants with these types of policies. I am not saying that this could not change at some point in the future if the political and social climate and the union and/or employer strategies change, but the record is quite clear that unless something changes, unions should not be optimistic about organizing significant numbers of employees of these firms by traditional means.

III

Corporate Investment and
Decision Making

6 Growing Problems for American Workers in International Trade

Lee Price

The American economy is rapidly becoming more integrated with the economies of other nations. Americans increasingly buy foreign goods, produce for foreign markets, travel abroad, work for foreign-owned companies, and so forth. From the viewpoint of American workers, these developments have profound effects on labor-management relations, employment, and income. If the present analysis is correct, only a reorientation of U.S. trade policy can make those effects positive.

Both exports and imports have grown more rapidly than domestic production, particularly since 1970. The share of U.S. production shipped abroad rose modestly from 7.5% in 1950 to 9.2% in 1970, but soared to 19.6% by 1980, before dropping back to 16.5% in 1982. The spurt in the 1970s was even more dramatic on the import side. Between 1950 and 1970, the ratio of imports to production climbed from 5.7% to 8.7%. The import ratio leaped to 21.4% by 1980 before dipping to 18.8% in 1982.[1] The increase in trade has occurred across a broad spectrum of manufacturing industries. By 1979, 42.3% of workers were employed in 2-digit manufacturing industries with an import share exceeding 10%, compared to only 13.2% of manufacturing workers as recently as 1972.[2]

Concerns of Workers: Stable Jobs and Improving Income

American workers have grave concerns about the effect of increased trade on their jobs, income, and relations with their employer—and they have good grounds for such concerns. International competition is putting increasing pressure on their wages and stratifying the distribution of income toward the most technically trained workers. Neither industries using new technology intensively, nor services, nor export promotion offers the prospect for more jobs with more trade. Moreover, increased trade has brought greater instability to the sales and employment of many manufacturing industries.

Increased trade influences wage patterns beyond the sphere of collective bargaining and probably intensifies the trend toward polarization of the distribution of income and skills in the U.S. labor force. For some time, the distribution of employment income has tended to become more unequal.[3] Some have accounted for this polarization by developments in technology *within industries* which stratifies the required skills and pay scales. Others focus on shifts in the labor force *among industries* toward services and high tech manufacturing that are said to have more stratified pay scales.[4] Increased trade favors more technically trained and skilled workers. Successful U.S. export industries generally tend to employ more of such workers, whereas those industries being displaced by imports tend to employ less-skilled workers.[5]

Increased U.S. participation in the international market can affect jobs as well as income. Jobs in both export and import industries have become more subject to the vagaries of foreign markets, exchange rates, and international credit. Robert Lawrence estimates that the U.S. manufacturing sector lost 513,000 jobs due to the decline in exports and as many as 240,000 more jobs from the rise in imports between 1980 and 1982. If correct, this combined drop in employment due to adverse shifts in trade would represent half of the 1.51-million decline in manufacturing employment that took place between 1980 and 1982.[6]

The situation is continuing to deteriorate for U.S. trade in manufactures. U.S.-manufactured exports slipped 3% from $144.0 billion in 1980 to a projected $139.3 billion in 1984. The volume of exports fell more than 3% because of inflation. In the same three-year period, imports are projected to climb 69%, from $131.5 billion to $222.6 billion.[7] Moreover, imports rose much more than that in volume terms because the real trade-weighted value of the dollar in terms of other currencies soared 52% between January 1981 and mid-1984.[8]

Unions have achieved a high degree of organization in industries with both gains and losses from expanded trade. High rates of unionization occur not only in industries troubled by imports such as steel and auto but also in industries with substantial net exports, such as aerospace, construction machinery, and heavy electrical equipment.

Although international competition has been affecting collective bargaining for some time, its effects are spreading and intensifying. Import competition has influenced bargaining in the textile and apparel industries for decades. More recently, to prevent even the stockpiling of imports in anticipation of a strike, labor and management in the steel industry devised the Experimental Negotiating Agreement to reach new contracts without the threat of strikes. The import surge during the 1959 strike in the steel industry had hurt both sides because some customers stayed with import sources after the strike ended.

International competition impinges on collective bargaining not only via the pressure of imports but increasingly via foreign rivals to U.S. exports and via U.S. multinationals' own foreign outsourcing. Two recent episodes, the six-month UAW strike at Caterpillar Tractor, which ended in April 1983, and a local agreement considered at a General Motors electric parts plant, represent case studies that probably could not have occurred ten years ago. Caterpillar emphasized throughout the negotiations that half its production is exported and that its chief competitor had become Komatsu of Japan rather than another U.S. company. Cat argued that Komatsu's labor costs fell well below Cat's U.S. costs and sought a substantial departure from the labor costs of the UAW pattern at other major companies. In the second case, union leaders at an IUE local in Warren, Ohio, were concerned because the work of their 7,000 members making wire harnesses for Packard Electric (a division of GM) was being shifted to several plants along the border in Mexico. Hourly labor costs at GM's Mexico plants stood at less than a tenth of Warren. Leaders of the local recommended ratification of a contract under which Packard would set up new plants in the Warren area at which the company would pay all new hires less than a third of the compensation package paid the current work force.

Both companies failed to achieve their goals in the latest bargaining round: the Caterpillar contract stayed within the pattern of previous key contracts of the UAW and the membership of the Warren local rejected the two-tier compensation structure. Since international competitive pressures in the construction equipment and auto parts industries shows no sign of abating, however, we can expect them to remain a part of future rounds of bargaining.

The now substantial international trade competition in these and other industries has implications for theories of collective bargaining similar to those often noted for industrial organization theories. As a matter of union strength, the percentage of the U.S. industry organized no longer suffices, any more than a concentration ratio of the top five producers' share of U.S. production necessarily reflects their oligopoly market power.

Discarding Myths to Develop Sound Policy

International trade has some undisputed benefits and some controversial effects. Everyone applauds both imports that have no domestic competition (such as scarce resources or agricultural products requiring a different soil or climate) and additional sales and jobs from exports. The major hitch comes with imports that compete with domestic products. On the one hand, consumers benefit from wider variety, lower costs, and the added stimulus to domestic producers to provide more competitive products. On the other hand, if allowed to surge, such imports can push many workers out of their jobs with little prospect for satisfactory employment elsewhere. The costs of that additional unemployment can easily exceed the benefits to consumers from more imports.

The trend of the U.S. economy toward further international economic integration appears inexorable. Any effort to reverse the tide by extracting the United States from its international economic ties would cause great damage to the U.S. economy as well as that of foreign nations. On the other hand, the future evolution of trade is not predetermined. In fact, the United States has a wide range of options for channeling the direction of continued integration. The direction chosen will influence the level and distribution of jobs and income and the health of the economy overall.

The U.S. debate over international economic policy has been dominated by free-trade advocates who downplay the growing problems for workers. These free-traders argue that the U.S. labor force as a whole has no grounds to be concerned because (1) wages are rising faster abroad; (2) the so-called high technology industries will boom to take up any slack; (3) the service sector employs most Americans and competes very well internationally; and/or (4) the biggest trade problem has been a failure to promote exports which the government is now correcting. Here I consider the validity of each of these contentions and come to some disturbing conclusions: wage differentials are becoming an increasingly important competitive factor in international trade; America's technology-intensive industries and its service industries are creating few new jobs in trade and have little prospect of doing so; and, finally, any sustained success in export promotion will aggravate problems in import-competing industries and will reduce total job requirements.

Despite the growing importance of trade, we have a very shallow understanding of the trends, on both a macroeconomic and sectoral basis. Where possible, I attempt to draw practical lessons for government policy and collective bargaining.

Narrowing Wage Gaps, but Rising Wage Competition

Traditionally, "internationalists" in the U.S. labor movement have hoped that helping to raise the pay of foreign workers would alleviate trade problems at home. Actual experience presents a paradox for this position: U.S. labor's trade problems have multiplied even as the gap between U.S. and foreign wages has narrowed. Accounting for this paradox goes a long way toward explaining the difficulties facing U.S. labor in international markets.

In recent decades, foreign pay scales have generally risen much faster than U.S. pay scales.[9] For example, manufacturing companies in the United States paid on average $2.41 an hour in compensation to production workers in 1960, $3.64 in 1970, and $12.26 in 1983. Labor costs in Germany escalated from 32% of the U.S. cost in 1960 to 56% in 1970 to 85% in 1983. At the same time, costs in Japan rose from 10% to 24% to 51%.[10] In 1980—before the major appreciation of the dollar—German, Swedish, Dutch, and Belgian hourly labor costs exceeded American costs by 22 to 33%. When the yen peaked in 1978, Japanese compensation attained a level equivalent to 67% of U.S. compensation.

In these comparisons, the magnitude of the labor cost gap two decades ago appears as striking as its rapid narrowing since then. To explain the paradox of rising trade problems despite a narrowing wage gap, one must explain why employers were willing to hire U.S. labor at ten times the cost of Japanese labor twenty years ago. The reasons for preferring U.S. workers despite their higher costs are vanishing faster than the wage gap itself. That accounts for the paradox that Japanese labor has become more attractive to hire even though its cost has risen five times more rapidly than the cost of U.S. labor.

Important "gravitational" forces have kept both production in the United States for the U.S. market and production for the U.S. market in the United States. These forces that have limited trade are now weakening. The U.S. market is losing the insularity that came from its uniqueness; foreign ingenuity is becoming more commercially successful; public investments in infrastructure and improving labor skills are making foreign production sites more formidable competition for the United States; the inertia of employers to produce for the local market is being replaced by a momentum to coordinate production internationally; and the costs to supply the U.S. market from abroad and foreign markets from the United States are falling.

Loss of Market Uniqueness

The relative prosperity of the U.S. economy itself once set this market off from the rest of the world.[11] Because the United States has had higher productivity across the breadth of the economy, it has enjoyed a higher standard of living. However, the gap is narrowing. Products once considered standard here but luxuries elsewhere have now become standard in Western Europe and Japan. As the consumption patterns of the other two areas have converged with those of the United States, products designed for the domestic market can be sold more readily in the other places and the products being designed for their markets have become more desirable in the United States.

Changes in the per capita gross national product provide a rough index of the convergence between the standard of living of the United States and that of Western Europe and Japan. The per capita product of Western European countries as a whole stood at 50% of that of the United States in 1950, 69% in 1960, 79% by 1970, and 86% by 1980. The per capita product of Japan in relation to the United States stood at 17% in 1950, 32% in 1960, 61% in 1970, and 73% in 1980.[12] Many of the newly industrializing countries (NICs) have also grown very fast relative to the United States, although they remain at much lower levels.

As the per capita product of these other regions has been catching up to the United States, their trade with the United States has grown rapidly. The rise in per capita production in the other regions is closely linked to the rise in wages and the development of mass markets and mass production there. As the scale of production in those regions has expanded, their unit costs have fallen and they can compete more effectively with U.S. production.

In addition, as the others' standard of living has come to more closely resemble that in the United States, mass production for those markets has become more up-scale and can more readily appeal to the U.S. market. Most of Japan's exports first succeeded in the local market.[13] The prosperous local Japanese market can now support, for example, mass production of autos and video cassette recorders in a variety and sophistication that could not have been supported two decades ago.

Improved Technological Prowess Abroad

Playing catch-up to the United States provides additional advantages for other countries, whether or not their standard of living is becoming comparable. They have the advantage of installing more up-to-date plant and equipment. In the case of some basic industries, foreign production levels have increased much more rapidly than U.S. production levels. In general, this indicates (but does not guarantee) that facilities in other countries are more modern than those here.

The synthetic rubber industry makes a good case study. U.S. production climbed from 1.6 million metric tons in 1963 to 2.6 million metric tons in both 1973 and 1978. In stark contrast, the rest of the world's production zoomed from 1.0 million metric tons in 1963 to 3.8 in 1973 and 4.1 in 1978.[14] Thus, while the United States had achieved three-fifths of its 1973 and 1978 production levels by 1963, the rest of the world produced in 1963 only a quarter of its 1978 level. It seems safe to assume that the bulk of capacity in the other countries was built in those fifteen years. Likewise, probably much of the U.S. capacity in 1978 was more than fifteen years old, although some modern facilities may have replaced outmoded former capacity.

For other industries, the comparison of 1963 production levels to 1978 production levels tells a similar story—high U.S. ratio and low ratio for the rest of the world (ROW). In crude steel production, the United States had a ratio of 80% while ROW had 50%; television sets: U.S. 83%, ROW 35%; and motor vehicles: U.S. 73% versus ROW 39%.

As other countries have been expanding their production capacities, they have also been working to improve the available technology. The data on expenditures on civilian research and development (R&D), number of scientists and engineers engaged in R&D, and number of patents issued reflect the growing technological prowess of foreign producers. In 1981, the United States devoted 1.69% of its GNP to civilian R&D compared to 2.30% for Japan and 2.53% for West Germany.[15] While the United States was devoting 31% of its R&D resources to military purposes, the other two countries devoted less than 5%.

Turning to total expenditures, we find that the combined spending on civilian R&D by West Germany, Japan, France, and the United Kingdom represented only 44% of the U.S. total in 1964 but 106% in

1979. Data on the number of scientists and engineers doing civilian and military R&D show the same trend. (Data on those in civilian R&D alone do not appear to be available.) The total for both types of R&D among the other four countries rose from 55% of the U.S. total in 1965 to 91% in 1979. These efforts are reflected in the growing proportion of patents issued to foreigners. The U.S. Patent Office granted foreigners 20% of all new patents in 1966 but 41% in 1982.

Importance of Public, Not Private, Capital Investments

The United States has accumulated a much larger stock of privately owned capital equipment per worker than most of the rest of the world. According to standard trade theory, that fact should make the United States competitive in capital-intensive products. In fact, differences in the capital required to make various products have little relevance in the modern international system. Companies from around the world can now obtain capital financing at roughly the same cost. In addition, multinational companies can put their equipment into place at roughly the same cost in any country.

To explain where a product is made today, capital intensity has far less importance than other factors. Although labor costs differ far more than capital costs across countries, labor costs do not represent the only major cost factor a company considers in deciding where to locate its production. The available labor must have sufficient skills. Absence of the necessary facilities for transporting parts, materials, and finished products can rule out many locations. Minimum requirements for electricity, fuel, and waste disposal further narrow the choice of sites.

Take, for example, a U.S. auto company considering whether to produce engines or to assemble vehicles in Mexico rather than the United States. Differences in the required capital per worker for the two operations would probably not tip the balance. Financing and installing the capital equipment should not vary much between the two countries. The real discrepancies come in labor costs, availability of skilled labor, and the infrastructure of transportation and public utilities. The Mexican advantage in the first can be offset by its disadvantages in the other two. As a result, Mexico may be more competitive in engine production if that entails sufficiently few skilled workers and less infrastructural support even if it requires more capital per worker than assembly.

The NICs of East Asia, Latin America, and elsewhere have been working to eliminate these obstacles to becoming competitive world producers of many manufactured products. They have ambitious projects to train labor, to build ports, roads, and rails, to generate more electricity, to acquire technology, and so forth. As these are accomplished, the relative importance of differences in labor costs grows.

End of Inertia

Sheer inertia has also kept production in the United States that might have been done elsewhere. Corporate bureaucracies make the decisions about where to locate production of most manufactured goods. If production in the current U.S. location is bringing a satisfactory return, a corporation may be slow to relocate abroad. Relocation brings new costs and risks: planning and overseeing the installation of new facilities in foreign lands, coping with a foreign government's policies, potential political upheaval, ensuring quality and timely delivery at greater distance, protecting against adverse shifts in exchange rates.

Despite their inertia, intensifying foreign competition is leading more U.S. corporations to consider foreign outsourcing as an alternative. The role of inertia can be seen in a comparison among the consumer electronics industry, the auto industry, and the "white goods" appliance industry. In all three cases, the U.S. companies have had market power through their control of distribution channels. As imports from Japan and later other East Asian nations began to take a growing share of the market for radios and TVs, U.S. companies shifted a large proportion of their production and/or parts sourcing to East Asia and Latin America. Faced with a similar loss of market share to imports from Japan, the U.S. auto companies appear to be moving toward a production/sourcing pattern like that in consumer electronics.

In terms of the relative costs of production and transportation alone there would appear to be as much basis for U.S. companies to have shifted "white goods" production abroad as for either of these other industries. Indeed, with its more stable product technology,[16] the "white goods" industry should be more easily established and operated at a distance. However, the import share for these products has remained modest. Between 1972 and 1980, the import share averaged less than 5% for refrigerators and freezers, less than 2% for air conditioning and commercial and industrial refrigeration equipment, and less than 1% for washers and dryers. In 1980, the three industries had product shipments of $13,543 million compared with imports of $281.5 million.[17] Thus, companies in those three industries have faced little pressure from imports to relocate abroad to supply the U.S. market.

Compressors, a key component of refrigerators and freezers, provide a noteworthy exception to the inertia of the "white goods" industry. In recent years, Japanese companies have developed compressor technology apparently superior in price and performance to the standard technology of compressors built in the United States. As the Japanese share of the compressor market has risen sharply, Whirlpool has decided to phase out its U.S. production, which employed about a thousand workers. It will either stick to its standard technology but reduce costs by moving production to its Brazilian affiliate or buy the compressors from Japan, Italy, or another U.S. company.[18]

Increased Feasibility of International Coordination of Production

The once strong tendency for the development of superior technology locally to contribute to production locally is breaking down. In the past the need for headquarters personnel either to adjust specifications rapidly or to oversee quality dictated that many products had to be made in the headquarters country. That is now changing with the declining costs and increasing ease of international transportation and communication. Companies based in the United States or elsewhere can now more readily link production in one country with markets in another.

Not long ago international telephone calls were expensive and would take hours to connect. Today, one can dial direct for most international telephone calls. To call direct from the United States to the major countries of South America in 1983 cost $1.18 per minute and $1.58 to those of East Asia. In 1960, the phone charge to both areas was $4.00 a minute—after the call was connected. In practical terms, the charge for a minute of telephone time to Brazil would buy ninety minutes of an American production worker's time in 1960 but only six minutes of his time in 1983. Leased private lines and voice-grade channels on satellites (which did not exist in 1960) have become even cheaper for heavy users.[19]

If telephone calls do not suffice to resolve a foreign production problem, a company today can send off an engineer relatively cheaply and expeditiously. By the same token, a foreign company can more readily send a market analyst to the United States or another export market. International flights of U.S. carriers had an average cost of 6.35 cents per mile in 1960 compared to 10.09 cents in 1982.[20] To put this in perspective, a 5,000-mile round trip could buy 86 hours of American production labor in 1982 but bought 239 hours in 1960.

Perhaps even more significantly, the number and convenience of international flights has dramatically increased. Take, for example, the flights between the two electronics centers, San Francisco and Singapore. The international edition of the *Official Airline Guide* (OAG) for March–April 1964 lists only three flights a week, each with an elapsed time of almost twenty-five hours. The OAG for September 1983 shows twelve direct flights and seventy-three connections a week. A daily one-stop flight has an elapsed time of eighteen hours.

These institutional pressures propelling the United States toward trade expansion appear to be accelerating. More nations are approaching the U.S. standard of living; the scientific base for other countries to develop superior technology is strengthening; the infrastructure and labor skills of those countries are also catching up; companies are losing their inertia for supplying the market locally; and the capacity to co-ordinate production in one country to meet the changing needs of another country is improving. These trends prompting greater trade also make labor-cost differences a more significant variable in decisions as to where to locate production across a wide spectrum of manufac-turing industries. We find further reasons to expect greater trade and competition as we now turn to technology issues.

Few Job Prospects in Technology-Intensive Trade

The development of new technology has important implications for trade-related employment. Although the United States enjoys a trade surplus in technology-intensive goods, recent studies indicate that that surplus is faltering.[21] Ironically, new technology may help the trade balance of troubled import-competing industries as much as successful export industries. That will occur, however, only if the technology reduces the employment requirements of the former industries.

To evaluate developments from an employment perspective, we should pay particular attention to industries with substantial employ-ment today and, with some overlap, to those with the promise for substantial employment growth in the future. We can also usefully distinguish "growth" industries from "mature" industries, according to the expected increase in demand for their output.[22]

Some mature industries are implementing technological change as sophisticated and as comprehensive as that of many growth industries. For example, the rapid increases in productivity of the auto and the textile industries indicate major changes in production technology. As mature industries, their productivity growth implies little if any increase in employment (beyond a cyclical recovery). As large employers, these industries can create large numbers of displaced workers with very modest increases in the share of imports or rise in productivity.

The electronics-based industries will no doubt see a rapid growth in sales to both producers and consumers in the United States. However, a serious question remains as to whether the boom in sales will translate into substantially higher U.S. employment. As noted above, the talent in foreign countries to develop technology on their own has grown immensely.

Even when the United States develops technology in advance of foreign competitors, production flowing from that technology may not take place in the United States. In contrast to traditional products, new products do not have specifically trained workers or fixed equipment to keep their production in the United States. Moreover, the major companies in this industry lack the bureaucratic inertia that has kept some industries' production concentrated in the United States. They already face stiff foreign competition and have large foreign operations. The 1977 benchmark survey of multinationals found relatively high foreign commitments by both the "office and computer machine" industry and the "electronics components and accessories" industries. The foreign affiliates of the first category had 42.2% of their parents' worldwide assets and 41.6% of their employees. The second category had 25.4% and 40.5%, respectively. These compare to the average of all manufacturing of 29.0% of assets and 31.1% of employees.[23] Thus, both electronics-related industries had a much larger share of employees abroad than the average for manufacturing.

Already available but not yet installed production technologies could substantially reduce work requirements in many U.S. industries. As the economy recovers enough to eliminate excess capacity and to improve the companies' cash flow, those technologies could be installed rapidly. That would improve the competitiveness of U.S. production, if the rest of the world does not move just as rapidly to improve its installed capacity. Such implementation of current technology would have a negative effect on employment in trade-competitive industries unless demand increases sufficiently to overcome the productivity gains.

Domestic Orientation of the Service Industries

The service sector has—and apparently will continue to have—far greater importance in the domestic economy than in international trade. On the one hand, service activities represent a large and growing proportion of employment and output in the U.S. economy. Between 1960 and 1983, the broadly defined services component rose from 38.3% to 49.5% of GNP and from 62.3% to 73.7% of nonagricultural employment.[24] On the other hand, international trade in services remains remarkably small and has grown no faster than trade in goods. Service exports represented 17.3% of total exports of merchandise and services in 1960 and 16.1% in 1982.[25] As for the future, although U.S. exports of services will expand, so will imports. Overall, there appears to be little prospect of significant net exports of services needed to generate additional U.S. employment in that sector.

Although some services are extensively traded internationally, most are not. Indeed, the rapid growth of employment in U.S. service industries has had little to do with international transactions. Six of seven service industries with the largest employment gains from 1967 to 1979 depend on the local rather than the international market. In an unpublished paper, Michael Urquhart of the Bureau of Labor Statistics has examined the growth of employment in services between 1967 and 1979. He compared actual 1979 employment in each industry with the level that would have occurred if 1979 employment had been distributed as it had been in 1967. He found that seven service industries had at least 500,000 more employees in 1979 than they would have had based on the 1967 employment pattern (table 6.1). All but finance have depended for their growth on the local market rather than the regional market. In the case of finance, the boom in foreign lending by U.S. banks no doubt did contribute to employment growth but we have no way of knowing the extent. In any case, further employment growth due to "exports" in that sector appears ruled out by the current retrenchment in foreign lending by U.S. banks.

Unfortunately, satisfactory data on international service transactions do not exist. Lack of separate data on U.S. *exports* of services hampers most studies of services in the international market. They estimate only the total sales by U.S. companies abroad rather than the U.S. value-added done in those industries for sale abroad. Thus, their estimates include foreign value-added that does not increase U.S. jobs.[26] The differences can be substantial. A study that did make the proper dis-

Table 6.1
Sectoral shifts in employment 1967–79

Sector	Employment		
	1979 Actual	1979 at the pattern of 1967	Difference
Health services	6,990,000	5,050,000	1,940,000
Eating and drinking establishments	4,235,000	2,994,000	1,241,000
Education	7,974,000	6,878,000	1,096,000
Business and repair services	3,717,000	2,737,000	980,000
Real estate	1,605,000	1,018,000	587,000
Welfare and religious organizations	1,563,000	988,000	575,000
Finance (banks, brokers, etc.)	2,425,000	1,868,000	557,000

Source: Michael Urquhart, "The Employment Shift to Services: Where Did It Come From?" *Monthly Labor Review*, April 1984.

tinction found that in 1974 U.S. service companies had total foreign sales of $50.0 billion but exports of only $7.0 billion. This compared with sales by foreign service companies in the United States of $28.8 billion of which imports by the United States comprised $7.9 billion.[27] Only from the perspective of U.S. companies' sales abroad versus foreign companies' sales in the United States did the United States have a substantial positive balance. However, from the standpoint of U.S. trade—on which jobs depend—the United States registered a slight deficit in the services industries that year.

The best available data indicate that international trade in services has been growing rapidly from a very low base. The activities most associated with the term "services" in trade policy discussions today fall into the category "other private services" which encompasses all separate payments for such diverse services as advertising, accounting, communications, data processing, engineering, consulting, health, and insurance. Although such activities comprised $835.1 billion of the U.S. gross domestic product in 1982, the United States registered total receipt of just $5.6 billion for its exports and paid $3.7 billion for imports of such services in 1982, according to the best available data, that of the balance of payments (considered incomplete by many).[28,29,30]

The International Monetary Fund compiles data separately for communications, nonmerchandise insurance, and technical services for construction and related industries.[31] The latest data (1982) show a

U.S. deficit in communications (exports of $1.51 billion versus imports of $1.89 billion), a deficit in nonmerchandise insurance ($0.18 billion versus $0.67 billion), and a surplus for construction-related services ($1.58 billion versus no more than $0.23 billion).

For the combined category of passenger fares, travel, and other transportation, the United States had receipts of $27.8 billion and payments of $32.1 billion in 1983.[32] Passenger fares and travel have increased at a faster clip than other transportation. In fact, foreign payments to the United States for passenger fares and travel grew from $1.1 billion in 1960 to $14.3 billion in 1983. However, the U.S. deficit in this category remained because comparable U.S. expenditures abroad climbed from $2.3 billion to $19.6 billion.

From a services employment perspective, the United States enjoyed a deceptively large surplus for fees and royalties: $7.7 billion versus $0.6 billion. Because fees and royalties compensate for technology previously developed and transferred, the jobs related to current payments may no longer exist. In addition, to avoid taxes charged on payments to their U.S. parents for profits or imports, affiliates of U.S. companies often boost their payments for royalties. Companies operating in the United States have much less incentive to overstate royalty payments. With enhanced foreign ability to develop technology for sale to the United States, the current U.S. surplus in this services category will probably decline in coming years, too.

For a number of reasons, the data examined above do not capture all U.S. trade in services. Unlike goods, services cannot be counted and valued as they cross the border; they are rendered in foreign countries or via telecommunications facilities. In addition, many services come as part of a package with goods exported or with investments, not as a specific service. Many U.S. sales abroad of such services as accounting, insurance, legal advice, and the like have generally been linked to U.S. manufacturing corporations' exports and foreign operations.[33] As previously noted, the technological strength of major foreign corporations has grown relative to the major U.S. firms in recent years. In fact, in recent years foreign corporations have made greater additions to their investments in the United States than U.S. corporations have added to their investments abroad.[34] (U.S. corporations still have far greater investments abroad than foreign corporations have here.) As foreign corporations invest in the United States, their local affiliates will no doubt buy such services from their home country. Thus, for those services tied to multinationals' investments, the U.S. export surplus will probably decline and so will the jobs that go with the services.

Modern computers linked by telecommunications satellites open a new era for services to be exchanged internationally. The evidence of such exports and imports so far consists of anecdotal reports. On the one hand, powerful or specially programmed computers in the United States are processing data for complex foreign projects. On the other hand, engineers in Pakistan have designed bridges for the United States and workers in Korea and the Caribbean have been key-punching data for American insurance companies. Although one cannot now predict how substantial the trade in such services will become, one can confidently predict that the United States will run a deficit in the more routine activities—which in the future may include the operation of computers themselves.

In summary, available evidence gives little reason to expect many net new U.S. jobs from increased trade in services. Both exports and imports of services are roughly balanced at remarkably low levels. Compared to the rest of the world, U.S. service industries generally have a reputation for efficiency, but so does U.S. manufacturing. Just as in manufacturing, we can expect growing U.S. imports of services that entail lower technical skills. The services sector has absorbed many workers who have lost their jobs in goods production and will continue to do so. But their new service jobs will largely supply the domestic rather than the international market.

No Net Job Gains from Export Promotion

Increased government assistance to exporters has become a common proposal for reducing employment problems from trade, but proponents of export promotion tend to ignore several key facts. First, any sustained increase in exports necessarily brings additional imports. As a result, attempts to create additional jobs in export sectors may not bring additional jobs to the economy as a whole and may aggravate employment problems in import-competing sectors. Second, the most important adverse effects of trade on employment come from the added instability of trade. Recent experience finds not only import surges but export declines beyond the reach of export promotion schemes.

As a practical matter, exports have been rising very rapidly in recent decades, but so have imports. They do not move in lockstep from year to year, but they have raced along fairly closely over the longer term.

U.S. exports and imports stood roughly at $20 billion in 1960, $40 billion in 1970, and $250 billion in 1981.

The exchange rate of the dollar relative to other currencies reflects the supply of and demand for the dollar. During the last decade of floating exchange rates, the dollar has gone through wide gyrations above and below the level suitable for stable flows of goods, services, and financial assets. Exports and imports ultimately move in tandem because U.S. exports raise demand for the dollar and U.S. imports increase its supply.[35] In any given year, exports and imports may diverge due to destabilizing shifts in exchange rates, different rates of growth between the United States and its trading partners, changes in the price of oil, and other factors. Nonetheless, any policy that succeeds in raising exports for a sustained period will also raise imports in the longer term.

Just as a successful export push would raise imports, a major reduction in the nation's overall imports would bring down exports. Thus, a policy to withdraw the United States from the world economy by scaling back overall imports would damage U.S. export industries. Oblivious to this effect, many in Congress expected to stimulate the U.S. economy with sharp hikes in most tariffs under the Tariff Act of 1930 (Smoot-Hawley). In fact, exports can be expected to fall as quickly and deeply after such action as new domestic production substitutes for the shunned imports. Thus, the domestic stimulus rationale for Smoot-Hawley was unfounded even if no other country had retaliated against the U.S. action.

Trade can reduce labor requirements for a given level of consumption because the labor required for an additional $1 billion of exports generally falls below the labor required to produce an additional $1 billion of imports. In this sense, trade closely resembles technological change. Walter Salant and Beatrice Vaccara have made the analogy and tied it to the risk of greater unemployment:

Both types of changes create the opportunity, when the resources displaced can be absorbed elsewhere, to attain a higher output or more leisure; neither contains any guarantee that the opportunity will be used instead of being dissipated in involuntary unemployment.[36]

Whereas technological improvement permits less labor to produce the same output, trade expansion allows less labor to bring the same output for consumption. Thus, like improved production technology, increased trade can either increase the nation's standard of living or raise its unemployment.

Trade has affected U.S. employment much more by bringing additional instability to the economy than by reducing the labor-to-consumption ratio with balanced growth of exports and imports. In the context of a stable, fully employed domestic economy, everyone would welcome the higher standard of living that would come from putting less labor into exports than would be required to replace imports. Currently, however, the U.S. economy has very high unemployment and trade is adding to it. As noted previously, some estimates attribute half the drop in manufacturing employment between 1980 and 1982 to the shift in trade.

The U.S. trade deficit, which ran close to $40 billion from 1978 to 1981, soared to $72.5 billion in 1983 and a projected $130 billion in 1984.[37] The trade problem results ultimately from the large American public and private borrowing requirements that, by Federal Reserve policy, are not being fully supplied by credit created in the United States. Due to the wide gap between its credit demands and supply, the United States has been draining the financial resources of the rest of the world. The large increase in the export of U.S. bonds has financed and provoked a large trade deficit and increased the value of the dollar 52% since 1980; it has also disturbed foreign countries by raising their interest rates. Their economies have slowed since they have not created enough additional credit to cover the drain to the United States completely. Some of the weaker creditor nations have declared mini-defaults due to their faltering exports, much higher interest costs, and a more costly dollar (in which most of their debt is contracted).

How long can these high levels of bond exports, exchange rate of the dollar, and trade deficit be maintained? Three scenarios seem plausible. In the first and most optimistic scenario, the United States begins to create enough credit for itself;[38] its net export of bonds and net imports of goods subside; the trade deficit narrows; and both the U.S. and foreign economies expand. In a second scenario, other countries create enough additional credit to cover the credit being drained off by the United States;[39] U.S. bond exports and the gaping trade deficit remain; but greater expansion occurs abroad and probably in the United States. The third and bleakest scenario represents a continuation of the current course: massive U.S. credit demands continue but accommodating credit is not forthcoming from any quarter; real interest rates, bond exports, dollar value, and trade deficit remain high; the world economy continues to constrict; mini-defaults become maxi-defaults; such a disruption of the world economy would probably increase demand for U.S. bonds as a "safe haven" and further widen the U.S. trade deficit until a run on the dollar ultimately ensued.

An employment-oriented trade policy would not push exports nor contract imports, but would work to smooth out the peaks and valleys in exports and imports. Unfortunately, to narrow the gaping U.S. trade deficit requires more than trade-specific measures. Only an overhaul of domestic monetary and fiscal policies would suffice. Short of that, measures to assist exports can stabilize employment even if they cannot increase the national employment permanently. Likewise, measures to stave off major import surges can provide some job stability.

Conclusion

This review of trade developments has found little room for comfort for American workers. Our examination has, however, revealed some useful lessons for trade policy to channel the increasing integration of the U.S. economy with the rest of the globe.

Powerful structural changes (such as improved transportation and communication, closing gaps in production abilities and consumption patterns between the United States and other countries) are propelling the internationalization of the U.S. economy. Technology developed in other countries is becoming increasingly competitive with that developed in the United States. The U.S. government can do a better job of improving its own infrastructure, the skills of its work force, and commercially competitive technology.

The fact that foreign countries have improved their technology-creating capacity is giving the United States more competition, but need not make Americans worse off. The new technology of others can improve the American standard of living. To avoid employment dislocation from the intensifying competition in technology, the government should encourage imports of the technology rather than the products of that technology.

On a sectoral basis, neither technology-intensive industries nor service industries can create many additional jobs in the international market. A job-oriented trade policy therefore cannot neglect the major manufacturing industries.

Major U.S. corporations—particularly the multinationals—are bringing in a very large proportion of U.S. imports. Reliance by U.S. steel companies on semifinished steel from abroad, by GM on small vehicles from Japan, or by Whirlpool on compressors from abroad would each have far-reaching implications for the future of their respective industries in the United States. Continued free rein for the multinationals will transform collective bargaining to the advantage of the companies in those industries. The results could be disastrous for organized and unorganized workers alike.

Although the United States cannot rely on trade to expand national employment, it can keep trade from badly aggravating unemployment by preventing surges in imports and rapid erosion of exports. That maintains jobs not only in the industry of the specific product but in its suppliers and their local communities. Since most service jobs depend on the health of local goods-producing industries, they should also benefit from a trade policy that lessens instability resulting from trade shifts.

Finally, the internationalization of the U.S. economy has made a sound domestic monetary and fiscal policy all the more critical for two reasons. First, the large trade deficit will persist until the United States can supply its own credit by raising the supply of—or reducing demands for—credit internally. Second, trade expansion and trade-stimulated improvements in technology reduce labor requirements. This effect has become particularly acute since unemployment has reached such a high level. Without vigorous efforts to expand demand (and reduce the work time per job), trade expansion will raise unemployment more than it will improve the standard of living.

Notes

The views expressed in this chapter are those of the author and do not commit his employer, the International Union, United Automobile, Aerospace and Agricultural Implement Workers. The author wishes to express his appreciation to Steve Beckman for his many discussions and comments on the issues of this chapter.

1. House Committee on Energy and Commerce, Staff Report, "The United States in a Changing World Economy: The Case for an Integrated Domestic and International Commercial Policy," Committee Print 98-N, September 1983, p.9.

2. Gregory K. Schoepfle, "Imports and Domestic Employment: Identifying Affected Industries," *Monthly Labor Review* 105 (August 1982): 15.

3. Peter Henle and Paul Ryscavage, "The Distribution of Earned Income Among Men and Women, 1958–77," *Monthly Labor Review* (April 1980): 3–10.

4. Robert Kuttner, "The Declining Middle," *Atlantic* (July 1983).

5. C. Michael Aho and James A. Orr, "Trade-sensitive Employment: Who Are the Affected Workers?," *Monthly Labor Review* (February 1981); Harry P. Bowen, "Changes in the International Distribution of Resources and Their Impact on U.S. Comparative Advantage," *Review of Economies and Statistics* (August 1983).

6. Robert Z. Lawrence, "Is Trade Deindustrializing America? A Medium Term Perspective," *Brookings Papers on Economic Activity I,* 1983.

7. U.S. Department of Commerce, Bureau of the Census, *Highlights of U.S. Export and Import Trade,* December 1980, tables 2 and 4, updated for 1984 through June by telephone, multiplied by 2.

8. U.S. Department of Commerce, International Trade Administration, *U.S. Trade Performance in 1983 and Outlook,* June 1984, pp. 27, 47.

9. The changing composition of U.S. trade partially—perhaps entirely—offsets this trend, however. U.S. trade with the newly industrializing countries, which have lower pay scales than those in Europe or Japan, comprises a rapidly growing portion of total U.S. trade. Thus, the weighted average of the labor costs of U.S. imports may not be rising relative to U.S. labor costs, even if the labor costs of every U.S. trading partner are rising relative to U.S. labor costs.

10. U.S. Department of Labor, Bureau of Labor Statistics, Office of Productivity and Technology, "Hourly Compensation Costs and Direct Pay of Production Workers in Manufacturing, Ten Countries, 1960–1983," April 1984 (unpublished).

11. Steffan Linder is credited with the theory that converging consumption patterns lead to increased trade, *An Essay on Trade and Transformation* (New York: Wiley, 1961).

12. Herbert Block, *The Planetary Product in 1980: A Creative Pause?* U.S. Office of Economic Research, National Foreign Assessment Center, Central Intelligence Agency, 1981.

13. James C. Abbeglen, "How to Defend Your Business Against Japan," *Business Week,* August 15, 1983, p. 14.

14. United Nations, *Statistical Notebook,* New York, various years.

15. National Science Foundation, National Science Board, *Science Indicators 1982.*

16. *Business Week,* June 20, 1983, p. 73 states that "product innovation in the major appliance business moves at a snail's pace."

17. U.S. Bureau of Labor Statistics, Office of Productivity and Technology, Division of Foreign Labor Statistics and Trade, "Manufactures Imports, Product Shipments, New Supply, and Import Penetration: 1972–1980," August 1982. Preliminary data through 1982 show little change from this flat import trend.

18. *Air Conditioning, Heating, and Refrigeration News,* December 16, 1982.

19. U.S. Department of Commerce, Office of Telecommunications, *U.S. International Telecommunication Rate History,* OT Report 75–77, November 1975; 1983 rates on file at Federal Communications Commission.

20. Civil Aeronautics Board, Office of Economic Analysis, Financial and Cost Analysis Division, "Comparison of Domestic and International Operations of the Major Carriers," July 27, 1983, and CAB, *Handbook of Airline Statistics 1973*.

21. Lester Davis, "Technology Intensity of U.S. Output and Trade," U.S. Department of Commerce, International Trade Administration, Office of Trade and Investment Analysis, July 1982; C. Michael Aho, and Howard Rosen, *Trends in Technology Intensive Trade*, Economic Discussion Paper 9, U.S. Department of Labor, Bureau of International Labor Affairs, October 1980; and data supplied by Howard Rosen updating the analysis of the latter through 1981. Two studies have found a rising trade surplus in technology-intensive industries, but made dubious distinctions between technology-intensive and non-technology-intensive industries. For example, they consider as technology-intensive many types of machinery (for example, farm, construction, general industrial) all of which have rising trade surpluses, but exclude auto, which has had an even greater growth in its deficit although it is probably equally technology-intensive. See Richard Cooper's comments (page 165) following Robert Lawrence, "Is Trade Deindustrializing America? A Medium-Term Perspective," in *Brookings Papers on Economic Activity* I: 1983, which follows the scheme of Robert M. Stern and Keith E. Maskus, "Determinants of the Structure of U.S. Foreign Trade, 1958–76," *Journal of International Economics* (May 1981): 207–224.

22. The popular terms and distinctions for industries, for example "high-tech," "smokestack," "sunrise," "sunset," and "basic," often confuse rather than improve our understanding of the underlying trends and alternatives.

23. Betty L. Barker, "A Profile of U.S. Multinational Companies in 1977," *Survey of Current Business*, October 1981: 40.

24. *Economic Report of the President*, 1984.

25. U.S. Department of Commerce, *Survey of Current Business*, June 1983.

26. Economic Consulting Services, Inc., *The International Operations of U.S. Service Industries: Current Data Collection and Analysis*, Washington, D.C., June 1981; U.S. International Trade Commission, *The Relationship of Exports in Selected U.S. Service Industries to U.S. Merchandise Exports*, USITC Pubication 1290, September 1982. The ITC conducted its own data survey and therefore has no excuse for the failure of its analysis to distinguish the extent that foreign sales by U.S. service firms were composed of U.S. value-added (true "exports") on the one hand and of foreign value-added on the other.

27. U.S. Department of Commerce, *U.S. Service Industries in World Markets: Current Problems and Future Policy Development*, December 1976, cited in Ronald Kent Shelp, *Beyond Industrialization: Ascendancy of the Global Service Economy* New York: Praeger, 1981.

28. Department of Commerce, *Survey of Current Business*, June 1983.

29. Estimates of U.S. exports of services often include income derived from assets held by Americans abroad—$80.0 billion in 1982. An analysis of the

effects of international developments on U.S. employment should not consider such payments.

30. Morgan Guaranty estimates that an additional $15–20 billion in U.S. service exports goes uncounted, *World Financial Markets*, May 1983: 4–5.

31. International Monetary Fund, *Balance of Payments Statistics*, Vol. 33, *Yearbook* 1982.

32. U.S Department of Commerce, *Survey of Current Business*, June 1983.

33. For example, Lester Davis estimates that U.S. exports of manufactures directly and indirectly created 4 million U.S. jobs in 1980, of which 1.5 million were in industries supplying services. "Domestic Employment Generated by U.S. Exports," U.S. Department of Commerce, May 1983.

34. U.S Department of Commerce, *Survey of Current Business*, August 1983.

35. On a long-term basis, U.S. imports usually tend to exceed its exports. The U.S. sustains a deficit in merchandise trade because it runs a surplus on its other international accounts, particularly the earnings of multinationals. U.S. multinationals earn far more abroad than do foreign multinationals here.

36. Walter S. Salant and Beatrice N. Vaccara, *Import Liberalization and Employment* (Washington, D.C.: Brookings Institution, 1961): 96.

37. Department of Commerce, International Trade Administration, *U.S. Trade Performance in 1983 and Outlook*, June 1984, p. 3

38. This can be accomplished without regressive cuts in social spending if progressive taxes are raised, other federal spending is limited, borrowing for mergers, speculation, and luxury consumption is curbed, and the stringent policies of the Federal Reserve Board are eased.

39. With its massive foreign borrowing, the United States in effect is mortgaging its foreign assets as did major European countries during the two world wars.

7   Union Involvement in Entrepreneurial Decisions of Business

Robert B. McKersie

A shift appears to be taking place in the traditional union reluctance to get involved in the entrepreneurial kind of business decisions. Until recently most unions have resisted the idea of joint decision making or, even on a more minor scale, being informed of key decisions. Except in wartime when the principle of "equality of sacrifice" moved unions into a much more central role (participation in the War Labor Board at the national level and in production committees at plant, company, and industry level), the guiding principle of collective bargaining and union-management relations has been "management manages and the union grieves."

It is my premise that we are on the threshold of an era of considerable experimentation with different forms of union involvement in entrepreneurial decisions. In many ways the current period (the early 1980s) is for union involvement in strategic decision making what the early 1970s were for the quality of work life. We see the past decade and the next one as a score of years that stimulated developments in the industrial relations system at levels above and below the traditional middle level of collective bargaining.

The possible involvement in entrepreneurial decisions presents for union leaders a whole host of issues and dilemmas; some are similar to the dilemmas posed by quality of work life but others are unique to the structure of decision making found in corporate boardrooms.

The Nature of Entrepreneurial Activity

Since my focus here is on the involvement of unions in entrepreneurial decisions, the term needs to be defined. Entrepreneurial decisions are operational—decisions that are needed to run the business; thus they affect employment over the long run. In other words, the focus is on the strategy decisions that affect the shape of the business—such events as purchasing, expanding or selling a plant, embarking upon a new generation of technology, starting a new product line, or divesting from an old product line or business.

Given this definition, then, a series of subjects (all interesting in their own right) fall outside our present purview. For example, union influence over pension funds can have wide repercussions for the union movement (such as investing in unionized firms, thereby enhancing employment opportunities), but this is not an operating matter for a given business (Sheinkman et al. 1980). By the same token, the definition excludes the role of the union in joining with management counterparts to approach government for the establishment of some type of industrial policy or, to cite another example, becoming a party to a proceeding before a regulatory body considering a new rate structure (as is often the case in the telephone and power industries). These roles do not involve the union in either approaching or confronting the company directly over investment decisions.

However, we should not draw too fine a line, since a union that finds itself in partnership with management before some kind of government tribunal may in the process find itself playing a more influential role with respect to the main areas of corporate strategy. Keeping these activities aside for the moment, we will concentrate on the key areas of entrepreneurial activity and examine the extent to which unions are or should be involved. A related category of joint activities (one that is becoming increasingly important) involves the "industry booster" role. For example, the bricklayers and sheet-metal workers unions are banding together with their respective industry trade associations to promote new projects and to pursue a program of "let's get more business for the benefit of both sides." Assuming management finds such programs congenial, there does not seem to be any reason for unions not to be involved in programs of this sort except for the opportunity costs of the time spent in such joint activities.

It is clear that these "big picture" roles for unions should not be excluded from any consideration of what the labor movement can or should be doing to foster members' interests. Indeed, playing a more decisive role in pension funds and helping corporations vis-à-vis government agencies and competitors (antitrust issues aside) represent very important opportunities for unions. These roles, however, do not impinge upon management discretion in operating a particular business and do not involve the union leadership in reconciling its traditional adversarial role with a new role of involvement and collaboration. Here we will be examining involvement in the matters of a particular firm that raise serious dilemmas and contradictions for unions, given their historical mission to serve as an independent representative of worker interests.

Reasons Why Unions Are Cautious about Involvement

A few factors give unions pause with respect to their involvement in entrepreneurial decisions. Some union leaders believe that "management should manage" because that is the best way for operations to run more smoothly and efficiently. If another institution is involved, there are bound to be time-consuming deliberations and efficiency may be impaired. Evidence for this point comes from research on German codetermination (Furlong 1977).

More fundamental for the union is the point that involvement may weaken the union's main function, namely, protecting worker interests. As representatives learn about business decisions, they may lose sight of the impact and consequences of these decisions for the rank and file.

A worker or union director may also get overwhelmed by the detail and by the technical information that comes to board members. From conversations with one observer of the German scene it is clear that some worker-directors are ineffective because they do not have the background or the style for dealing with volumes of financial material.

Moreover, it is possible for a labor leader to get caught up in the glamorous process of the boardroom, to be thinking more about the ideology of participation rather than about the bread-and-butter issues, such as job security, that are of direct interest to the rank and file. It can be very seductive to meet with top management in elegant surroundings.

The modus operandi of corporate boards is foreign to most workers and union leaders. The culture of decision making by assent or consensus based on formal presentations, often by staff and functional specialists, is quite different from the town-meeting style of most unions where actions are taken after open debate, often with considerable emotional energy. Robert Stern (1983), who has studied the behavior of worker-directors in employee-owned firms, has reported that the biggest surprise to newcomers is that boards do not take votes—often the meeting has moved on to the next agenda item before the union representative realizes that silence means support for the management position on the pending item. Batstone and colleagues (1983) found that only 10% of the items presented to the British Post Office Board (composed of an equal number of management and union directors) contained any information about options or alternatives.

Another danger is that the participating labor leader may get coopted or silenced into assent and become totally discredited with his membership because of board decisions that appear to be unfair to the rank and file. Again it is possible to cite an example from abroad. In the instance of British Steel, where labor directors have been involved for many years, the labor director from Corby could not say anything to the rank and file about the impending shutdown of the steel mill in that community. Management directors expected him not to reveal the essence of top corporate deliberations. When it was announced that the plant was going down, he found himself in a very difficult position. The book by Brannen and colleagues (1976) elaborates this theme by presenting other examples of how worker-directors who knew about impending closures were completely ineffective in advocating the interests of the rank and file. Unfortunately, their role was one-way: to report to management the feelings of the rank and file (in effect giving management information so that management could push forward) but not to give the local unions information so that they could oppose the cuts. In one situation the worker-director's role was even more embarrassing because the worker-director had implied to his local people that if they became more efficient they would survive—which, given the general market conditions, was not possible.

This last point relates to the reality that when a business does not fare very well the union will share the blame for the bad consequences: "The news may be bad and the messenger may be killed." Moreover, one has to ask why some corporations are now willing to allow labor leaders to come into the boardroom when they resisted this step vehemently just a few years ago. One explanation is that when things are going well business wants to keep a free hand for fear that it would give unions a bargaining advantage. When things are going badly, business likes to have the company of union leadership as a way of educating the union membership about the difficulties. One official in the UAW remarked that as a result of briefing sessions with management he had come to learn "more than I want to know." In some field research I did in Britain, it turned out that the labor leaders in the shipyard industry who had the best picture of the future of that industry (by being taken on some tours and being given some information on a confidential basis) were the same leaders who did not want to have anything to do with participation.

Another variant of the same message comes out of the experience of Studebaker—a company that was willing to share considerable information and to involve UAW officials in some of the intricacies of the business. When the company went down, there were hard feelings on all sides. As Thomas Donahue (1976) has said, the union movement has to be careful when management comes bearing information and invitations to participate in decision making. "Usually management wants to share trouble but not success."

Even where the business is successful and the decisions that union leaders had some role in shaping or at least monitoring work out well, it may not be clear to the rank and file that their representatives should be credited with the good results. It is difficult for workers in assessing something as complicated as investment strategies, for example, to know what the "shadow" performance would have been. In other words, just how much worse would the overall situation have been if the union had not been involved in the entrepreneurial decisions? Basically the assumption of U.S. collective bargaining has been that a labor leader survives by delivering concrete gains and opposing management decisions that would have adverse consequences for the rank and file.

One problem with the increased participation that often accompanies concession bargaining is that the employment gains involved may only be evident over the long run; consequently it is difficult for the union to show concrete short-run gains compared to what would have happened if the union had maintained its adversary posture. For example, a labor leader does not get much credit for protecting jobs when the rank and file do not know their jobs were in jeopardy or do not know the extent to which their jobs are going to be cut back. The potential bind that develops from involvement at the top is the core dilemma for union leaders in all aspects of collective bargaining; specifically, collaboration with management can create severe internal political problems for union leaders.

Moreover, the evidence from industrial relations systems that have had the most experience with participation (especially Scandinavia and Germany) is that workers do not place a high priority on having their representatives involved in the global decisions of the business. This conclusion is borne out in a comprehensive study by the *International Research Group* (1981) and by Chamberlain (1981, 100) who makes the point as follows:

Experience from Denmark indicates that democracy at the shop floor level is a sort of system which is considered more meaningful from the workers' point of view than the representative democracy. At the same time, the interest of trade union officials runs in the reverse direction: greater attention to more formal systems of joint decision-making in the upper reaches of the enterprise.

This same reversal of interests is illustrated in Germany. Workers are more concerned with co-determination in the workplace, union officials with co-determination on the supervisory board.

This view is supported by surveys of worker interest in participation in the United States (Witte 1980; Kochan, Katz, and Mower, chapter 13, this volume). These surveys consistently show that workers assign considerably higher priorities to gaining a direct say on issues affecting their specific jobs at the level of the workplace than over broad corporate policies and how the business is run.

Reasons Favoring More Involvement

We can divide the reasons favoring greater involvement into three broad categories: philosophical, increasing the size of the pie (sometimes referred to as integrative bargaining), and neutralizing the power strategies of management.

Philosophical Rationale

For some labor leaders, having a role in entrepreneurial decisions is seen as a means for achieving certain broad social objectives. Walter Reuther, concerned about pricing and profits of the automobile companies, often asked for a "look at the books." Significantly, during the 1958 negotiations he went beyond his usual request to see the books and proposed that the companies reduce selling prices by $100—and if subsequently the companies had to restore prices to make a normal rate of return (after meeting the union demands), then the parties would submit all these matters to arbitration.

Close to this purpose is the "destatusizing" that comes when workers get involved at close range with the executives of the corporation. Herb Rebham, vice-chairman of the Volkswagen board and top union leader for the International Metal Workers Confederation, makes the point as follows: "The fact that a guy who used to work on the assembly line sits on the compensation committee is interesting. We know all the perks." (*Wall Street Journal*, July 1, 1980)

A larger purpose [and one supported by the work of Bluestone and Harrison (1982)] is the use of involvement to prevent inappropriate disinvestment and the loss of economic vitality for a community. Rank-and-file workers, especially if they are senior, may not have the same stake in preserving the viability of the enterprise as the national union leaders who are committed to a healthy union—the latter may have the same interests as the community in keeping a business functioning and fostering employment, union membership strength, and economic activity for future generations.

The philosophical rationale has been well summarized by Brody (1980) who argues that the purpose of participation is to "democratize the whole process of decision making at the corporate level so that the voice of workers will be heard in corporate councils."

Integrative Solutions

Another stream of thinking about the rationale for union involvement views typical labor-management relations as being stuck in a low-trust syndrome. As a result, there are many "missed opportunities." Due to low trust, management does not share information about its intentions and may slowly walk away from a facility—a type of gradual disinvestment process. On the other side, the workers and the union, seeing the slow march to extinction, act in a very defensive and adversarial manner. As a result, both sides find themselves in a very unsatisfactory state of affairs, unable to break out of the "prisoner's dilemma." Many examples of these mutually destructive cycles have come to light as part of the recent rush of plant shutdowns and the resulting recriminations. Union: "Why didn't you tell us you were at the brink?" Management: "We didn't think you would listen."

Countering Management Power

By far the most important reason for union leaders to get involved at the strategic level is to blunt containment power strategies being followed by some corporations. One of these might be called "creeping decertification," wherein a company seeks to keep all of its new plants unorganized and gradually shifts production out of its unionized plants into its newer plants. The purpose then of union involvement at the strategic level is to deal with such a policy at its origin.

Another managerial power strategy is the whipsawing of plants on the basis of the principle: "The low cost operation gets the business" (Buss 1983). Unions have lived through an earlier era of workers being pitted against one another within the plant and as a result developed safeguards—the seniority system and a contract to prevent management from playing workers off against one another. Unions currently find themselves forced to develop similar kinds of safeguards to deal with competitive threats coming from a higher level, namely, cross-plant comparisons. Historically, the union response to management's strategy of divide and conquer has been to take wage costs out of competition via the standard rate, the master contract, or pattern bargaining. The ability to sustain these policies has broken down in a number of industries and an alternative route to the same end is through involvement at the highest levels of the corporations.

Involvement in Entrepreneurial Matters at Different Levels

We will now consider union involvement in entrepreneurial matters at three levels. Let us first consider the lowest level, that of the work group or the department. For the U.S. system of collective bargaining, additional involvement in entrepreneurial decisions at this level may not seem as critical as it would be in other systems. As a result of the detailed labor contract and the way in which plant-level labor relations are conducted, unions already have considerable influence—what some analysts have referred to as job power or job-control unionism, as described in this volume by Michael Piore. Notwithstanding this already high degree of involvement at the bottom tier of the system, as the quality-of-work-life movement develops, some workers are assuming increasingly managerial types of functions at the workplace, such as specifying how new technology should be introduced. In some advanced forms of participation, workers are also involved in planning the layout of new departments and in shaping the organization of work.

There are several implications for unions of the rapid growth of quality-of-work-life and other forms of plant-level participation. One of these is the need for unions to place any effort to improve productivity at the plant level within the context of corporationwide employment prospects. It is important for a union to ascertain whether the net effect of a program of involvement at the work-group level will be negative because the prospect is one of static or shrinking employment or whether it will be possible for more work and employment to be made available to the work group and department involved.

Similarly, a union that actively participates in a cooperative quality-of-work program at the workplace may find it necessary to ensure that it will not be weakened corporationwide because of a "union-free" policy. In other words, from the viewpoint of the union the trade-off must be, "We'll run the risk of modifying our traditional stance at the local level if we receive some assurances about our role on a corporationwide basis." This is, in essence, the linkage that Irving Bluestone and other officials of the UAW presented to General Motors in a showdown over the "southern strategy" and the requirement that the concept of quality of work life had to be coupled with GM's acceptance of the union at its new plants.

At the middle level, greater involvement in entrepreneurial kinds of activities is currently arising out of the need to ensure that the terms of concession agreements are being honored and implemented. Examples of safeguards that have emerged out of concession bargaining are discussed by Cappelli and McKersie (chapter 11, this volume) and therefore only two examples are cited here. In some agreements there is a commitment that the funds saved will be reinvested in the plants involved. In order to ensure that this is happening, a union needs to receive detailed information about investments or to have a "look at the books." Enforcing the principle of equality of sacrifice also requires having considerable information on white-collar and managerial compensation and employment policies.

Thus again there is a direct linkage between what takes place at the middle tier of the industrial relations system and involvement at the highest level. Specifically, workers will not be motivated to engage in concession bargaining to save their jobs unless they can be assured that the competitive gap has a reasonable chance of being closed as a result of the new arrangements. This means the release of detailed information about the position of the plant vis-à-vis competition and suggests continuing involvement by the union in some type of process suitable for monitoring the economic performance and future prospects of the enterprise.

Finally we come to the highest level, the strategic level of the firm, where union involvement in entrepreneurial issues takes on its most controversial form. At this level, we need to distinguish the *channels* from the *substance*. Concerning substance, two general subjects are of interest to the union: (1) organizational security, that is, the union's representational rights at existing and prospective plants; and (2) the employment prospects for its members. The driving rationale for a union's involvement at the strategic level relates to its need to improve or protect its organizational status and/or the employability of its members.

Channels fall into two categories: (1) having a vote or directly influencing the decision (such as representation on some type of board); and (2) receiving information or being consulted about impending developments. The latter approach includes a range of styles and techniques by which union leaders and union members learn about relevant economic information.

Different Forms of Involvement

Before examining in detail one of the most talked-about ways for unions to get involved, namely, membership on the board of directors, we should make several distinctions. First, there is an important difference between formal and informal procedures for involvement. For example, some unions are given information regularly via briefing sessions, while others only learn about developments in informal off-the-record discussions. Some union leaders prefer the latter method, since it provides them with more political maneuvering room and if they so choose, to remain aloof, thereby avoiding certain disadvantages that might come from having been put on formal notice about unpopular developments.

The second distinction is whether involvement takes place on a case-by-case basis or whether it occurs as a result of a more regular procedure. The arrangements that have emerged from concession bargaining to ensure that the terms of the contract are honored fall into the first category of specific involvement to achieve the essence of the agreement.

A trend appears to be emerging with the establishment of top-level communication sessions. These mechanisms are agreed to in the collective bargaining contract but the sessions themselves are extracontractual. In the case of Ford and the UAW, this is called the Mutual Growth Forum, for Boeing and the IAM the concept is an annual technology briefing and for AT&T and the CWA the communication vehicle is called the Common Interest Forum. The latter has three stated purposes:

1. providing a framework for early communication and discussion between the parties on business developments of mutual interest and concern to the parties and their constituencies;

2. discussing and reviewing innovative approaches to enhance the competitiveness of the company and improve employment security;

3. improving understanding and relationships between the parties and avoiding unnecessary disputes by cooperatively addressing significant changes and developments in the union or company environment.

Presence at the Board Level

Thus far Chrysler and Pan American serve as the two prominent companies where union presence on the board has been agreed to as a quid pro quo for concessions. Significantly, the number of companies with union- or worker-designated directors is increasing steadily in connection with employee stock ownership plans. Eastern Airlines, Western Airlines and a number of trucking companies are going this route. In order to talk about the subject with a larger base of experience, however, we need to turn to European examples.

The presence of a union representative on a board seems to work better when the approach is not overly adversarial. Thus, in Germany where relations between management and the union are arms-length but not antagonistic, the codetermination model seems to work reasonably well. In the United Kingdom, by contrast, especially in the Post Office where an experiment was tried with worker representatives both at the regional and national levels, the experiment was judged a failure and discontinued after two years. In fact, very few of the important decisions were made at the board level and management proceeded to subvert the whole intent of the experiment because it viewed the worker/union members as only representing one interest group. Since union representatives had been thrust into its midst, management never brought issues before the board and decided most matters in committee. In turn, the unions adopted a very strong bargaining stance which further intensified the tension in the boardroom (Batstone et al. 1983).

This case illustrates the point that it is not desirable to force participation at the highest level. As illustrated by the Post Office example, participation in a boardroom only works when the union leader is respected and the other board members see some advantage in having this person as a member and where the board has accepted the fact that representation is a permanent rather than a temporary phenomenon. For example, it is reported that Chrysler Chairman Iacocca and

UAW President Fraser have high respect for each other and that Fraser's participation in the deliberations of the Chrysler Corporation has worked because of their personal rapport and mutual respect.

A second important point is that it appears to be preferable for the union to have a *presence* rather than *parity*. The rationale for only the minimal participation of one or two worker/union members is that the trade union point of view can be presented and then the board is challenged to reconcile it with the other perspectives that are relevant. The problem with parity, as in the case of the British Post Office experiment, is that it assumes that only two interest groups are involved. In such a situation, management maintains that it is acting in behalf of all constituencies—with presumably the other half of the board representing only the employees. This leads to a very difficult and asymetric process. One purpose in having a union representative participate in board deliberations is to improve the *quality* of the decisions. It takes no more than one or two union representatives on a board to achieve this result. Another way to view the presence of the union is as a mechanism for referral of a pending proposal back to the staff of the corporation for more work. Under such a concept, if the worker representatives are not ready to proceed, they do not have the opportunity to veto but do have the opportunity to send the proposal back for further consideration.

Finally, there is the opportunity for innovative proposals to surface and be considered because of the new perspective involved. It has been reported that Fraser was able to keep some plants of Chrysler open because he saw an opportunity for changes to avoid a shutdown. Similarly, worker representatives in British Steel were able to help with the transition arrangements and made valuable suggestions about how a plant should be shut down and worker interests considered in an integrative manner. A recent report on employee representation on company boards in Sweden noted: "Employers appreciate the contribution made by employee representatives. One such survey by the SAF of their affiliates indicates that 20% said the work of the board improved as a result of employee participation. Few had negative comments" (Eiger 1983).

Differing Views of Two Unions

Not all union leaders desire involvement at the strategic level. A good illustration of how two unions, both in the key manufacturing sector, can differ with respect to the desirability of involvement at the strategic level can be seen in the approaches taken by the steelworkers and the autoworkers.

In the case of the autoworkers, a number of important developments illustrate substantially greater involvement over the past several years. First, a member of the UAW is on the Chrysler board. For the other companies, there are regular forums in which key UAW leaders are briefed about worldwide employment developments. In the 1982 negotiations, the union, with General Motors, developed the important principle of the "pass-through," namely, the linkage between a wage reduction and a price reduction. While this concept did not appear in the final agreement, it did illustrate the willingness of the union to become intimately involved in the business matters of the corporation.

By contrast, the steelworkers have not been involved in any comparable way. Indeed, they passed up the opportunity to receive detailed profit information because they felt the whole business was "too complicated." When officials of the union are asked about whether they might have played a role in reinvestment decisions in some of the mills that have been slowly depreciated, they answer as follows: "We knew what was going on but we saw no need to get involved or to challenge the investment decisions made by management." For a while after the 1979 contract was signed, the union did ask for a report on maintenance expenses and major investment decisions from each of its locals. However, from what can be judged, little has come of this program. Rather, the emphasis of the steelworkers union has been on the industry level and achieving assistance from the government in the form of import protection and relaxation of regulations. For example, as a result of the tripartite committee that functioned during the Carter administration, a major change was made in the implementation date of the pollution control program.

Feasibility Considerations

If a union leader desires to have more involvement, it is much more appropriate for this to take place at the level where key entrepreneurial activities take place, namely, at the corporate level.[1] Thus, where collective bargaining takes place at either the industry level (as in basic steel) or plant by plant (as in the case of the majority of bargaining units in manufacturing and services), supplemental channels of involvement will be needed to achieve a strong union presence at the corporate level. This is illustrated by our findings on quid pro quos in concession bargaining. Only those unions that bargained on a companywide basis were able to get a quid pro quo from management, because they could deal with the firm at the level at which strategic decisions are made (Cappelli 1982).

The second factor favoring involvement is the presence of a small number of dominant employers in an industry. Typically in oligopolistic industries investment decisions are large and discreet and the stakes are high for the unions involved. By comparison, in industries comprising many small employers, such as garments or retail food, the union needs to play a role at the industry level in order to help stabilize the industry generally rather than worrying about the fortunes of a particular enterprise or scrutinizing investment decisions company by company.

The third point is that the union must have the company and/or the industry reasonably well organized if there is to be any prospect of involvement in entrepreneurial matters. Few, if any, employers will voluntarily open up their councils to union influence. Consequently, the involvement only happens where the union has the presence and the bargaining power to command attention.

Given the reluctance on the part of employers to allow unions to play any kind of substantial role, unions face another dilemma over the approach they take to achieving greater involvement. If a union comes at the matter in an adversarial or power fashion, it is unlikely to get anywhere. This is the reason that the UK shop stewards movement at the Lucas company in Great Britain, which offered an elaborate list of capital budgeting ideas and new products for operations slated to be phased out, got nowhere. Probably the same thing will happen in the United States to the ideas being proposed by a union-community coalition at McDonnell-Douglas on the West Coast. On the other hand, if a union approaches the task of achieving greater involvement in a cooperative fashion, it may walk away empty-handed. This is where "corporate campaigns" or other pressure tactics are likely to play a role. Pressure may be needed to get access to strategic decisionmaking, but once in place unions may need to be able to demonstrate they can play both a representational and an integrating role.

There are no easy answers to this dilemma. This is why experimentation is so important. It is also the reason why we need to learn more about the role of legislation (such as in Germany and Scandinavia) in fostering this process.

Labor Law Perspectives

Public policy has a strong bearing on the extent to which there will be greater involvement by unions at the top level of corporations. There are several dimensions to this part of the discussion.

One issue is whether workers and their union representatives by virtue of assuming managerial functions (whether at the plant level via something like autonomous teams, or at the highest level by participating fully in board-of-director deliberations) become, for National Labor Relations Act purposes, a part of management and thereby lose standing as an employee group or representatives of a bona fide bargaining unit. This may be labeled the "Yeshiva trap." In this landmark case for labor law, the U.S. Supreme Court held in 1980 that the faculty of Yeshiva University were managerial employees and therefore not entitled to bargaining under the National Labor Relations Act. At the point where workers and their representatives come to play a central role in governing the business, some would argue that they lose the very ground on which the National Labor Relations Act gives them bargaining rights.

Another issue involves the scope and dividing line of mandatory and nonmandatory subjects for collective bargaining. Clearly, entrepreneurial decisions fall within the nonmandatory realm of the National Labor Relations Act. Thus a union cannot require that these subjects be bargained over and cannot bring these matters to an impasse. This may not be a major impediment, however, given the point that a bargaining or power approach to these strategic areas is not functional in its own right. An employer who insists on opposing union participation on legal grounds would probably oppose the union equally as hard on other grounds, were this to become a mandatory subject of bargaining.

However, there may be ways for public policy to foster more involvement by unions in strategic matters, short of making union participation a mandatory subject of bargaining. Charles Morris (1977) has proposed that the National Labor Relations Act be revised so as to provide for the requirement of consultation on selected strategic and entrepreneurial matters. This would be one step in the direction of a type of legislative framework that exists in several Scandinavian countries as well as on the Continent. Certainly we in this country are not ready to have legislation that would require the presence of worker/union representatives in various management councils, but we may be at a point where some type of consultation and disclosure and communication of information to workers and union representatives about important strategic matters would be appropriate.

Conclusion

What does this all add up to? First, we appear to be entering a period of considerably more experimentation with various forms of involvement, either the formal, periodic variety or informal briefings and consultation on a less regular basis.

The focal point for union involvement in strategic issues will vary between the industry level and the corporate level depending on two variables: the structure of the industry and the structure of bargaining. A small number of oligopolistic employers implies that the corporate level is probably the key point for engaging strategic decision making while in a highly competitive industry the focus for union involvement is at the industry level. In so doing, the union helps stabilize the industry and regulates competition over industrial relations policies and practices across employers (the garment trades example of avoiding cutthroat competition over wages) and the union avoids the dilemma of promoting the competitive prospects of one firm against another.

Where a union bargains on a single-company basis it may already have direct access to corporate strategic decisions via informal contacts. However, where it bargains on a plant-by-plant basis or on an industrywide or employer association basis, a vacuum may be created at the corporate level where key decisions are made and the union lacks any presence, communication channels, and influence.

Moving to the other side of the equation, since employers will resist involvement of unions, unions will need to exert bargaining power to achieve recognition and influence over strategic decisions; however, once access is gained unions must be able to demonstrate they can play both a representational and an integrative role. To this end, presence is better than parity on a board of directors.

Finally, American labor law poses a number of specific constraints on the development of more union involvement. While a wholesale change in the law to require union involvement or to make this a mandatory subject of bargaining is probably neither advisable nor feasible, perhaps providing consultation as well as information and disclosure rights would be a step in the right direction.

Notes

1. Coping with multinational corporations capable of allocating investment resources and shifting production across national boundaries presents special challenges to a union, as illustrated by the following quotation: "The investment decisions for Spain and Austria aren't made by Opel, they're made in Detroit. And since co-determination ends at the border, we can't co-determine" (*Wall Street Journal*, July 1, 1980). Lee Price discusses this and other challenges to the labor movement caused by the internationalization of the world economy (chapter 6, this volume).

References

Batstone, E., et al. *Unions in the Boardroom*. Oxford: Blackwell, 1983.

Bluestone, B., and B. Harrison. *The Deindustrialization of America: Plant Closings, Community Abandonment, and the Dismantling of Basic Industry*. New York: Basic Books, 1982.

Brannen, P., et al. *The Worker-Director*. London: Hutchinson, 1976.

Brody, D. *Workers in Industrial America*. New York: Oxford University Press, 1980.

Buss, D. "GM vs GM: Unions Say Auto Firms Use Interplant Rivalry to Raise Work Quotas," *Wall Street Journal*, November 7, 1983, pg. 1.

Cappelli, P. "Concession Bargaining and the National Economy." *Proceedings of the Industrial Relations Research Association*, 1982.

Chamberlain, N. *Forces of Change in Western Europe*. U.K.: McGraw-Hill Book Company, Ltd., 1981.

Donahue, T. "Trends in Industrial Relations." In *Proceedings of the International Conference on Labor Trends*. McGill University: Industrial Relations Centre, 1976.

Eiger, N. "The Education of Employee Representatives on Company Boards in Sweden." In *Working Life in Sweden*. Swedish Information Service, Swedish Consulate General, N.Y., No. 27, 1983.

Furlong, J. *Labor in the Boardroom: The Peaceful Revolution*. Princeton, N.J.: Dow Jones Books, 1977.

International Research Group. *Industrial Democracy in Europe* Oxford: Clarendon Press, 1981.

Morris, C. "The Role of the NLRB and the Courts in the Collective Bargaining Process: A Fresh Look at Conventional Wisdom and Unconventional Remedies." *Vanderbilt Law Review* 30:4 (1977):661–87.

Sheinkman, J., et al. *Pensions: A Study of Benefit Fund Investment Policies*. Industrial Union Department, AFL-CIO, 1980.

Stern, R. "Community Participation in Economic Crisis: Unequal Power and the Theory of Community Distortion." *Proceedings of the Industrial Relations Research Association*, 1983.

Witte, J. *Democracy, Authority, and Alienation in Work: Workers' Participation in an American Corporation*. Chicago: University of Chicago Press, 1980.

Discussion, Part III

Leslie Nulty: There is no question but that heightened international competition is forcing unions to take a more global view, but this has been traditional in some segments of the U.S. labor movement. Unions in the garment industry have long been concerned with the way that industry is managed, for example. In our union, dealing with a highly competitive industry, if the union were to promote the welfare of a particular firm, it would risk putting all the other firms, where we also have members, out of business. Therefore, a union needs to take an industry perspective and focus its energies on involvement at the industry, not the corporate level. In the retail industry, for example, for several years we have had a joint labor-management committee which provides a forum for discussion of industrywide issues.

Whichever way unions go, we are going to be forced into more strategic thinking. Picking the right strategic decision will be tough, especially in a period of high unemployment. A brief anecdote shows how hard this is. We had a case where two of our locals faced demands for concessions from similar employers in two different areas. One local agreed to concessions in return for employer neutrality in organizing in areas where the company is expanding. In another case the union held firm and did not grant concessions. In the first case the union grew by leaps and bounds as it organized areas of expansion. In the second case the union is also doing well because, although the first employer pulled out, another even more successful one came in. Our members were protected by strong successorship language. These two locals took very different strategic points of view but both came out ahead.

John Carmichael: I would be interested in seeing some experimentation in representation on boards. I think you have some other examples (besides Chrysler), such as the plywood factories in the West. I think we might proceed here in ways somewhat similar to the ways the labor movement came into QWL. In 1972–73, the early stage, there was no pell-mell change. Initially, it was the UAW who started the experiments. That was a good ten years ago so it certainly has been a slow development. I don't know of any companies that are inviting us into the boardrooms, but given the opportunity, I think we'd want to experiment so we can evaluate it.

Sam Camens: I think we have been groping around in our discussion trying to find a way to get us out of this economic, social, and political mess. But now these studies and this discussion are getting right to the point because they are hitting on the macro issue, that is, whether we are going to have a national industrial policy and a strong set of basic industries in this country. To me, we have to start with a policy at this level. Then everything else can fall into place.

Furthermore, we cannot separate what we as unions want to be like on the shop floor from the values of our larger society. For me it all comes together on one issue, namely, do we want to save the democratic process? I don't think we are talking about killing the goose (overthrowing capitalism) but whether we are going to have a democratic society and whether the values of a democratic society are going to be extended to the workplace. We must have a right to participate in all decisions that affect us, and we need to recognize it and fight for it. It is something for everybody to understand, and we had better not waver on these matters. It is a role that we must understand and have to find answers on how to do it.

I, as a union leader, could not give workers an answer in Youngstown, a city completely devastated by steel-plant shutdowns. The shutdowns affected 10,000 steelworkers who are looking for answers. We have a right to participate in such grave social decisions. Everybody around us was raising the issue of whether we are moving across traditional union lines to get involved. We have no choice but to do so. Look at what the U.S. Steel Corporation is trying to do now, to have the British Steel slabs imported into Fairless Works. That is the beginning of the end of the hot-steel process in this country. We have a right to be involved, and that is what our members expect us to do. [Ed. Note: U.S. Steel abandoned its proposed joint venture with British Steel several months after this discussion took place.] Most unions fail to realize that basically their members do want to participate in all such decisions that affect them. The whole concept of a democratic society now stops at the industrial gate. Once you open that up, you would be surprised to see that workers want to be involved in the decision-making process on everything that affects them in their workplace.

We have to extend the whole concept of the right to participate at the strategy level so that we can be part of corporate decisions. We had a chance to be involved through the Tripartite Steel Committee set up under the Carter administration. That committee produced the trigger-pricing concept. With union input at the very top level we were able to participate. We now have to start to take the initiative to save the industrial base in this country, but we are not going to do it unless the union movement takes the initiative as a total democratic concept, to be involved on the plant floor and at the strategic level, and not only once in three years through collective bargaining.

Donald Ephlin: As to how we represent our members, there are no barriers as to what is off limits. Whatever is legal we should try to do. Getting control of outsourcing in our industry was our first priority. It is unfortunate that we have to do so much through collective bargaining. Controlling costs, saving plants, and so forth, are not within the limits of collective bargaining. Our long-term strategies have been representing our people, getting their fair share, and protecting members' rights. Participating on the board, what does that do for us? Without the union there, the outside directors and the people on the board hear only from higher managers. I spoke to the Ford board of directors, and the first one who came out and said what a good job we were doing there was an outside director. Regarding entrepreneurial decisions and going beyond the norm, I do what I can to protect workers first; the many people getting displaced are important. But we are also helping to sell cars; we sent people out on the road and we got Ford to use the UAW logo in their ads. It is all geared to sell cars, which is in our best interests, and it is also not bad for the labor movement. It ties in with the mood of today. I think we have to use whatever weapons we can and somehow increase our political support. We must get into new areas as quid pro quo's for economic restraint. I think we have to do more of getting into decision making. General Motors did not invite us into QWL either. And as for the right to speak at the Ford board, well, they didn't offer that to me either; I took it.

Herman Starobin: Lee Price said we can't compete with third-world labor. This is even more true in the labor-intensive industries. Full employment used to be defined as 4% unemployment. Now, Feldstein [chairman of the President's Council of Economic Advisors] has it up to 7%. Will it go to 10%? What happens to the structure of the American economy? Aren't we really describing the process of becoming a third-world country? The primary interest of the nation-state is to protect the interest of its people, but neither the United States nor Canada seems to be doing that. I agree with Sam. A major element of the responsibility of governing, in protecting the interest of our people, includes a full-employment policy. We all know how the infrastructure (roads, bridges, sewers) has fallen apart. There has to be greater control of multinationals with limits on imports and some control on the movement of capital across borders.

Doris Lackey: We as labor organizations need to think about how we leverage our financial power. The financial institutions in this country are the ones that most directly affect the big economic decisions, and we need a voice there. Some unions are finding ways to do this. For example, there was significant movement between the textile workers and J. P. Stevens after several unions threatened to withdraw funds from Manufacturers Hanover, a bank that had financial involvement with Stevens. Manufacturers Hanover influenced Stevens in a way that the textile workers could not. In another instance, the steelworkers threatened to withdraw their accounts from a Pennsylvania bank if it continued to withhold funds owed to other workers for back pay from a firm that closed down. The bank paid. It also agreed to target investments to help revive the area's economy. When we talk about corporate strategy, we have to realize that we have it within our power to influence whether and how these institutions help finance industry's activities. Our pension funds, our investments, and our treasuries provide tools to get their attention.

Michael Bennett: Organized labor should take advantage of boardroom openings as soon as possible. Certainly USW in Youngstown would have taken the opportunity if it had been available. The outcome would have been no less severe and the tragedy might have been avoided. Besides the boardroom, though, we need to get involved in decision making at the plant or division or other relevant operating levels of a company as well. For example, I am talking with GM management at both the division and the plant level under the auspices of the job security clause we negotiated into our contract. In Flint, Buick made the decision on the front- versus the rear-wheel drive and where to build it. At least sixty presentations were made to GM at the corporate level to convince them to build this product in Flint, and we eventually succeeded. Those efforts came out of the joint local union and management meetings. The idea for the union is to be a social conscience in these meetings.

Richard Prosten: An attempt has to be made to expand union involvement in order to deal with a process that has been under way since World War II of building megacompanies through acquisitions and expansions. It is this process, to a great extent, that has changed the urge of unions to control companies. The corporate structure is not now responsive to collective bargaining, especially decentralized collective bargaining, if it ever was. The corporate decision-making process has changed, as well as our ability to influence it.

Michael Bonn: I agree with Sam Camens on the issue of the number of jobs that are lost because we do not get involved. In our union we have local autonomy, and our local is trying to force the banking industry to invest in our valley instead of taking the money overseas. Think of the implications nationwide if we and other locals were able to do this. We would rebuild our industries rather than wait for some national political or industrial policy to come along.

Charles Sabel: The description of the world that Lee Price presented, one of American basic industries surviving in the face of lower wages worldwide, has gone forever. But no amount of wage cutting will ever save those industries in their present form. The tragedy of the labor movement is that it assumed that management would make the right decisions. American management has not solved its competitive problems and it has hurt itself as well as labor. The groups (that is, management and the government) that labor has trusted are themselves desperately confused. There is no guarantee that the United States will emerge successfully from its economic crisis. The outcome depends on who takes the initiative. Americans—management, labor, and government—are lousy planners compared to Europeans, where governments have been more involved in strategic planning, and union participation and corporate planning have been more common. But Americans are especially good at finding innovative solutions at the local level. If labor doesn't help find an answer, there is no guarantee that someone else will.

Thomas Kochan: This has been a remarkable discussion. Two or three years ago you could not have gotten a group of labor leaders and academics in a room to talk openly about the issue of whether unions should get directly involved in basic management decision-making processes. The discussion would have ended with a consensus that "codetermination was perhaps all right for Europe," but American unions believe in using collective bargaining and are not interested in participating in management for both philosophical and historical reasons. But here we are going much farther, recognizing that the issue is not whether codetermination is appropriate but rather noting that there are various channels—industry levels, corporate levels, and perhaps others—for achieving union influence over basic management decisions. We are now talking about these as strategic, not philosophical, issues and debating feasibility as practical matters. I think this represents considerable progress for both academics and the labor movement.

IV

Labor Market and
Technological
Developments

8   White-Collar Employment

Paul Osterman

In recent years considerable scholarly energy has been devoted to examining innovations in the pattern of the U.S. labor market and U.S. labor relations. High on the list of topics are technical changes such as robotics, the implications of growing foreign competition for domestic markets, and shifts in the nature of collective bargaining. Each of these concerns, and several others, is important for understanding the evolution of the labor market and labor relations, and each deserves the attention it has received.

Nonetheless, an important aspect of labor markets and industrial relations has been absent from most of the recent research. As is well known, white-collar employment is now the largest single job category—in 1981 it accounted for 53% of employment—yet virtually all research has been devoted to blue-collar jobs. This limited attention would be unfortunate even in a period in which white-collar employment arrangements were relatively stable, but such is very much not the case now. There is substantial evidence that the internal and external labor markets for white-collar jobs have been subject to considerable change and various pressures. Hence it is all the more important to understand the nature of this sector of the labor market.

My purpose is to describe briefly some of the findings of my research on white-collar employment. This research has taken several forms. I conducted a set of intensive interviews with some large Boston-area white-collar employers.[1] These interviews were designed to map the internal labor markets—job ladders, training procedures, hiring requirements and the like—for several representative white-collar occupations. Second, I examined the impact of technical change upon white-collar employment through a large national sample of industries for which I have information on employment levels, wage levels, and the extent to which mainframe computers have been deployed. Finally,

I have analyzed national surveys of white-collar employees with an eye to understanding the nature of white-collar careers.

Technical Change

It is difficult to pick up a newspaper or magazine without reading about technical change in the office. Computers and word processing have already invaded offices in large numbers, and other technologies, such as electronic mail and teleconferencing, seem poised for a similar assault. It is important to discount much of the talk of the "office of the future" as something of a media creation, particularly since observations reveal much less change than one would suspect from the attention the topic has received. Nonetheless it does seem clear that a significant wave of technological change is upon us.[2]

Much of the discussion of this technological change has a somewhat schizophrenic quality. One often hears two different and seemingly contradictory arguments. First, many commentators claim that the widespread introduction of computers and computer-driven technologies threatens to render obsolete the skills of today's workers. Related to this claim is the belief that our educational system must train youth in "computer literacy" and other higher-level technical skills. All of this implies that computers and other innovations will demand more training than our labor force possesses. It is even sometimes argued that the technical backwardness of the American labor force is in some sense responsible for the difficulties we have had in meeting foreign competition.

Set against this is a quite different interpretation. This is the argument, sometimes made by the same commentators who propagate the first view, that technical change is de-skilling the work force. The argument here is that computers and other innovations are replacing skilled labor and are lowering the skill requirements of jobs. This is seen as a special danger in the case of computers because of their capacity to "think" and hence perform functions hitherto reserved for people. Related to the de-skilling argument is a concern about the labor-displacing effect of the new technologies.

Both the "up-grading" and the "de-skilling" interpretation of computers and other new technologies are intuitively appealing, and both are widely accepted in the press and in academic circles.[3] Yet on their face the two views conflict. It is possible, of course, to reconcile the two perspectives. For now, however, it is simply worth noting that the general failure to recognize the contradictory nature of two widely held interpretations is good evidence of considerable confusion on the subject.

The issues raised by this topic are complex, and it is by no means clear what the new technologies actually portend. It would be both presumptuous and premature to claim an answer to the problem. However, it is possible to examine the logic of the positions and bring some preliminary evidence to bear.

The logic of the de-skilling position seems to be the most compelling, at least as judged by its claim to the bulk of academic and union writing on the subject. Clearly, there is a tendency for employers to substitute unskilled for skilled labor, and clearly the urge to subdivide jobs is a powerful one. At the same time it is important to understand that there are important limits to the argument:

- First, it is also true that employers possess a powerful drive to minimize costs and it may be that minimum labor costs are achieved with a relatively small labor force of skilled workers working with computers compared to a larger labor force of unskilled workers working with (or "for") computers. In this case there would be displacement but not de-skilling.

- Second, employers seek to reduce turnover whenever possible since quitting imposes hiring and training costs. Excessively subdivided or de-skilled jobs will often raise the quit rate and hence the logic of the division of labor is unlikely to be taken to the extreme.

- Third, the long-term effect of technical change has historically been to upgrade skill levels. The American labor force today clearly holds more skilled jobs, and is a more skilled labor force, than fifty or a hundred years ago. Of course, this may be small consolation to workers who have difficulty making the transition to higher skills required by technical change.

- Finally, computer technology also provides the wherewithal to expand or broaden jobs. For example, in some insurance companies before computerization several different clerks divided the tasks of opening mail containing claims, assembling the client's file, and determining the appropriate outcome. Because files have now been computerized all of these tasks are now combined into a new, and broader, job.

As this last observation suggests, fieldwork turns up evidence of both division of labor and recombination of jobs. This suggests that in significant measure the impact is a matter of choice to the firm and is subject to a variety of forces. My interviews suggest three major influences upon how firms design jobs in response to the possibilities offered by new technologies.

Government Regulation

The first influence is government regulation, particularly affirmative action. As we will see in our discussion of job ladders, firms have altered their internal labor markets and job specifications in several ways in response to equal employment opportunity (EEO) pressure. If new technologies are likely to lead to high turnover and low mobility in predominantly female jobs, the EEO implications of this are likely to be considered. Having said this, however, it is important to recognize that EEO is a consideration but is unlikely to be decisive.

Human Resource Policies

The second, and more significant, influence is what might be termed "human resource policies." The interviews strongly suggest that firms differ in their commitment to internal careers, training, and stability of employment. Some companies are strongly wedded to the concept that employees enter the firm at the bottom of the job ladder and the ladder is closed to entry at higher levels. These firms "train their own" and make considerable efforts to reduce turnover. In these circumstances the firms are reluctant to degrade jobs via new technologies and instead seek to broaden job content and to retrain the work force if necessary. By contrast other companies are more willing to hire from the outside at all levels of the job ladder and view turnover as much less problematical. It is under these conditions that de-skilling is most likely.

The determinants of variations in policies are somewhat obscure. For newer firms, particularly in the high technology field, the ideology of the founder seems important. Stable and predictable markets are also significant, and older firms in secure market niches adopt this ideology. It will be interesting to observe whether high technology firms can maintain their character in the face of growing competitiveness in their markets.

Union Avoidance

Finally, union avoidance is a clear motivation in some cases. It is quite apparent that white-collar employers are concerned about unionization among clerical and other lower-level white-collar employees. Most frequently this concern is reflected in wage determination, and the interviews developed considerable evidence of wage compression, that is, cases in which low-level white-collar wages were increased relative to those of managers in order to avoid unrest. Furthermore, as we will see, temporary help services are another common union avoidance technique. However, firms are also aware that job redesign is a potentially difficult issue. The examples of the most complete de-skilling occur when firms can also find a new labor force, suburban housewives or rural residents, for instance, for whom the redesigned jobs do not represent a setback. The most common example is movement of data-entry tasks to rural areas where long days in front of a cathode-ray tube (CRT) are acceptable. When such a labor force is unavailable, firms appear to be more cautious in their introduction of new technologies. Other instances in which de-skilling is prevalent is when the core of the union is composed of craft workers who are vulnerable to new technologies. In these cases the twin management urges of division of labor and limiting the power of the union converge and de-skilling is very likely.

Beyond the de-skilling versus upgrading argument there is another aspect of job redesign that is often overlooked. Technological change permits the reallocation of tasks among different jobs. This is a considerably more complex issue than the simple de-skilling concern, but it may, in fact, be more important. I have in mind a situation in which a production process is accomplished by several jobs, each of which contains a series of tasks. With the introduction of the new technology some tasks may be eliminated and some new ones added, but in addition some tasks are reallocated from one job to another. Studies by the Communications Workers of America suggest that such a process is under way for various technical jobs in the Bell system where new technologies bring unionized craft within the abilities of exempt (nonunion) employees.

Under this circumstance the de-skilling argument loses clear meaning. One job may be de-skilled in that it loses some tasks, but another job is upgraded because it gains new ones. An observer standing above the fray might conclude that the net effect is little change in overall skill level, but in fact important distributional considerations are involved. There may be a systematic pattern to who gains and who loses in the process. Specifically, some unions are concerned that tasks are reallocated from union members to supervisors or nonunion employees, and in this circumstance an important aspect of union response is to attempt to track the change in job tasks. Beyond the union issue, reallocation of work may occur between blue- and white-collar jobs, between men and women, and the like. Taken as a whole, this pattern of task reallocation is a consequence of technological change that is potentially very important and has too frequently been overlooked.

Displacement

The impact of new technologies was examined through econometric studies as well as fieldwork. This approach has, of course, the advantage of greater generality, although it is often purchased at the cost of a textured understanding of the process. Nonetheless the results are quite suggestive.

We studied whether the introduction and expansion of mainframe computers displaced clerical and managerial labor. Employment and wage data were collected on an industry basis for two years (1972 and 1978, years chosen because of their similarity in terms of the business cycle) and merged with industry data on the number and size of mainframe computers (including minicomputers but not micro or word processors) in those industries in the two years. We can thus determine how changes in employment levels varied with the extent of increases in computer usage.[4]

Despite the intensity of interest in the topic, no national study using "hard" data (as opposed to case studies) has hitherto been available. Two additional aspects of this effort are also significant. First, we examine employment levels of both clerks and managers. Traditionally attention has been focused on clerical employment, but in our view the fate of managers is linked to that of clerks. A great many of those identified in occupational statistics as managers supervise clerks, and therefore substantial loss of clerical employment should also affect them. The results of the study support this view. Second, we examine both the short- and the long-run impact of an expansion in computing power. In the short run we expect that the displacement effect would dominate, as computers are substituted for clerical and managerial labor. We expect that this effect will be larger than any short-run offsets, such as the need for some clerical labor to work directly with computers and the fact that computers may lower product prices and hence expand overall output. However, we also believe that in the long run the impact may be reversed, because computers may lead to a reorganization of the firm as the additional computing power permits an increase in information management, central control, and bureaucracy.[5] This re-organization—an increase in the amount of "managing"—may lead to some additional clerical and managerial employment.

The results of the study support most of these expectations. Between 1972 and 1978 the average industry increased its number of mainframe computers from 638 to 1,146, and the average size increased from 69 to 352 kilobytes. In the same period, the increase in computer power decreased both managerial and clerical employment. For managers a 1% increase in computing power (defined as the number of computers times their size) decreased employment by 0.12%; for clerks a 1% increase in computing power decreased their employment by 0.18%. Clearly the overall impact was one of displacement and employment loss. This impact was, however, composed of both a short-run and a long-run effect. In the short run the displacement was very large, but several years later this was somewhat offset by new hiring. There is, however, no reason to believe that the individuals initially laid off were the ones who were subsequently hired as partial replacements.

The most important conclusions from this study are that computers do in fact lead to employment reductions for both clerical and managerial employees. Hence concerns about displacement are justified. It is also important to understand that these results do not refer to microcomputers or word processors, but they certainly are suggestive in this regard.

Changing White-Collar Working Conditions

More than technology has changed in the white-collar world. Many of the most dramatic developments have occurred in the internal labor markets (personnel policies) of employers. These changes significantly affect the working conditions, promotion opportunities, and earnings of white-collar employees. In this section I will first describe the structure of internal labor markets for several representative white-collar occupations and will then take up some specific changes that have occurred in recent years. These will include the growing use of temporary help services, job posting, and increasing economic insecurity of white-collar work.

The Structure of Internal Labor Markets

Very little is known about the structure of white-collar internal labor markets, in part because of the bias in the literature toward blue-collar work and in part because of the tremendous heterogeneity of white-collar occupations, which makes generalization difficult. In our interviews we asked a series of questions designed to map the internal labor markets of three representative white-collar occupations: clerical workers, low-level managers, and computer programmers. We will focus here on three aspects of these job ladders.

1. *Entry Rules.* Internal labor markets vary in how open or closed they are to entry from outside the company and how easy it is to move into them from elsewhere in the firm.

2. *Skill Level.* Some job ladders require considerable skill and hence barriers to entry are a significant problem while in other cases entry skill requirements are not steep.

3. *Nature of the Skill.* The nature of the skills vary along several dimensions. Some skills are very firm-specific, that is, the skills are useful only in the company in which they are learned. As a result mobility is restricted. Other skills are more general. In addition, the role of technical proficiency versus personality attributes is an important unresolved issue with respect to white-collar employment.

The results of examining these and other aspects of white-collar internal labor markets have been reported elsewhere, but several points are worth noting here.[6] First, there is considerable variety in the extent of openness in white-collar internal labor markets. Managerial ladders are virtually closed to the outside except at the entry position but are fairly open to entry from elsewhere in the company. By contrast, computer programming job ladders are very open to the outside, and there is a great deal of interfirm movement. Their technical requirements, however, make them very difficult to enter from elsewhere in the company at any but the bottom position. Clerical positions are open to both outside and inside entry at virtually all levels of the job ladder.

Perhaps of greatest interest for our purposes is the nature of the skills involved in these occupations and the opportunities for training. First, not surprisingly, clerical jobs are the least skilled (as measured by time required to learn the job and entry-level education requirements), computer programmers are the most skilled, and managerial jobs lie in between. Once we examine the nature of the skills rather than the levels, however, there is considerable similarity across occupations. None of the occupations are very firm-specific, and movement among firms is possible in all cases. Second, although personality (measured as ability to get along with others) is never as important as technical knowledge, it is an important attribute in each of the three occupations.

Finally, and this is a central point for those concerned with retraining displaced workers and the ability of previously excluded groups to enter white-collar occupations, the evidence suggests that it is possible in each of these occupations to hire relatively unskilled individuals and train them so that they perform at an acceptable level of proficiency. Our evidence on this point is that a subgroup of firms in our sample expended considerably more resources than average on internal training and also tended to have job ladders that on average were more closed to outside entry. They compensated for the training expenditure by paying lower-than-average wages for each occupation. However, their entry-level hiring requirements were below average, and they hired a less-skilled work force. Furthermore, to the extent we could measure it, the content and nature of their jobs did not differ from those in other firms.[7] The significance of all this is that since firms that are willing to adopt a training-internal promotion strategy can economically employ "non-traditional" workers in white-collar jobs, there is no intrinsic reason, other than custom or habit, why these jobs should not be available to a broader spectrum of the labor force than is now the case.

Temporary Help Services

In virtually all of the firms we interviewed, the volume of temporary help was increasing. This finding is confirmed by national data. According to the Bureau of Labor Statistics, in 1983 2.5 million Americans worked as temporary employees, an increase of 25% from 1977.[8] Data from the trade association, the National Association of Temporary Services, also confirms this impression. According to their figures gross revenues in the industry increased from $612 million in 1971 to $5.3 billion in 1981.

These figures are an understatement—our interviews suggest that many firms are establishing in-house temporary pools that would not be included in the data. These in-house services are run along the same lines as the stand-alone services. Finally, it is worth noting that use of temporary help is not limited to clerical employees but is growing for a variety of occupations including engineers and computer programmers.

The use of temporary help arrangements clearly represents an effort by employers to circumvent the restrictions placed upon them by the formal and informal rules of internal labor markets. Temporary help provides flexibility in terms of employment levels and job assignment often absent with permanent workers. It is commonly the case, particularly for clerical workers, that union avoidance also is a motivation. This is signaled by the fact that the few firms that were not planning to establish their own in-house temporary services were those in which a large fraction of the labor force was already unionized or (in management's view) in danger of unionization. In these firms the in-house approach was unattractive since the substandard conditions seemed likely to lead to unionization of the temporary labor force. In these circumstances management found outside temporary services more desirable.

It seems apparent from the interviews that the trend toward increased use of temporary help services is likely to continue. The economic environment of the past decade has made firms extremely chary of increasing their permanent work force. Furthermore, even in the absence of formal contractual obligations it is difficult for employers to use their permanent workers in as flexible a way as they would wish. This is partly due to reputational constraints and the morale of those employees the firm wishes to retain. Furthermore, the growing willingness of courts to intervene in the employment relationship—for example, the recent developments concerning discharge and at-will employment— also make temporary help services more attractive. When firms use off-premises temporary help services, the personnel problems become those of the other company. When firms use in-house services, they seek to recruit workers with a set of expectations different than those of regular full-time employees. Under both circumstances the firm can deploy labor with very little constraint.

Job Posting

A second recent development concerns the growing use of posting systems in most white-collar settings. These systems have grown out of affirmative action pressure, pressure that has been more effective than is generally believed.[9] One goal of government enforcement has been to achieve "appropriate" proportions of target groups within each occupation. In our context the difficulty firms often face is a shortage of women in higher-level occupations. In order to provide themselves with a defense for these shortages and, in some cases, in a genuine effort to overcome them, firms have introduced job-posting and bidding schemes. Under these programs all jobs up to a certain level are posted, and all employees are eligible to apply.

Although job posting appears to change the nature of the job ladders dramatically, in practice the effect is considerably less sweeping. Some firms require managers to interview inside candidates but permit them to hire anyone, including outsiders. Other firms limit the number of jobs posted. In still other firms more mundane considerations block the effectiveness of the posting system. For example, the time lag between posting and closing of jobs is so short that only through informal word-of-mouth channels are most jobs really available. Finally, educational and experience requirements often place jobs out of reach. The consequence of all this is that job posting, which on its face is a revolutionary change in white-collar industrial relations, is most commonly used for clerical employees to move from one clerical job to another across departments. It is a mechanism for lateral, not vertical, mobility. However, there are a few firms that can demonstrate that posting has led to increased upward mobility, and it is clear that in most firms posting and affirmative action have created a set of expectations, and an institutional structure, that over time may be of consequence.

Economic Insecurity

The final structural change in the nature of white-collar work has been growing economic insecurity. In part this might be implied by developments discussed previously—labor-displacing technological change and increasing use of temporary help services—but more is involved. The growing economic difficulties are somewhat subtle in their effects and need to be carefully described.

With respect to the most common indicator of insecurity—unemployment rates—the pattern is mixed. In the recent economic downturn white-collar workers suffered along with everyone else. Table 8.1 shows the unemployment rates of white-collar workers, by occupation, for selected years. White-collar unemployment rates are relatively high by historical standards, and this fact is probably responsible for the plethora of startled newspaper and magazine articles about white-collar layoffs and the like. However, it is also important to note that white-collar unemployment rates have *not* risen relative to blue-collar rates. Regres-

Table 8.1
Unemployment rates by occupation and sex for selected years*

	Professional	Managerial	Sales	Clerical	Blue-collar
Men					
1967	1.0%	0.8%	2.2%	2.2%	3.8%
1973	1.7	1.2	2.5	3.0	4.8
1978	2.0	1.7	3.0	4.1	6.2
1981	2.2	2.1	3.4	5.1	9.8
Women					
1967	1.9	1.8	4.7	3.5	7.7
1973	2.9	2.5	5.2	4.5	7.7
1978	3.5	3.4	5.5	5.1	9.7
1981	3.4	4.1	5.9	5.9	12.7

Source: *Employment and Earnings* (Washington, D.C.: Bureau of Labor Statistics, various years).

sion equations that estimate the relationship between the unemployment rates of the different occupational groups, as a whole and separately by sex, find no time trend after controlling for the blue-collar unemployment rates. If anything, the results show a slight downward trend for several of the occupations. Hence by this measure white-collar insecurity is high in recent years because of the general economic downturn, not because of any structural shift in the nature of white-collar work.

In another respect, however, the economic circumstances of white-collar workers have worsened. Table 8.2 shows for selected years the fraction of white-collar workers, by sex and occupation, who worked part-time. The data permit us to distinguish between those who work part-time for voluntary reasons and those who work part-time for economic, that is, involuntary, reasons. As regression equations controlling for the business cycle confirm, there has been an increase in the fraction of white-collar workers working part-time for involuntary reasons (although the fractions involved remain small).[10] Distinguishing voluntary from involuntary reasons is important because these findings belie the common notion that part-time work has increased because the labor force composition has changed in a way that leads more workers to desire part-time employment or because preferences have somehow changed. Rather, it seems apparent that part-time work has increased against the will of many white-collar employees.

Table 8.2
Fraction of occupational employment part-time due to voluntary and involuntary decisions

	Professional		Managerial		Sales		Clerical	
	Voluntary	Involuntary	Voluntary	Involuntary	Voluntary	Involuntary	Voluntary	Involuntary
Men								
1967	.055	.005	.023	.006	.115	.009	.085	.010
1973	.060	.009	.024	.006	.105	.016	.091	.012
1978	.057	.013	.022	.007	.113	.017	.108	.020
1981	.054	.014	.027	.013	.103	.028	.111	.027
Women								
1967	.211	.009	.112	.011	.409	.036	.171	.014
1973	.200	.018	.119	.013	.447	.058	.199	.022
1978	.189	.026	.101	.016	.425	.063	.199	.030
1981	.187	.029	.105	.016	.411	.088	.197	.037

Source: *Employment and Earnings* (Washington, D.C.: Bureau of Labor Statistics, various years).
Note: Unemployment rates for 35–44-year-old white males were 1.6% in 1967, 1.8% in 1973, 2.5% in 1978, and 4.0% in 1981.

Conclusion

It would be desirable to emerge from this survey with a firm sense about the future of white-collar work, but that is not possible. The future is clouded and evidence points in several directions. In some ways technical change and computerization clearly pose a threat to the existing middle- and upper-level white-collar work force, but on the other hand for lower-level workers new promotion opportunities may emerge. Furthermore, the impact of technical change may involve substantial reallocation of tasks. Our evaluation of this process depends upon who gains new work and whose jobs are narrowed.

Similar ambiguity exists concerning structural changes in white-collar work. The spread of temporary help services and the growth of involuntary part-time work represent worsening of structural conditions, but even here there are some offsets, such as the emergence of job-posting systems. Finally, our evidence that a wide range of workers can be successfully trained for many white-collar jobs suggests that these occupations may potentially be sources of employment for people who in other times would have found work in the declining blue-collar sectors. Hence, even if white-collar work is "degraded" from the perspective of the occupation, it may represent upgrading viewed from the perspective of the labor force.

If we cannot confidently predict the direction of white-collar work, we can at least describe some of the factors that will shape the ultimate outcome. Four considerations come to mind: (1) the future pattern of technology; (2) the success of new forms of managerial organization; (3) government regulation; and (4) unionization.

Much of the recent scholarly energy devoted to studying technology has emphasized that specific technologies do not inevitably impose particular job designations upon employers. Whether jobs are narrowed or broadened remains discretionary. This perspective is a healthy antidote to earlier tendencies toward technological determinism, but it is often overstated. The range of economically efficient production configurations is limited by the technology at hand. There is little point in denying this. On the other hand, more discretion lies in the hands, and minds, of those who design specific technologies, and it is here that the greatest uncertainty rests. What new devices will emerge from the research laboratories is an open question and in fact is subject to political and social intervention. It would seem that the decisions of manufacturers and vendors should be the focus of serious research.

The second significant factor is the success or failure of some of the new management models that have emerged in growth sectors. In many respects the organization of white-collar work in newer, high technology firms differs from that found in older, traditional industries. Jobs are more loosely defined, there are greater opportunities for intra-firm mobility, and lifetime employment is an espoused goal if not always a reality. It seems fair to say that the working life of most white-collar workers is richer and more satisfying in these firms than elsewhere.

The open question, however, is whether this model is viable in the long run or whether it merely reflects the luxury of high growth rates combined with the sensibility of a younger generation of managers. The crucial question is what will happen when growth slows and competition bites. At that point we will learn whether these firms represent a model of the future or a transitory pattern.

The third consideration is whether government regulation once again becomes aggressive. This is particularly significant in the case of affirmative action efforts because such a large proportion of the white-collar work force is female. As we noted in our discussion of job posting, government regulation can alter the pattern of internal job ladders and hence can exert a significant impact upon the nature of white-collar work.

Implications for the Labor Movement

The final determinant of the future shape of white-collar work is the success, or lack thereof, of the union movement in organizing white-collar workers. It is apparent from our research that employers are deeply concerned and have structured compensation systems and hiring practices in order to minimize the opportunities for organization. At the same time it is also well known that major organizing efforts are under way, particularly among clerical workers but also sporadically among others, such as engineers. It is very difficult to predict the outcome of these efforts. Obviously the organization of white-collar workers is not impossible (as witness many European countries), but here one senses that the outcome rests not so much on any particular event but rather on whether the union movement or economic conditions can alter the world view and self-image of many white-collar workers. Many of the successful clerical organizing drives have occurred on college campuses or in other nonprofit organizations where the general atmosphere is conducive to the notion of unions. Much less success is apparent in the private sector. Success probably requires that the individualistic orientation of white-collar workers be left behind and that a group consciousness emerge. Existing studies of the union organizing process (which emphasize the attributes of individual workers) provide little guidance on how this occurs.

A transformation of white-collar employees' attitudes may depend crucially upon whether the union movement can creatively develop innovations in what it offers employees. Aggressive employers seem able to compete with unions on wages and benefits. It is at least possible that unions need to shift to developing an agenda around the issues of technological change, upgrading and de-skilling, innovative job ladders, sex discrimination, autonomy and professional standards, and a variety of other issues that have generally received little attention. Whether such an agenda will in turn require organizational innovations is a topic that must be carefully considered.

Of all these issues perhaps the most pressing is the formulation of a union stance with respect to technical change. In general, the historically most typical response seems to be essentially reactive and defensive. Unions have less often sought to influence the design and deployment of technology than they have attempted to protect their membership from decisions already made by management. Such a stance may be effective in situations of considerable union strength or when technical change is incremental. However, neither of these preconditions is applicable in our case. There is at least an argument to be made that unions must seek to match management expertise concerning the options inherent in particular technologies. It may even be that unions should move backward in the chain and seek to influence vendor decisions. This may imply national political action on the subject of technical innovation.

This discussion is meant to be speculative and provocative. We cannot be confident of the answers or even feel that we have asked the right questions. Nonetheless I hope I have demonstrated that the white-collar labor market is dynamic and fluid, that there is much to understand, and that interesting and important discoveries are possible.

Notes

1. The industries represented in the survey were banking, insurance, utilities, electronics manufacturing, and consumer goods manufacturing.

2. It is worth noting that this is not the first such wave. At least for clerical workers, the introduction of the typewriter early in the century was equally

significant. There is still considerable debate in the literature about whether this improved or worsened working conditions.

3. The major advocate of the de-skilling position is Harry Braverman, *Labor and Monopoly Capital* (New York: Monthly Review Press, 1974). His argument has been applied to a variety of settings by different authors. For an application to the computer programming occupation see Joan M. Greenbaum, *In The Name of Efficiency* (Philadelphia: Temple University Press, 1969). For the upgrading argument see Robert Blauner, *Alienation and Freedom* (Chicago: University of Chicago Press, 1964).

4. The results of this study are reported in Paul Osterman, "The Impact of Computers upon the Employment of Clerks and Managers" (Department of Economics, Boston University, March 1984, Mimeographed).

5. Hence the common complaint that computers really increase the amount of paperwork and reports. In the paper cited in note 4 I develop a more careful explanation of how this might happen.

6. Paul Osterman, "White-collar Internal Labor Markets," in *Internal Labor Markets*, ed. Paul Osterman (Cambridge: MIT Press, 1984), and Paul Osterman, "Internal Labor Markets and the Mismatch Hypothesis, A Study of White-collar Employment," *Proceedings of the Industrial Relations Research Association* (1982), 436–460. Another relevant paper is Paul Osterman, "Employment Structures Within Firms," *British Journal of Industrial Relations* 20 (November 1982) 349–361.

7. A good example of the two approaches can be found in the case of computer programmers. The most common strategy has been to hire these workers on the external labor market. This seems to make sense both because the skills are technical and because firms that train their own face the danger of seeing their workers pirated. A few firms, however, have taken a different track. They have established a ladder out of secretarial and clerical positions into programming training courses. They avoid the danger of pirating by permitting only fairly long-term employees to apply and by teaching company-specific programming skills. In other words, they do not train these workers to be general-purpose programmers but rather to work only on company procedures. It is also interesting to note that this points up the ambiguity of the de-skilling argument. From the perspective of the programming profession the work has been de-skilled, but from the perspective of the former clerical workers upgrading has occurred.

8. *Personnel Journal* 62 (February 1983): 124.

9. See Paul Osterman, "Affirmative Action and Opportunity, the Impact of the Contract Compliance Program Upon the Turnover of Female Employees," *Review of Economics and Statistics* 64 (November 1982), 604–612.

10. Positive and statistically significant coefficients on time trend variables (in a regression in which the dependent variable is the fraction of employment, by occupation and sex, comprised of involuntary part-time workers and in

which the independent variables were the time trend and the unemployment rate) were found for men in professional, sales and clerical work, and for women in the same three occupations. Only managerial employment was exempt from this trend. In similar equations in which the dependent variable measured *voluntary* part-time work the only statistically significant coefficients on the time trend variables were negative for women in professional and managerial work and positive for men in clerical work.

9 Computer Technologies, Market Structure, and Strategic Union Choices

Michael J. Piore

There have accumulated over the last ten years a variety of case studies on the impact of computer technologies upon the job structure. These studies have produced confusing and contradictory results. Some suggest that computer technologies are like other forms of mechanization and automation: they reduce the total number of workers required to produce a given output; they reduce the skills associated with manual blue-collar work; and, on balance, they reduce the relative numbers of blue-collar jobs, shifting the structure of employment toward managerial and technical workers. Others seem to suggest exactly the opposite: the old distribution between blue-collar and white-collar work is blurred. Computer technology requires a close collaboration between skilled blue-collar workers and new technical workers who program and manage the new equipment. Thus, manual labor seems if anything to be more highly valued than before. And in some workplaces total employment actually expands.

These contradictory results are generated by the fact that computer technologies are actually being used in two very different types of production situations. One of these is mass production, which involves very long runs of standardized products. The prototypical case is automobile assembly. Here, computer-aided technology is designed, as mechanization and automation have always been, to eliminate labor. In car assembly, for example, robotics has been introduced in painting and welding, jobs that were difficult to man effectively because of extremely unpleasant and dangerous working conditions. In welding, the machines also ensure levels of quality that workers are unable to maintain consistently. The chief advantage of computer-controlled, as opposed to conventional, machines is that they can move around and position themselves with a flexibility and agility that heretofore only a human being could do. The people who previously did the work are no longer required; they are replaced by the technician who programs and maintains the machines. The programs are complex and difficult to work out, but little initial knowledge of the production process is required, since the program can be debugged through a process of trial and error in the initial stages of what is inevitably a very long production series and the cost amortized over subsequent units of output.

The second kind of production situation is the introduction of computers into shops where the product design changes frequently and where, as a result, there are much shorter production runs. In these shops the computer-controlled equipment offers many of the advantages of mechanization and automation previously available only in mass production. Under the older technologies the economies were obtained through the use of highly specialized equipment dedicated to a particular set of operations, and only in mass production were the runs long enough to pay back the investment in equipment of this kind. With computers, it is no longer necessary to specialize the equipment in this way. Instead of junking the hardware each time the design changes, it is simply reprogrammed.

In this second type of use, however, there is a tremendous premium on getting the program right the first time around. The production run is not long enough to debug a faulty program through trial and error in the process of production. A technician skilled in programming alone is not equal to the task. The collaboration of an experienced workman who knows the production process and can anticipate trouble is required. Either the workmen must be taught to do the programming themselves or the programmers must learn how to communicate with skilled workers and utilize their knowledge. Very often, an experienced worker must also watch the programmed machine in operation, spotting it when it begins to go wrong and intervening to stop it and sometimes perform the operation manually before irreparable damage is done to an expensive part or to materials. Again, to underscore the point, the machines could in principle be programmed correctly to operate without the aid of skilled workers: the problem is that the production run is too short to make that kind of programming economical. Industries in which this is the case range from specialized machinery operations to the use of computer-aided sizing, marking, and cutting in the garment industry.

This suggests that the impact of the new technologies on the job structure is going to depend very much on an aspect of the economy that has received very little attention by economic analysts—the length of production runs. What will be the distribution of output between mass production and short-run batch production? That distribution depends upon the structure of product markets.

Market Structures

Historically, mass markets for single standardized products did not occur naturally—they were created and maintained by a specific set of organizations and institutions. The central institution was the modern corporation that organized the market for individual commodities and controlled the supply and the price of basic material inputs so that supply conditions were predictable and stable enough to invest in the highly specialized equipment dedicated to a particular make and model. At the macroeconomic level, a variety of governmental institutions, ranging from the Federal Reserve Board to the unemployment insurance and Social Security systems, worked to sustain aggregate demand, creating a stable set of background conditions that would validate corporate policies in individual markets. Industrial unionism as it evolved in the postwar period has also provided important institutional support for mass markets at both the micro and the macro level. At the micro level, industrial unions have provided a way of reconciling workers' rights and a concern with worker welfare in mass production with stability and continuity in the production process necessary to validate the kinds of technologies involved in mass production. At the macro level, the wage determination structure in which the settlements of the industrial unions are key has been a central element in maintaining the stable, long-term expansion of purchasing power required to sustain mass markets.

In the last ten years, however, background conditions necessary to validate traditional forms of mass production have deteriorated. Several factors seem to have intervened to render the institutional structures that had been successful in earlier decades increasingly inadequate to the task. First, the domestic market for the major durable goods around which mass production had been centered became saturated. Virtually every American family has at least one car; many have two or more. The potential markets for household durables have similarly been filled. This, moreover, is the case not only in the United States—in other industrial countries as well mass producers can clearly foresee the saturation of domestic demand. As a result, beginning in the late 1960s and increasingly in the 1970s, the major industrial producers began to compete with each other for their own markets and those of the developing world. As they did so, the markets of many producers became smaller and, even more important, increasingly unstable and uncertain, making investment precarious in the large-scale, specialized equipment that mass production requires. The competitive pressure breaking up mass markets was further intensified by the entrance of newly developing countries. The role of the Asians has been particularly damaging because they pursued labor policies that suppressed their own wage levels, and in expanding world productive capacity, they contributed little to world demand for consumer durable goods. The Latin American countries have pursued a more benign policy, expanding production and consumption in a more balanced way.

The second factor breaking up mass markets in the last decade has been the great increase in the overall uncertainty of the general economic climate. Wide fluctuations in the prices of primary materials, especially oil, have made demand highly volatile. As energy prices have fluctuated, automobile demand has shifted unpredictably from small, fuel-efficient cars to large, traditional ones and back again, confusing manufacturers as to what to produce. The confusion has been augmented by unusually sharp fluctuations in national economic activity, by variations in the rate of inflation, by the high levels of interest rates and the unpredictably long period over which these levels have been maintained, and by the deregulation of a number of markets that government policies had previously stabilized. Finally, and this is very important, since 1971 major international currencies have been freed to fluctuate relative to each other; the value of the dollar has moved widely, and unpredictably, relative to the value of the currencies of our major trading partners.

Computer technology, and the particular contribution it makes to batch production, has aided the adjustment to this more volatile economic climate. But those developments have probably also added to the volatility because they have enabled small-scale producers with specialty products to pick off bits and pieces of demand at the edges of what would previously have been the basic market for mass production. The mini-mills have done this in steel. Small Japanese and Italian producers have done this in machine tools. A similar phenomenon is occurring in chemicals. And some observers have argued that this is an important factor in the success of Japanese automobile manufacturers in the U.S. market. Thus, since the new technology points in two contradictory directions and the market structure determines the direction in which the job structure will actually move, recent economic trends have been decisive. They are clearly pushing toward a revaluation of the skills of experienced workmen and a breakdown of the traditional division of blue-collar and white-collar responsibilities, toward a more collaborative relationship between the two kinds of workers, if not the actual integration of the two kinds of responsibilities.

Union Strategies

What conclusions can one draw about the role of trade unions in American society—what are the implications for union strategy? The answer is that this very much depends on how market structures evolve over the coming decade. If we can re-create the predictable, smoothly expanding mass markets of the earlier postwar decades, there will be a shift back toward mass production and older union strategies will again become viable. But if this does not happen, trade unions will have to invent new strategies and structures appropriate to the emergent flexible production structures. It is impossible now to say which of these alternatives is more likely. But I think it will be very difficult to re-create the background conditions required for mass production and, hence, that trade unions must think through the implications of these changes for their role in American society.

To appreciate what would be involved in the moving from mass production to flexible production, it is useful to go back to fundamentals and look at the basic role of unions in the two systems. I detect a certain reluctance to do this, a reluctance covered by the phrase "Our job is to do the best we can for the workers we represent." But this should not obscure the fact that worker organizations play an organic role in the production process, and that role determines *how* they are able to go about protecting and enhancing worker welfare. The nature of the production process determines what union strategies and tactics are consistent with the economic constraints under which business firms operate and which ones can, therefore, be successful in organizing the labor force and winning material concessions.

Under mass production, competitive advantage comes from pressing to achieve economies of scale. Producers have for this reason sought (1) to organize the steady expansion of the markets for their product; and (2) to stabilize the economic environment and the central parameters of business decisions so as to minimize the risk of the large investments in specialized equipment that mass production entailed. Their labor relations policies have, almost from the inception of the large corporations, been motivated by the desire for this stability. The major instruments that have been used to achieve stability in labor relations are high and rigid wages, and in mass-producing industries these long predate unions. Big business has consistently believed—at least up until last year—that the gains from such stability would outweigh by far the short-run advantage they might achieve by pushing down wages temporarily when they were in a position to do so. Ford introduced the $5 day in 1914, over twenty years before the UAW appeared on the scene. U.S. Steel, along with virtually all manufacturing corporations, maintained its wage levels for the first two years of the Great Depression. The wage reductions that the companies finally introduced in the fall of 1931 were, from the companies' point of view, a disaster since they did not regenerate profits and they created the atmosphere of discontent and betrayal that, when the recovery made it feasible, led to worker protest and industrial unionism. The new unions restored the stability that mass production required, in part by reintroducing high and stable wage levels, in part by collective bargaining practices designed to ensure internal equity and industrial democracy.

The new collective bargaining practices were also linked closely to and oriented toward mass production. Bargaining takes place around a set of defined rules and procedures governing wage determination, work practices, discipline, and job assignments all linked to a clearly defined and carefully specified set of jobs, unambiguously assigned to particular workers. There is also a clear demarcation of responsibility between the union and management. The union negotiates a set of rules with management in the collective bargaining process: the contract is implemented by management and the implementation is overseen by the union. All of this, however, is only really possible when there is a well-defined production process with a clear set of work tasks and responsibilities that can be identified in advance, and that in turn implies that there is a single set of standardized products.

What will be the unions' role under flexible production technologies and shifting markets? In this world too it will be essential to maintain high, stable wages. But the reasons for such a wage policy are different. The new world will be—indeed, it already is—one of very intense competition. The competition is creative and leads to economic growth and prosperity if it takes place around new product designs and new techniques of production to go with them. (Think, for example, of the high fashion garment industry.) But in the short run, any business can probably stay afloat by cutting wages and selling the old products at lower cost. For the economy, and possibly the firm, this will lead to economic stagnation. To prevent this from happening, to channel competition into product and process innovations, wages need to be taken out of competition. It is difficult to imagine this happening without strong trade unions.

Unions are also necessary for a second, even more fundamental, reason. Effective product and process innovation requires the maintenance of a sense of community among producers in which tight collaboration is possible. I have emphasized the collaboration between skilled blue-collar workers and white-collar technicians required in programming machines for a shifting product mix. But the scope of the community required in this kind of environment is much greater than simply the community between labor and management. In the intense competition that accompanies this kind of production and the rapid shifting among product designs and processes, everyone's fate is subject to luck and everyone eventually loses a round now and then. Often, there will be a run of such losses. Competition of this kind is thus tolerable only if there is some kind of safety net: in the garment and construction industries, for example, the fluidity with which people shift from worker to supervisor or even to employer status and back again, and the way in which the current winners use the losers as subcontractors, is part of that safety net and sustains a sense of community. In these industries, unions are important—in many cases the key—institutions in defining and maintaining this community. In these dispersed industries, and in large companies as well, the barrier that unions erect to "sweating" is also a key in the maintenance of community and cooperation.

But the way in which unions operate under flexible technologies has to be very different from the way they operate in mass production. As the product becomes more variable and work tasks and responsibilities change frequently and in unpredictable patterns, it becomes much more difficult to define a set of jobs in advance and to write rules to govern the variety of issues and contingencies likely to arise in the shop. General principles, as opposed to specific rules, come to govern labor-management relations; wage determination and work allocation tend to center on concepts such as skill or craft as opposed to a set of particular jobs. The line between worker and managerial responsibility and between union and employer roles becomes a good deal more ambiguous. When general principles as opposed to specific rules govern work relations, the line between contract negotiations and contract administration is also more difficult to draw because there is much wider room for interpretation, and hence for negotiation, in the application of a previously accepted principle to a specific situation. The contrast between industrial relations in the work situation emerges most clearly in industries like construction, where pay is based on craft, the contract is reinterpreted on every major project by the business agent, work assignments are fluid and constantly changing, supervisors are members of the union and sometimes the contractor is a member as well, and where the worker can often lay out a job better than his boss can. But even in industrial unions, shop practice tends to drift in the direction of construction as one moves out of the mass-production parts of the industry toward areas of more specialized production.

The changes in market structure and technology associated with the computer are already creating pressures on industrial unions and the employers with whom they bargain to experiment with new forms of collective bargaining. The quality-of-work-life programs in the automobile industry can be interpreted as moves in this direction. The requisite changes may, however, have to go even further and break distinctions that are not only matters of practice but also of law. The traditional definition of the bargaining unit, for example, which excludes the supervisors and technicians who under computer technology in batch production collaborate so closely with skilled blue-collar labor that their jobs tend to merge, loses its original logic. The notion of managerial prerogatives loses much of its original logic as well, as the line between conception and execution becomes blurred. The close collaborative relationships here clearly begin to resemble patterns of industrial relationship in some European countries where there are works councils in the shop and union representatives on company boards of directors.

What remains problematic under these collective bargaining arrangements is the relationship among workers in different shops and enterprises. The problem is well illustrated by an example my colleague Harry Katz reported from a QWL shop in the auto industry. A worker pointed out an empty bay in the factory formerly devoted to an operation that a year ago had been shifted to another plant because it was too expensive to perform in-house. "If they were going to do that today," the worker said, "they would sit down with us and we would figure out how to cut costs enough to remain competitive in-house." Looked at one way, this is a poignant example of the new spirit of Japanese-style, labor-management collaboration. But it is also a situation in which management is able to play off workers in different units of the same company against each other in ways that undermine worker solidarity. The union will clearly have to find ways to limit that competition if it is to survive. And the QWL experiments have yet to suggest ways of doing this.

The business organization itself, however, may change in shape and structure under the impact of the changing market structure in ways that make that task easier. The two industries that at least historically have been more clearly characterized by the small-batch production the emergent economic climate seems to favor are garments and construction. These industries are characterized by small productive units, and the productive apparatus is built up by linking these units in shifting structures of complex subcontracting arrangements. The small size of the typical unit and the way in which the units combine depends on the flexibility of the product design and the variability of the markets to which the industries cater. Both these industries, it is true, have recently evolved in the direction of larger, more stable organizational structures, but this does not necessarily detract from their irrelevance as organizational models. Productive centers that seem to have been most successful in the specialty markets growing at the edges of the older mass-production industries, such as Japan or central Italy, have organizational characteristics similar to those that have historically dominated in garments and construction. This suggests that the union structures of those two industries (and certain parts of the trucking industry) may provide models for, or at least ideas about, new forms of union organization that will be more relevant to the economic climate. Again, there are legal issues arising in this connection that will probably have to be reexamined if the new organizational forms appropriate to this kind of economic structure are to be successful. The secondary boycott provisions of the NLRA, for example, have an effect that is altogether different in dispersed industries than under mass production; for this reason the garment industry is actually exempted from many of those provisions.

It may be a mistake, however, to expect in the future exact parallels of the past. Large corporations appear to be responding to the shifting market structures by developing the flexibility that has characterized garments and construction internally or by establishing new linkages with their suppliers and customers. They are decentralizing power and responsibility so as to make the various units of the enterprises relatively more autonomous, forcing them to compete with each other for various aspects of corporate activity but also enabling them to combine and recombine with each other to perform one or another corporate task in new and different ways. At the same time, the shifting technology and requirements for flexibility have forced large corporations for the first time to lay off numbers of higher-level managers. Those managers have themselves often found jobs with customers and suppliers. But the vagaries of the economic climate are creating paradoxical situations where the laid-off managers sometimes later reappear working for the original company, either as consultants or temporary help, because business unexpectedly spurted or because their new company merged with the old one. The uncertainties about managerial careers that these changes are generating could create the anxieties and discontents that have been conducive to the organization of blue-collar workers, but they also raise questions about the relevant organizational entity. Clearly, a shop or even a plant is no longer the relevant bargaining unit—perhaps the enterprise itself is too small a unit. The corporation in its current form arose to organize mass production. Historically, batch production occurred in dispersed enterprises linked through shifting subcontracts. The new corporate forms may thus prove unstable—increasing use of subcontractors and consultants may be a sign that the corporation itself will eventually dissolve. This may point toward organizing a new occupation like computer programming on a craft basis across industries. But perhaps both the organizational structure and the anxieties that current employer practices are generating militate in favor of new organizational categories. Is it possible, for example, to organize middle-level managers as a class across industries? Could workers in several different companies who normally do business with each other be organized in a single unit?

It is much too early to see clearly the future direction of the economy. We seem to be drifting in an environment of unstable markets toward new, flexible production techniques. These techniques and the markets in which they arise are producing major organizational changes. But the new organizational forms are still fluid, and it is unclear which, if any, will survive. There will clearly be a place in the new world for unions. Indeed, it is unlikely that a dynamic, growing economic system can be built around flexible forms of production and shifting markets without strong worker organizations. Such organizations are required to channel competitive pressures away from sweating and into innovation and to create and preserve the sense of community between workers and employers that is critical to the innovative process. But the worker organizations that do this will be different from those that operate under mass production, and unions will have to experiment to discover organizational forms that fit the new environment. The period of experimentation may be prolonged by the fact that what ultimately works will depend upon the forms that business organizations ultimately take, and these are still unclear. The wider the range of experiments that unions tolerate or actively encourage, the better the chance that they will create an organizational form compatible with the solution that does eventually emerge.

But the foregoing ignores an important and alarming possibility— U.S. business may not be adequate to the task of self-reorganization. American corporations no less than American labor—indeed in certain respects much more than labor—have been oriented toward mass production. The corporation may simply be unable to escape a heritage institutionalized in its standard operating procedures and reinforced by the system of professional education on which it draws. If this is so, the economy will continue in the 1980s, as it did in the 1970s, to slip progressively farther behind in world competition. Successful readjustment would require the intervention of new actors. This contingency is admitted in the developing political debate about the need for an "industrial policy"; but the phrase as used in the debate is really empty. Industrial policy seems to mean that the government should do *something*. But nobody has a compelling idea of what the government should do or why it should be better able to see it and do it than business itself. The labor movement has been advocating trade restrictions, but if our argument is correct about the relationship between new technologies and market structure, such restrictions will just push us farther beyond the situation which we already find so difficult. The domestic market is just too small to sustain mass production; to escape the pressures the economy is under, we would need more international trade, not less. To the extent that our problems are the result of the failure of our domestic producers to adjust to the changing climate, trade restrictions will paradoxically only increase the advantage of our more adept foreign competitors.

But perhaps the labor movement may be able to generate an industrial policy of its own. The new, flexible forms of production require a variety of complementary activities that are of much less importance under mass production—more extensive vocational training, employment and hiring services for moving skilled workers and technicians around in the economy as markets and products shift, research and development for the new products and processes that respond to these shifts. Were flexible production to develop within the large enterprises inherited from the age of mass production, those enterprises would presumably provide these things themselves. But if they cannot adapt, then flexible production will have to develop in federations of smaller enterprises, and in these federations the provision of communal services of this kind is problematic. Outside the mass-production industries, American unions have often based their power upon exactly this kind of role within the market. The garment unions used to run industrial engineering departments capable of advising small firms of the latest technologies and of actually laying out their plants for them; the construction and maritime unions have always been critical in vocational training and hiring halls. These activities have not only been central to the successful operation of their industries but have given the unions the leverage required to police employers as well. Ultimately the American economy could come to depend on the capacity of trade unions to assume these roles in a much wider range of industries and situations. If this older trade union tradition can indeed be successfully revitalized, it might constitute an attractive organizational alternative even if the large corporations do manage to meet the challenge of the new competitive environment.

Note

The argument of this chapter was developed in collaboration with Charles Sabel and is elaborated in our forthcoming book, *The Second Industrial Divide*. The research upon which it is based was financed by the International Labour Organization through a grant to Boston University.

Discussion, Part IV

Reginald Newell: I tend not to view computer technology in such polarized terms as do Osterman and Piore. It transforms skills of workers down to the lowest common denominator. I think robots epitomize technology in the auto industry as do computer-aided design systems in the aerospace industries, and now they are moving toward flexible machining systems and perhaps eventually to unmanned factories of the future. In describing the application of new technology to batch production, the skilled blue-collar worker now assumes the task of programming. This does create displacement because at least two employees are now replaced by one. The new equipment involves a big investment, and it is easier to teach a skilled mechanic programming functions than to teach these tasks to a semiskilled machine operator. In the short run the expenses created by these changes are uneconomical, but there is no question that over time it will have a negative impact on the number of employees and the distribution of skills. We in the labor movement are going to have to respond to these developments by redefining the scope of the bargaining unit from one based on the specific jobs performed to one based on a broader definition of the work performed.

Osterman and Piore talked about Taylorism in our job structures. Many people talk about this as if narrow job definitions were solely a union demand when in reality they were also the product of management demands and management's application of traditional industrial engineering principles. Unions will not be opposed to changing the structure of jobs as long as the changes are done in a way that does not erode the security and skills of their members or the jurisdiction and the security of the union.

Jack Golodner: Paul Osterman's white-collar study sounds like a reprise of earlier decades when new technology was brought in. In the 1920s and 1930s we had a movement toward mass unionization of blue-collar workers, while today we are poised for a similar event among white-collar workers. In the past there were not as many white-collar workers at the lower-skill levels where female workers predominated. But among some professional workers organizing did occur—in such sectors as entertainment, journalism, and education. There was evidence that white-collar people have no intrinsic characteristics that discourage them from unionization, but the conditions simply did not exist for clericals and other white-collar workers to unionize in large numbers. Today the conditions do exist, and the question is whether unions will take advantage of them.

Osterman notes that management has done such things as introducing new technology, which is likely to encourage unionization by creating insecurity and de-skilling. Clerical and janitorial jobs, for example, are increasing, whereas the growth in professional jobs has leveled off. There is a growth in underemployment among white-collar workers; part-time workers cannot get full-time work, and many people are forced to work below their potential.

When we talk about the growing sophistication of equipment, of course, we must also talk about more training. But I equate this to the task of learning to drive a car. Far from making it more difficult to drive, technological advances have made it easier. The modern car is far more complex than the Model T but certainly takes less skill to operate. The same thing is happening in the office. Operations are becoming simpler, and people feel more vulnerable to the effects of mechanization as a threat to their jobs. The impact of telecommunications, for example, gives people the sense that their work can be done in different regions, perhaps by temporary workers. Data processing, for example, can be done by workers in New York or in the Caribbean. Jobs become simpler to perform and easier to shift around. At the same time management is becoming increasingly dependent on a few key operations, and I think management recognizes this. Among the higher skill levels, differentials between union and nonunion pay are decreasing, as Anil Verma and Thomas Kochan pointed out. Management is recognizing the need for that small number of skilled workers who are employed in key jobs and is willing to compensate them well. I think this offers great opportunities for us on the union side, but I wonder if we are recognizing them. We have to organize these key jobs, not just expendable jobs. We should note that the first to be organized in earlier years were the highly skilled. Today, it is the teachers, artists, and other professionals who are setting the example of unionism for the other, lower-skilled white-collar people. I think it behooves us to keep this in mind when we think about organizing office workers.

Computer technology makes it both possible and necessary to increase the size and scope of employing institutions. The loss of autonomy, the difficulty of rewarding individual effort, the declining influence individuals have over their product or service, all point out to these workers that they are just numbers in these larger organizations. There is a growing feeling of hopelessness and an inability to cope that goes along with it. The international response to these developments has tended to be more government regulation and control over the workplace. White-collar workers are beginning to understand that decisions are being made that lie outside of their individual control; and historically unions have provided a voice for working people. I think they are beginning to realize that they can also have a voice through white-collar unionization.

Nancy Mills: I am not a Luddite, but I think it is important to say clearly that technological progress does not necessarily mean social progress. More questions need to be asked, such as, who benefits from the progress? If not workers, why not? Who benefits in a monetary way as well? There is no question that employers want to use new technology to maximize profits and minimize costs. But if all the benefits go to the company and none to the workers, then I am against it. We ought to be sharing in some of the benefits. Another issue is safety in the office—women working in front of cathode-ray tubes. We as trade unions need to examine that issue. And there is a much bigger economic issue. Robots don't buy sneakers. If we are displacing workers, they are going to go into lower-paying jobs if they get jobs at all. What then happens to the economy if they can't buy sneakers or houses? I am concerned that the labor movement must look at those issues, and I don't see that happening.

Andrew Martin: I would like to ask Golodner a question in regard to Piore's work. What change in organizational models seems likely to be necessary? You said you saw lots of opportunities for unions. Do you think those opportunities could be exploited effectively through existing models or are shifts necessary?

Jack Golodner: We need an attitude change. The base of the labor movement is still with blue-collar workers. It is politically difficult to cater to the present and look toward the future, to take dues from the present members in order to address the needs of potential members, especially when current members feel their jobs are being threatened.

Maybe the recent football strike provides an indication of the sorts of things we are likely to get involved in. Professional football players are one of our highest-paid groups of employees, but they were striking because of an issue caused by technological change. They were concerned with fairness in the distribution of the tremendous increases in profits that owners were getting from television. The same issue was involved in the Screen Actors Guild strike over their portion of the profits from video cassettes, cable TV and the like. These cases illustrate that there are new issues out there of concern to professionals and other white-collar workers. We simply have to understand what they are, and some unions are creating new departments to deal with professional and white-collar workers. So in some ways we are beginning to explore new models.

Leslie Nulty: I recently moved from manufacturing to retail. The combination of computerization and high-speed telecommunications gives the employer a far better handle on sales turnover, inventory, and such matters and gives him the ability to control and manipulate data with astonishing accuracy. I think this is a very serious area and unions better get a handle on it. It may have run away too far already since it provides the control that many employers want.

We in the retail industry are also concerned with the high turnover of workers. Contrary to what is often published, retail employers want high turnover among their full-time employees to limit their pension liabilities and other fringe benefit costs. So here we have a sector, where for all of the talk about career paths for white-collar workers, employers are systematically trying to eliminate the possibility of career paths and long-term employment.

Charles Sabel: The issue brought out by Osterman and Piore has been somewhat lost in the discussion. There is no question but that computers are used to de-skill people and increase managerial control. Managers never had the technology to achieve that before. But it is being applied in different ways in different firms in different countries. The question is, can we use the computer to perform the same work more cheaply or can we use the computer to creatively do things that we couldn't have done before? It really depends on the background of the particular markets. If you make a list of the conditions that influence how new technologies get used across countries, you find real national styles emerging. In some countries it is not being used to displace or de-skill workers because it is too politically or economically expensive to kick labor around that way; employers have to try to develop new skill opportunities with the new technology. There is an endless list of horror stories where labor is weak or is not taking an active role in thinking through how technology is used. This raises the question of alternative organizational forms for the use of technology and for the role of unions. For example, it is an interesting finding that the line between white- and blue-collar work is getting increasingly blurred. Outside of the United States, you can see alternative strategies that work to the advantage of unions and the labor movement. The question is, how can the U.S. labor movement take advantage of these developments?

Jack Joyce: We keep hearing that wages must be taken out of competition. But how can you do that in the world described by Piore?

Michael Piore: It is unlikely that we will be able to do so by moving to larger production units supported by expanding markets. That is what allowed us to create the institutions through collective bargaining to take wages out of competition in the past. To the extent that we are moving to a world of more varied or specialized products in which markets change much faster, we have to think about behaving more like the high-fashion garment industry than like autos. In that kind of world, there is enormous competitive pressure. One year a firm is going to produce a style that doesn't sell. If we try to compete on the basis of the lowest labor cost, it is going to be a continuous, downward spiral.

Peter Doeringer: If you look across the spectrum of issues pulling at the trade union movement, each one represents an attempt on the part of employers to gain more flexibility. This might be viewed as a sign that unions have been successful in the past, but the basis of their success rested on their ability to limit the effects of competition. Unions are no longer able to do this. So now management searches for flexibility and so far has done so by going it alone. As a result, management has gained the initiative in certain areas with respect to advancing nonunion human resource management systems. In terms of where we are going, the trade union movement is now about where it was early in the century. Those unions that are successful in the future will realize that they have to participate in the search for flexibility as well. In the last round of bargaining, the employers won. How do unions win the next round? We must recognize why there is a drive for flexibility and try to turn that more to the unions' advantage.

V

Developments in Collective Bargaining

10   Collective Bargaining in the 1982 Bargaining Round

Harry C. Katz

The 1982 round of collective bargaining is worthy of close analysis because it involved the negotiation of a large number of major collective bargaining agreements. Moreover, many observers believe these negotiations mark a turning point in industrial relations in the United States.[1] In particular, attention has been focused on the "concession bargaining" that characterized negotiations in a number of industries. These concessions have in some cases been accompanied by an increase in the amount of labor-management cooperation occurring at the plant level through quality of working life (QWL) or similar types of programs. Speculation has arisen over whether these developments represent a shift away from the "adversarial bargaining" that has traditionally characterized U.S. labor relations.

On the other hand, other observers have suggested that these negotiations and movements toward greater cooperation merely represent a natural and temporary adjustment in response to the severe economic pressures that labor and management face in these industries.[2] Thus, a debate appears to be developing over whether recent bargaining behavior represents something fundamentally different from what would have been expected based on established patterns of collective bargaining.

The research reported here focuses on nine of the key industries engaged in major contract negotiations in 1982. Our purpose is to present an intensive and qualitative examination of the process and outcomes of these negotiations. This analysis looks at three interrelated dimensions of 1982 bargaining in the nine industries: the environmental economic pressures upon each industry; any changes that emerged in the bargaining process or procedures; and the various outcomes that comprised 1982 contract settlements.

One hypothesis guiding the research is that any changes in collective bargaining are likely to be more permanent if they involve alterations in the bargaining process. Aspects of the bargaining process such as bargaining structure (whether bargaining occurs at the industry, company, or plant level) or bargaining tactics (whether direct communication occurs with the work force during negotiations) tend not to be easily reversed and thereby have implications for future negotiations.

Bargaining outcomes also differ in terms of their implications for future negotiations. For instance, pay criteria such as a cost-of-living escalator (COLA), once introduced into a contract, tend to reappear in subsequent settlements. Similarly, union jurisdictional issues tend to undergo only periodic revision. This contrasts with the level of wage settlements where there exists less continuity over time. So, pay criteria and union jurisdiction, for example, can be classified as bargaining outcomes that are likely to affect more than just the terms of any single agreement. It is for these reasons that this research looks at the bargaining process as well as outcomes and tries to distinguish between one-time changes and those bargaining outcomes that are likely to influence future negotiations.

Sample and Methodology

Two criteria influenced the selection of industries to be included in this study. First, we attempted to choose negotiations likely to have a major impact on the nation's economy. Second, we included industries that face a variety of different economic pressures. Specifically, within the sample are two industries (oil refining and electrical products) that continued to undergo relatively favorable (or at least what could be termed stable) economic conditions over the 1970s. While these industries suffered with the rest of the economy through a cyclical downturn in the early 1980s, they did not face a major increase in competition as did other industries in the sample. Therefore, we do not expect these industries to see major changes in bargaining outcomes or process of lasting significance.

A second set of industries are the primary focus of analysis since they represent industries that had intensified competition in their product markets in the late 1970s and early 1980s—auto, steel, rubber, trucking, airlines, and meat-packing. A number of these industries also traditionally had relatively centralized collective bargaining structures. This second set of industries will probably experience the greatest degree of change in collective bargaining in 1982.

The clothing industry is the third category—an industry that has historically faced high levels of competitive pressures thorughout the post–World War II period. In this industry labor and management constantly had to adapt to the threat of competition. Thus, the first and third categories provide good comparison groups for the negotiations in the second category because they represent cases where we would expect bargaining to be characterized by a continuation of trends from previous years.

The analysis of these select negotiations is highly qualitative. The data mix industry-level and firm-specific sources of information. We reviewed the economic characteristics of these industries over the post–World War II period and used published data to identify industry-level trends and characteristics. We then identified a key firm within each industry and collected case-study data on internal bargaining system characteristics and the effects of these system characteristics on the negotiations process. Wherever possible, we interviewed industry association representatives and trade union leaders to obtain additional qualitative information on the characteristics of bargaining during this round as these individuals saw them.

Findings

Table 10.1 summarizes our findings. An X is placed in each category box where we found a significant development within 1982 bargaining in an industry. Sometimes the development involved the introduction of a new bargaining outcome or change in a bargaining process that affected only one major company or agreement in the industry. In other cases the new development pervaded the whole industry.

Table 10.1 illustrates that a variety of economic pressures were influencing outcomes in the 1982 bargaining. Industries such as trucking and airlines felt the effects of both domestic nonunion competition and regulatory change while, in contrast, the automobile, steel, and clothing industries were under pressure from heightened international and nonunion competition. It is interesting to note that all industries in the sample, except for electrical products and oil refining, were facing competitive pressure from nonunion firms. In some industries, such as trucking, airlines, and meat-packing, nonunion firms emerged as full-fledged competitors. In contrast, in auto and steel, nonunion competition emerged only in segments of the industries—auto parts and specialty steel (mini-mill) production.

Table 10.1
Collective bargaining pressures, process, and outcomes

	Environmental economic pressures			Bargaining process			Bargaining outcomes					
Industry	International competition	Domestic nonunion competition	Regulatory change	Changes in degree of centralization	Shift in role of IR function	New forms of communication or tactics	Compensation level concessions	Changes in pay criteria	Work rules	Job security	Union jurisdictional issues	Labor-management cooperation
Auto	X	X		X	X	X	X	X	X	X		X
Steel	X	X		X		X	X		X			X
Trucking		X	X	X	X	X	X		X		X	
Airlines		X	X		X	X	X	X	X	X		X
Rubber	X	X		X		X	X		X			
Meat-packing		X		X			X	X	X	X		
Clothing	X	X										X
Electrical products										X		
Oil refining						X						

Furthermore, the overall distribution of X's reveals that more changes occurred in bargaining processes and outcomes in industries that were facing economic pressure from one source or another. Note that bargaining in both the electrical products and oil refining industries had few significant process or outcome developments. Settlements in the electrical products industry followed a pattern set in the three-year GE-IUE and UE agreements that included a continuation of COLA increases plus additional 7% wage increases in 1982 and 3% wage increases in 1983 and 1984. In oil refining, contract settlements also provided relatively high pay increases and few innovative features. The pattern in this industry was set by the two-year agreement at Gulf that provides a 9% wage increase in the first year and a 7% increase in the second year.

Settlements in the clothing industry were also relatively strong, and any innovations that occurred involved modest improvements in contract terms and not concessions. Contracts in men's and boys' clothing followed a pattern that provides a continuation of the existing COLA formula plus pay increases of 19% over the agreement's 38-month term. A novel feature of bargaining in the female garment industry was the introduction of a COLA escalator in ILGWU contracts.

To determine whether the developments recorded in table 10.1 amount to incremental or fundamental alterations in the course of bargaining, two issues must be considered. First, it is important to distinguish between developments in bargaining processes and outcomes that are likely to have lasting implications versus bargaining outcomes that appear to be temporary and easily reversible adjustments. Second, the changes adopted in a few industries or firms within a given industry appear to add up to the search for a fundamentally new industrial relations system. In these cases, the important point is to understand the interaction between particular new items within settlements. Within these cases, it is the holistic nature of the modifications adopted in bargaining that contain the roots of long-run, fundamental change in collective bargaining.

The press has focused on the compensation level and work-rule concessions included in 1982 bargaining. Notable compensation concessions that occurred in our sample include: the postponement or deferral of COLA increases in the auto, steel, rubber, and trucking industries; the pay freezes adopted in meat-packing; and the dollar pay cuts introduced at Braniff, Pan Am, Continental, and Republic airlines.

Work-rule revisions accompanied many of these concessionary wage settlements.[3] As part of the new Master Freight Agreement, for example, over-the-road truck drivers with less than full loads will make local pickup stops and perform duties previously assigned to "local drivers." Important changes in work rules and compensation occurred in some firms within the industry that negotiated separate company agreements outside of the Master Freight Agreement. In one company, for example, the traditional pay system based on miles driven and hours worked was replaced with a percentage-of-revenue pay system.

Airline industry bargaining in 1982 also led to important work-rule changes in at least thirty-nine different bargaining units of the eighteen major unionized carriers. At United, for example, pilots agreed to reduce crew size from three to two in exchange for new job-security protections. Indeed, pilots negotiated changes in pay for nonflying time or some similar scheduling provision in at least fifteen of the eighteen major carriers.

More generally, the central characteristic of managerial efforts in 1982 negotiations appears to have been a push for increased flexibility in human resource management. This was frequently manifested in proposals for such things as broader job classifications, more managerial discretion in the allocation of overtime, more liberal subcontracting rights, restrictions on voluntary transfers or other movements across jobs, and similar matters.

These pay and work-rule concessions will exert significant impacts on costs and employment. The concessions are also consistent with a national slowdown in the rate of compensation increases. Annual compensation adjustments over the life of the contracts for all settlements covering 1,000 or more workers averaged 3.6% in 1982 in contrast to the 7.9% rise in 1981.[4] Yet it is our view that the majority of these pay and work-rule revisions may be temporary and easily reversed if economic conditions improve within particular industries. With regard to these changes we agree with observers who point out that similar types of changes have occurred in these and other industries during previous economic recessions. It is perhaps only the magnitude of the reduction in the rate of pay increases and the scope of work-rule changes that set 1982 apart from the outcomes of bargaining in previous recessions.

The tendency for pay and work-rule provisions to be addressed more aggressively by employers during periods of slack demand or intensified competition has been well documented in the collective bargaining literature. Slichter described the intensified competition between union and nonunion plants that occurred during various recessions and the Depression of the 1930s.[5] Similarly, the recession of 1958–59 produced another round of managerial efforts to take a hard line on work rules and to regain some of the prerogatives that were incrementally lost during the expansionary period of the war and immediate post–World War II era.[6] The productivity bargaining literature of the 1960s and early 1970s represents another installment in the discussion of how work rules are subject to periodic buyouts of existing practices.[7] Finally, the 1972 recession prompted at least one observer to document the cases of "reverse collective bargaining" that occurred during the downturn.[8] All of these can be seen as earlier examples of some of the developments in plant-level collective bargaining that occurred in the recession of the early 1980s.

Bargaining Process Changes

To see whether *new* things emerged in the 1982 bargaining round, one must look at other aspects of bargaining. One area where fundamental changes did occur concerns alterations in the bargaining process. Important modifications during the 1982 bargaining round occurred in the degree of centralization in bargaining structures, shifts in the role of the industrial relations function, and the emergence of new forms of communication and tactics in bargaining.

Decentralization in Bargaining Structure

Economic pressures produced the decentralization of long-standing bargaining structures in a number of industries in the 1982 bargaining round. This decentralization took the form of an erosion of intraindustry (intercompany) pattern bargaining in the auto, rubber, and meat-packing industries. Within the trucking industry the influence of the national Master Freight Agreement declined as regional and company modifications and deviations from the national agreement emerged. Within the steel industry the number of companies covered by the Basic Steel Agreement dropped from eight to seven. More broadly, the Wage Policy Committee of the United Steelworkers (USW) established different bargaining goals for "distressed industries," such as basic steel, and "healthy" industries, such as nonferrous metal or containers, where the USW also represented workers. This produced a weakening of the interindustry (intraunion) pattern bargaining that had traditionally characterized USW negotiations.

In the same industries a second form of decentralization emerged through a downward shift in the level at which issues were resolved involving a movement from national to company- or plant-level resolution. Examples of this shift occurred in the rubber, steel, and auto industries where plant-level modifications in work rules were frequently introduced as part of efforts to lower costs and keep business in-house.

This decentralization in the structure of bargaining reversed the centralized and pattern bargaining that had emerged in the postwar period. The earlier centralization of bargaining structures had been facilitated by extensive union coverage in these industries. In effect, then, intensified competitive pressures in the late 1970s and early 1980s have forced decentralization as part of the process whereby wage and work-rule concessions have been introduced in response to the new competition and associated erosion of union coverage.

Management Structure for Industrial Relations

A second bargaining *process* development in the 1982 round involves shifts within management structures and changes in the position of industrial relations staffs. Industrial relations staffs in a number of firms were moved into the more general human resource management staff area and integrated more closely with operating management functions. This showed up in 1982 bargaining through the direct intervention of operating managers in negotiations in several firms in the trucking and airline industries. In some cases the top industrial relations executives were replaced. For example, in the airline industry five out of twenty-three vice-presidents of industrial relations were fired in 1982 alone.

Within many firms, those holding the traditional set of professional industrial relations staff functions were resisting changes being urged upon them by other professionals in the broader personnel/human resource management function or resisting pressures coming from top management to reduce the growth in labor costs.[9] Meanwhile, for over a decade, within the firm, areas of personnel that lay outside of industrial relations had been expanding in scope, responsibility, and importance as the pressures of government regulations increased, and labor market demand for managers, technical workers, and other professionals also intensified. Furthermore, the industrial relations staffs were being asked to encourage the spread of communication and worker-participation programs that had often developed in nonunion plants within these firms.

In short, by 1982 industrial relations managers had become isolated within the management decision-making hierarchy; the criteria they had used for building and later maintaining their power and influence within management were becoming less relevant for coping with the emergent competitive pressures. Thus, in order to achieve significant changes in bargaining in 1982, a transformation in the behavior of industrial relations professionals within the firm had to be achieved or, if this was not possible, a change in the individuals making the key bargaining decisions was needed.

In General Motors these pressures led to reorganization of the corporate personnel and industrial relations functions, and the creation of a new strategic planning group within the industrial relations staff. In a trucking company we observed the formation of a strategic planning group which involved the vice-president of human resources and operating managers directly in collective bargaining negotiations.

Communication Strategies

The decentralization of bargaining structures and response to economic pressure also often involved extensive efforts to change the expectations of rank-and-file-workers. A strategy frequently used to achieve this change in expectations was to increase the flow of information and communications concerning the state of the firm and industry competitive conditions. These new communications efforts were used frequently to gain acceptance for bargaining outcomes that more closely tied compensation and work practices to the productivity and cash flow requirements of the firm. The need to change expectations while at the same time avoiding the occurrence of a strike posed a challenge to both management and union officials to mix their previous emphasis on stability with a new emphasis on achieving modifications in labor costs.

Examples of more direct communication between workers and management that occurred in 1982 include the direct mailing of a final management offer at American Airlines and more informal communications between labor and management in the airlines, trucking, auto, and rubber industries. In the trucking industry, for instance, corporate managers in some companies conducted meetings with their drivers across the country to discuss the implications of deregulation and nonunion competition. In the auto industry more direct communication occurred both before and after the settlement. Before the new agreement, General Motors experimented with a film shown to the rank and file that was eventually stopped after union opposition. As part of the new agreements at Ford and General Motors, "mutual growth forums" now occur where workers and managers discuss business pressures and forthcoming decisions.

Bargaining Outcome Changes of Lasting Significance

Like these bargaining process changes, there were also a number of other changes in bargaining *outcomes* in the 1982 round that are likely to have lasting effects.

Pay Criteria

One outcome was the modification of the pay criteria used to set pay levels. In the auto, airlines, and meat-packing industries there was a shift away from the use of a COLA formula mechanism and a shift toward profit sharing and other "contingent" compensation mechanisms that more directly tie pay to company performance. At Ford and GM, for example, the 1982 settlements introduced a profit-sharing formula. Meanwhile, a variable earnings plan was introduced at Braniff (before its bankruptcy) and extended at Eastern Airlines in agreements covering the ground crew. At Eastern, stock ownership was an important part of the pilots' new contract and later extended to the ground crew and flight attendants. This shift in pay criteria reverses traditional negotiating practices which, in the process of taking wages out of competition, had placed heavier emphasis on wage comparisons or formula escalators than on either the firm's profit level or cues from the local labor market.

Employment Security Guarantees

Bargaining in 1982 also entailed heavy emphasis on job security and the introduction of explicit employment guarantees in a number of agreements. At American Airlines, harking back to the type of productivity bargaining that occurred in the West Coast longshoring industry, lifetime job guarantees were provided to existing workers. Agreements to experiment with pilot employment-guarantee projects also were included in the national UAW contracts with Ford and GM.

In addition, plant closing moratoriums were adopted in the auto and meat-packing industries while prior notice of plant closing was introduced into the electrical products industry. In the trucking industry, a form of employment guarantee was provided through limitations introduced on management's ability to create nonunion subsidiaries, a case where union jurisdictional issues became an important bargaining outcome.

One way to interpret these employment guarantees is to see them as the parties' response to heightened uncertainty regarding the future course of employment in the face of increased product market competition. In the past, with more stable product demand, labor was content to set the wage level and let management adjust employment levels. Now, labor is less sure what employment level is implied by any given wage settlement and has shifted toward trying more directly to determine employment.[10]

Worker Participation and Labor-Management Cooperation

Another important aspect of 1982 bargaining settlements concerned efforts at worker and union participation and labor-management cooperation. Particularly noteworthy are developments within the auto, steel, airlines, and clothing industries. These efforts included programs to provide greater information sharing between labor and management. For example, at Ford and GM "mutual growth forums" have been established, as have greater informal communication channels between union and management officials at both plant and corporate levels. Chrysler and Pan Am added a union representative to the company's board of directors. In the steel industry, labor-management "participation teams" are active in a number of plants.

Interrelationships among Process and Outcome Changes

An interesting issue concerns the interrelation between these worker participation programs and other contractual changes. It is our view that taken together, in a few cases the scope of the participation programs and accompanying modifications to collective bargaining amount to an effort by labor and management to search for an alternative industrial relations system. The changes under way in the auto industry are one such case, and the new contract at American Airlines serves as another, though more limited, example.

In the auto industry labor and management appear to be moving away from the traditional labor relations system that placed heavy emphasis on the contractual resolution of disagreements and involved substantial standardization in pay and work rules across companies and plants within each company.[11] Now, more variable and flexible pay has been introduced at the national level through the adoption of profit sharing; at the local level experimentation with pay-for-knowledge schemes at a few plants reveals the beginnings of a similar shift. Movement to a more informal and decentralized relationship between labor and management has been encouraged by the direct communication between workers and management that has been occurring as part of quality circles, mutual growth forums, and other more informal exchanges. The greater information and advance warning regarding business plans and new technologies now provided to union officials in some plants has reinforced this shift.

Although worker-participation programs were initiated in the auto industry in the early 1970s, the recent programs involve something fundamentally new. The novel aspect of recent events in the industry is that these programs now interact extensively with work practices and traditional bargaining issues. Work-rule changes that involve the broadening of job classifications and more flexible job assignment procedures are now typically linked closely to the enhanced communication union leaders and workers receive as part of the participation process.[12] This increased communication and information exchange appears to be emerging as a partial substitute for the security traditionally provided through the written contract and seniority rules. In a handful of auto plants there is continuing experimentation with work teams and single job classification systems accompanied by worker and union direct participation in production and business decisions. Notably, these team systems involve many of the flexible procedures appearing in some nonunion companies that have experimented with advanced behavioral techniques in worker involvement and communication.

The intriguing issue concerns whether this experimentation develops into an extensive transformation of the conduct of labor relations. In the process, many of the contractually based and arms-length aspects of the traditional American labor relations pattern might well be replaced by a participatory relationship in which workers are more directly involved in problem-solving processes. Needless to say, the implications of this sort of transformation for the American labor movement are enormous.

Another interesting development involves the collective bargaining settlement reached at American Airlines. The settlement package included extensive job security for existing employees, lower wages for new hires, and provides for greater work-rule flexibility in the new contract. This agreement does not go as far as the novel experimentation under way within the auto industry and in some ways follows earlier examples of productivity bargaining. Yet the agreement does provide a major departure from bargaining in the airline industry and provides an example where the workers were willing to trade highly valued past practices in exchange for explicit employment guarantees. The issue is the extent to which this agreement signals the workers' willingness to go even further in revising traditional labor relations practices.

A common element in the American Airlines and auto settlements is that management has gained enhanced work-rule flexibility by giving workers increased communication, participation, and employment guarantees. This may be a road that other unions will choose to follow in the years ahead in the face of heightened competitive pressure. Thus, events in these industries should be closely monitored.

Summary

Three conclusions emerge from this study of 1982 bargaining in nine key industries. First, innovative bargaining did not occur everywhere—industries under economic pressure exhibited a diverse pattern of significant change but industries that were facing relatively good economic conditions continued past bargaining patterns. Second, wage and work-rule concessions were a common feature of bargaining in industries facing heightened economic pressure, and in a number of cases these concessions were accompanied by changes in the bargaining process and other bargaining outcomes that will likely have implications for future negotiations. And finally, in a few cases the scope of innovative bargaining appears to add up to the search for an alternative industrial relations system that involves enhanced participation and communication and moves labor and management away from their heavy reliance on job-control unionism and formal contractual procedures.

Notes

This research is part of the project on the "U.S. Industrial Relations System in Transition," funded by the Sloan Foundation.

1. Audrey Freeman, "A Fundamental Change in Wage Bargaining," *Challenge* 25 (July–August 1982): 14–17; and "Labor Seeks Less," *Business Week*, December 21, 1981, 82–88.

2. Daniel J. B. Mitchell, "Recent Union Contract Concessions," *Brookings Papers on Economic Activity* 1:1982, 165–204; and John T. Dunlop, "Working Toward Consensus," *Challenge* 25 (July–August 1982): 26–34.

3. These issues are discussed more fully in Thomas A. Kochan and Harry C. Katz, "Collective Bargaining, Work Organization and Worker Participation: The Return to Plant Level Bargaining," *Labor Law Journal* (August 1983), pp. 524–530.

4. U.S. Bureau of Labor Statistics, Bulletin 83–41, "Major Collective Bargaining Settlements in Private Industry, 1982."

5. Sumner Slichter, *Union Policies and Industrial Management* (Washington, D.C.: Brookings Institution, 1941), 345–369.

6. See the symposium on "The Employer Challenge and Union Response," in *Industrial Relations* (October 1961). See also George Strauss, "The Shifting Balance of Power in the Plant," *Industrial Relations* 2 (October 1962): 65–96.

7. For a summary of the productivity bargaining developments during this period see George P. Schultz and Robert B. McKersie, "Stimulating Productivity: Choices, Problems and Shares," *British Journal of Industrial Relations* 5 (March 1967): 3–18.

8. Peter Henle, "Reverse Collective Bargaining: A Look at Some Union Concession Situations," *Industrial and Labor Relations Review* 26 (April 1973): 956–968.

9. These issues are discussed more fully in Thomas A. Kochan and Peter Cappelli, "The Transformation of the Industrial Relations and Personnel Function," in *Internal Labor Markets*, ed. P. Osterman (Cambridge, Mass.: MIT Press, 1984).

10. Peter Cappelli, "Concession Bargaining and the National Economy," in *Proceedings of the Industrial Relations Research Association*, ed. Barbara D. Dennis (Madison, Wis., 1983).

11. Harry C. Katz, "The U.S. Automobile Collective Bargaining System in Transition," *British Journal of Industrial Relations* (forthcoming), and Harry C. Katz, *Shifting Gears: Changing Labor Relations in the U.S. Automobile Industry* (Cambridge, Mass.: MIT Press, forthcoming).

12. Kochan and Katz, "Collective Bargaining."

11 Labor and the Crisis in Collective Bargaining

Peter Cappelli and
Robert B. McKersie

The term "concession bargaining" has become a catchall expression to describe a number of recent and important developments in the process and outcomes of collective bargaining. Rollbacks or concessions in wages and contract provisions have caught the attention of the public, but there have been a great many other changes that may be more important for the future of bargaining. Perhaps the most general development associated with these changes has been a broadening of the bargaining agenda to include employment levels and strategic business decisions. We continue to use the term concession bargaining because it has become generally accepted in the literature. But a wider description of its characteristics should help expand future discussions beyond the issue of wage rollbacks.

Field Guide to the Species

How do we go about deciding when we have a bona fide case of concession bargaining? There seems to be a rather large gray area between these developments and those that could be considered within the realm of "normal" collective bargaining. Concession bargaining can be defined as those cases where employment levels become explicit bargaining topics. Here, unions are making explicit reductions in labor costs (through wage cuts, work rules, and the like) in an effort to improve employment security. In previous periods, employment levels were not an issue in bargaining mainly because they remained reasonably stable. Employment adjustments occurred incrementally and temporarily if at all. Increased competitive pressures now are driving the concession process by threatening the viability of higher-cost operations, many of which are unionized, and the employment security of the workers in those operations. The rapid deterioration of the economic environment leads to one manifestation of concession bargaining—negotiations being reopened before contracts expire, presumably because the situation demands immediate attention. In terms of outcomes, concession bargaining has been evidenced by attempts to produce sharp, nonincremental changes in the terms of the agreement. These include drastic reductions in the trend of compensation and benefits and the elimination of favorable contract provisions without compensating union gains elsewhere. The union is typically left worse off in terms of the contract's provisions although better off in terms of employment security (as contrasted with the absence of concessions). In many cases, the union may also secure gains in areas such as union security or in gathering corporate financial information—areas that do not increase current labor costs—in return for granting labor-cost concessions.

Union firms are not the only ones facing these pressures, and union workers have not been alone in making concessions to save jobs. Wage and benefit cuts have occurred in nonunion, white-collar compensation (Bureau of National Affairs 1982), in executive compensation (Dun's 1982), and in nonunion, blue-collar pay. Union supporters would argue that, at least in the unionized case, workers have some influence over how the cuts are made. But management might counter that high union wages, above the market-clearing level, helped bring about the need for concessions in the first place. It is also important to note that in many cases firms are asking for concessions and striving to engage unions in this process when in fact the economic situation is not adverse and employment is not threatened. A survey conducted by *Business Week* found that 11% of the firms that had asked for concessions were taking advantage of the current environment and did not really need them (*Business Week* 1982). One union official commented that when unions asked firms to document their need for concessions, the incidence of concession negotiations fell off significantly (by about two-thirds). The arguments below, however, relate to the majority of cases where the economic pressures are real and the threats to employment that drive concession bargaining are genuine.

We have an estimate of the extent of collective bargaining affected by concession agreements in 1982 for the major industries in the United States (see table 11.1), derived from data collected by the Bureau of National Affairs (BNA). Their data include all cases where parties were negotiating over labor-cost concessions, not necessarily where agreement had been reached (Cappelli 1982). Eight industries have seen the spread of concession bargaining to 30–50% of the unionized sector:

Table 11.1
Concessions by industry group

SIC code 2-digit	Number of concession negotiations	% of unionized affected (estimates)	
10	3	6	Metal mining
11	0	0	Coal mining
12	1	3	Bituminous
13	0	0	Oil extraction
14	1	2	Nonmetalic minerals
16	1	8	Heavy construction
17	17	18	Trade contractors
20	16	20	Food
21	0	0	Tobacco
22		3	Textile mill
23	8	30	Apparel
24	1	5	Lumber
25	0	0	Furniture
26	3	5	Paper
27	6	22	Printing
28	1	28	Chemicals
29	2	25	Petroleum products
30	5	44	Rubber and plastics
31	1	35	Leather and products
32	5	20	Stone, clay, glass
33	27	40	Primary metal
34	1	1	Fabricated metal
35	17	35	Machinery—nonelectric
36	4	45	Electrical and electronic
37	31	48	Transportation equipment
38	0	0	Instruments
39	3	33	Miscellaneous manufacturing
40	0	0	Rail transportation
41	0	0	Local passenger transportation
42	4	15	Trucking
44	0	0	Water transport
45	19	50	Air transport
46	0	0	Pipelines–nongas
47	9	7	Transportation services
48	1	1	Communication
49	0	0	Electricity, gas, sanitary

Table 11.1 (continued)

SIC code 2-digit	Number of concession negotiations	% of unionized affected (estimates)	
50	5	1	Wholesale—durables
51	2	0.5	Wholesale—nondurables
52	0	0	Retail building supplies
53	0	0	Merchandise stores
54	3	0.3	Food stores
55	1	0.7	Auto dealers
56	0	0	Apparel stores
57	1	0.1	Furniture, furnishing stores
58	0	0	Eating, drinking establishments
59	10	0.7	Miscellaneous retail

Source: Tabulation derived from Bureau of National Affairs data base.

apparel, rubber, leather, metal, machinery, transportation equipment, air transportation, and trucking.

BNA lists in its data file approximately 450 cases of concession bargaining in 1982. The *Business Week* survey estimates that 36% of the unionized firms they surveyed had engaged in concession bargaining. As this is written, it is too early to tell what the activity rate was for 1983, but our guess is that the incidence of concession agreements is falling. BNA figures indicate that the number of concession cases was declining toward the end of 1982 and suggests that the amount of concession activity followed the worsening economic climate from 1981 to 1982 with a time lag—increasing as the economy declined and receding as the downturn slowed in late 1982–83.

Historical Comparisons

Activity akin to concession bargaining has been observed before. Peter Henle (1973), for example, documented several concession cases in the 1960s, but one has to go back to the twenties and thirties to find anything comparable to the current period of adjustments. Instances of concession bargaining since the Depression have been confined to individual industries undergoing severe structural change. This was the case for shoemaking in the 1950s when markets opened to foreign competition (Shultz and Myers 1950) and for meat-packing in the

1950s and 1960s as it responded to the growth of nonunion packing in the South (Juris 1969).

Explanations for the Surge of Activity

The reasons for the upsurge in activity can be traced to a number of developments that have placed substantial economic pressure on many industries in the United States. Changes in import penetration, enlargement of the nonunion sector, and deregulation have placed substantial competitive pressure on many industries, especially manufacturing, to cut costs through concessions (Cappelli 1982)). The importance of economic pressure was the determining factor in the twenties and thirties as well. Jean McKelvey (1933, 505) makes that point clearly:

The greater number of cooperative ventures have been launched in industries or establishments facing new conditions of competition because of technological innovations, the tapping of fresh sources of cheap labor or shifts in demand—changes which have taken place with an unprecedented suddenness and intensity during the post-war decade. On the other hand, it is equally significant that unions in such sheltered trades as building and railway transportation have shown little disposition to modify restrictive working rules or to cooperate with employers in increasing output and eliminating waste. In their case no competitive pressure has called for concessions in the interest of industrial efficiency.

This current period of concession bargaining, like the Depression, has been one where structural economic changes have not been confined to isolated industries. The severity of the recession has exacerbated the structural changes in specific industries and simultaneously affected those industries where the core of union membership is concentrated. These industries have been under pressure to cut costs in order to meet new competitive pressures, and concessions have been an obvious way to do that. Labor costs are a large proportion of total costs in most operations, and from the firm's point of view, they represent the most variable and controllable costs.

It is the speed with which economic conditions decline as well as the depth of the decline that helps determine the extent of concession bargaining. In industries that have been declining for some time, such as the textile and garment industries, the economic aspects of bargaining have been adjusting for quite a while and the process of adapting to the worsening environment has been more gradual. One could draw an analogy here to a dam that holds back pressure until it finally breaks, leading to a big collapse; contracts that adjust continually and gradually to economic changes may avoid that sudden collapse.

Important developments were also occurring at the plant level, which increased the likelihood of concessions there. Many industries were experiencing a long-term reduction in capacity, changes in product line, or a need to replace capital equipment—all of which made existing plants vulnerable to shutdowns. Plant shutdowns, as opposed to layoffs, made the whole work force vulnerable to unemployment and put great pressure on local unions to avoid such circumstances. Firms faced with excess capacity could use the threat of plant closings—which in many cases were inevitable—to secure labor-cost concessions from the unions (Cappelli 1983). We have examples in some industries where firms forced plants to compete with each other to retain existing production levels on the basis of labor-cost concessions.[1]

Whether unions have an incentive to agree to concessions depends on whether lower labor costs will improve the firm's competitive position, leading to great employment security for existing workers and possibly recalls for those laid off. The likelihood of this happening depends on the elasticity of demand for the firm's product—the responsiveness of demand to reductions in relative prices. This helps explain the generally lower level of concession bargaining in the public sector. Revenue there is fixed in the short run, and lower costs generally will not lead to larger budgets from which additional employment can be funded. There is less incentive for the unions to agree to concessions because the size of the "pie" available for distribution cannot be increased.

Major Elements of Concession Agreements

Table 11.2 presents a breakdown of the main concessions agreed to in 1982 and is drawn from the BNA sample. A tremendous variety of arrangements lies within these categories. There are many ways to cut labor costs, and employers tend to pursue them in the order in which they are easiest to secure. Changes in work rules tend to be the least damaging change for unions to agree to, and one finds that firms almost always include demands for work-rule changes in concession bargaining. The survey conducted by *Business Week* found that management is apt to go after changes in work rules first (57% with 19% undecided). Fringe benefits are the next easiest to adjust, and wage rates are the

Table 11.2
Union concession agreements providing for specified changes

Work-rule changes	56%
Wage/fringe freezes	52%
Wage/fringe cuts	48%

Source: Tabulation derived from Bureau of National Affairs data base.

most difficult. Wage and fringe benefit freezes are easier to secure and are much more common than outright cuts. Unions have generally been most reluctant to change the basic structure of compensation. Wage and cost-of-living formulas, for example, have remained intact although their levels have often been reduced.

Problems for the Unions

There is clear evidence that concession bargaining has made life difficult for most union leaders. The pressures associated with concessions create conflicts within unions, both between the membership and officials and between different levels of union administration.

Members and their leaders may differ on the need for concessions and on the potential benefits. We have seen cases where the members were eager to make concessions and their leadership was urging them not to, arguing that concessions were not needed, and cases where the leadership had to convince the members that a firm was genuinely in trouble and would go under if concessions were not made. Union leaders are often in the position of being blamed for unnecessary concessions if the operation survives and blamed for not making concessions if the operation closes.

Conflicts also occur between different work groups in the same organization. Workers in the packing division of a food products company, for example, were asked to make substantial changes in manning levels and job duties in order to bring new products into the plant, saving jobs for workers in other departments. The packaging workers turned down the proposal and were bitterly attacked by the others.

Local unions involved in multiplant operations may have workers in different plants competing with each other to remain open. In the rubber industry, for example, the workers at one plant were prepared to make substantial changes to save jobs, but some union leaders in other plants feared that these concessions would then be forced upon them and voted the changes down, thereby jeopardizing the viability of the first plant.

National and local union leadership may also conflict. Local leaders are concerned with protecting local jobs through concessions while national leaders are concerned with protecting the master or pattern agreements across plants, a pattern that would be eroded by plant-level concessions. Several years ago when concession bargaining had just come on the scene, there was more of a tendency for national leaders (aware of long-term economic developments) to see the need for concession bargaining while local leaders, being somewhat more isolated, were inclined to resist it. More recently, as the economic decline slowed and some signs of improvement have appeared, the situation has reversed. Many locals are eager to engage in concession bargaining, often due to fear or panic created by the recent run of plant closings, whereas national leaders may be more aware when companies have turned the corner and no longer need concessions. They may also feel at this point that plant-level concession bargaining is being used to whipsaw the union.

Changes in the Process of Bargaining

In general, one can see a number of defining characteristics associated with the process of concession bargaining. First, there has been relatively little industrial action associated with concessions, perhaps because the important issues have been ones of fact rather than principle: how bad the company's financial situation is, for example, what the employment consequences associated with certain decisions are, and so forth. As a result, information about the firm and about the economic environment has become more important than ever before. Second, and partly in response to this, there have been important changes in bargaining on the management side. Kochan and Cappelli (1983), investigating this change, note that management has been bypassing its industrial relations staff during concession bargaining, coming to the table with a stream of accountants and finance officers to provide the detailed information used in concession arguments. The existing industrial relations staff are often blamed for the current crisis and for the fact that labor costs have gotten out of hand. Further, they may not feel comfortable seeking concessions and risking the stable relations that they have developed over the years. The management bargaining team now is sometimes headed by the CEO, reflecting the seriousness that top management attaches to securing concessions. A final change concerns management's efforts to get its point across to the rank and file. In concession bargaining, management is no longer willing to let union leaders transmit the management position to their members. Management is now going directly to the workers and stating its case for concessions, often with elaborate, multimedia presentations. A case study of one auto parts company, for example, finds the chief executive officer addressing the workers and laying it on the line that concessions are needed to "protect your jobs."

Union Gains from Concession Bargaining

It is often possible for unions to secure improvements in other areas of relations with management in return for labor-cost concessions. The most important gain that unions seek is improved employment security. While cost cuts always improve the competitive position of a firm, the practical question is whether that improvement has any immediate effect on employment—often it does not. Judging the net effects of concessions on employment security is very difficult because it is impossible to know what the situation would have been like in the absence of concessions. Circumstantial evidence suggests that the effects vary. They depend on the nature of the problem and whether cuts in labor costs are sufficient, perhaps as part of a package of changes, to put the operation on the road to recovery. Where the problem is not due to cost competition, labor-cost concessions will make little difference. This was the case in the tire industry when the shift to radial tires made bias plant and equipment obsolete, as table 11.3 indicates. In cases where cost competition is the problem, the labor-cost differential addressed by concessions may be dominated by other components of operating costs. Decisions about the viability of individual plants are often of this sort. Plant labor costs are often outweighed in importance by considerations of capital and equipment costs, access to markets, and local taxes. Labor-cost concessions are likely to have a greater influence on improving job security when the cost differences driving competitive pressures are relatively small and can be equalized by concessions. Improvements in job security seem most obvious when operations are pulled back from the brink of being closed. The timing of concessions here makes it appear that they were responsible for saving the operation.

Table 11.3
Concessions in the tire industry

Year	Location	Status after concessions
1977–78		
10/3/77	Firestone, Akron	Closed
1/11/78	Goodyear, Akron (Plant 1)	Closed
1/24/78	Goodyear, Gadsden	Open
3/29/78	Goodrich, Akron	Closed
5/18/78	Seiberling, Barberton	Closed
11/14/78	Mohawk, Akron	Closed
11/16/78	Mansfield, Mansfield	Closed
6/7/78	Uniroyal	Sold
1979		
4/16/79	General, Akron	Closed
5/7/79	Goodyear, Akron (Plant 2)	Closed
6/11/79	Mohawk, West Helena	Closed
1980		
2/4/80	Goodyear, Los Angeles	Closed
2/10/80	Uniroyal, Detroit	Closed
6/27/80	General, Peru	Open
7/7/80	Uniroyal, Chicopee Falls	Closed
10/30/80	Firestone, Middlesville	Closed
1981		
2/22/81	Cooper, Texarkana	Open
3/27/81	General, Akron	Closed
4/2/81	Mercer, Newark	Closed
5/19/81	Firestone, Memphis	Open
7/16/81	Goodyear, Topeka	Open
8/13/81	Firestone, Akron	Closed

Source: Information obtained from the files of the Rubber Manufacturers Association.

Of course, concessions always run the risk of putting people through considerable sacrifice and raising their expectations, only to see plant closings and layoffs in the end. Whether this process is worth the effort depends not only on the chance of improving employment security but also on the alternatives available to the current work force. In the air transport industry, for example, we find that pilots, who really have few alternatives for similar earnings elsewhere, are much more ready to negotiate over concessions than are machinists, who can more easily find equivalent work in other industries. It is important to note that even where concessions do not save operations, they may buy time for that operation, and this in itself may help displaced workers to make job transitions more easily.

Under certain conditions, management may agree to improve other aspects of employment relations as a means of securing union approval of concessions, particularly where the firm needs such concessions to stay in business. Just how badly management needs these labor-cost concessions will determine how much they are willing to give a union in order to secure concessions. The BNA sample of concession cases finds that union improvements were secured in about one-third of the cases where labor-cost concessions were agreed upon. These union improvements are most likely to occur first, where firms are under the greatest economic pressure to cut costs and secure concessions (that is, where firms have the greatest incentive to secure union cooperation), and second, where the union can deliver relatively large labor-cost savings because, for example, it covers a large proportion of the labor force. Of the cases in the BNA sample where unions won improvements in return for granting concessions, only 4% were at the plant level (the sample of concession cases was split almost evenly between plant and higher levels of bargaining). Further, virtually every one of the concession agreements secured at the corporate level included significant union improvements, suggesting that the level of negotiation plays an important role in determining union gains in concession bargaining. Management has less incentive to secure concessions at the plant level, and therefore less interest in granting quid pro quos to help secure them, because fewer workers are involved in plant negotiations and the operation of the firm as a whole rarely hinges on the plant-level negotiations. Further, the power to grant these improvements in areas outside of the traditional terms of the contract is usually held only by central management. Indeed, most important quid pro quos deal with changes across the firm (such as union recognition or outsourcing restrictions) and are not within the control of plant-level management.

The range of potential improvements that unions can get in return for concessions is constrained by the economic pressures facing the firm. Improvements in current wages, benefits, and work rules, for example, would all raise current labor costs, which would reduce employment security for union members and defeat the purpose of negotiating the concessions in the first place. The improvements that unions can gain are therefore likely to be in areas other than those that raise *current* labor costs. These include virtually every other aspect of the employment relationship, however.

Symbolic improvements. These include management actions that essentially leave the union no better off but demonstrate that it still has bargaining power. Perhaps the best examples are equality-of-sacrifice provisions in the auto industry, which force management to suffer employment and wage cuts similar to those that the unions have accepted. The UAW, for example, forced GM management to rescind an improved executive bonus plan instituted just after the union agreed to new concessions. Similar actions occurred at International Harvester. Equality-of-sacrifice provisions may give unions power over unorganized white-collar workers. After these provisions were introduced at GM, for example, some white-collar workers there invited the UAW to discuss with them the advantages of organizing (Dun's 1982). Other examples include management "pledges" to consider union interests in future actions. These symbolic gestures serve a political function for the unions by demonstrating to their members that the union is not being pushed around by management and that the crisis is a genuine one whose burden is shared by management.

Job security. Some improvements attempt to improve job security directly. At Xerox, for example, the company exchanged employment security and no-layoff clauses in return for a union agreement to modify work rules significantly. United Airlines made a similar trade with their pilots. The most common of these cases, however, are those where employers agree not to go ahead with a planned closing or layoff in return for concessions.

Implicit job security. These changes indirectly improve job security by influencing business decisions that affect employment. Promises to limit outsourcing at Ford, for example, or to guarantee plant investment in the rubber industry, create the circumstances that will improve job security. One could also argue that improved Supplemental Unemployment Benefit (SUB) plans, the guaranteed income stream arrangements at selected Ford and GM plants, improved severance payments, and the like, all increase the fixed costs of labor (given the same level of costs) and make layoffs less likely.

Contingent compensation. Arrangements of this sort promise improvements in future compensation in return for current labor-cost concessions. They include not only stock-ownership plans and profit sharing, particularly common in air transport, but also arrangements that tie future wages to improvements in the firm's economic performance. At American Motors, for example, wage concessions are to be paid back based on improved company performance.

Say in company decisions. Formal arrangements to involve the unions in company business decisions have been the most publicized although perhaps the least common form of union gains. They range from putting union leaders on company boards in return for concessions, as at Pan Am, Chrysler, and McCreary Tire, to shop floor participation plans such as the job committees in the auto industry. These arrangements are often limited to particular issues at a given time, such as decisions about equipment purchases and subsequent manning levels.

Union security gains. These improvements cover a whole range of issues, all of which help to meet the union's particular needs with respect to its bargaining relationship with the employer. They include union recognition arrangements, such as the one between the United Rubber Workers and Goodrich (where the company agrees to remain neutral in any election campaigns); prohibitions on double-breasted operations secured by the Teamsters' Master Freight Agreement; and continuous information about company performance and future plans, such as the ones meat-packing companies are providing at the plant level to the United Food and Commercial Workers. Arrangements of this sort help to meet the union's current problems and improve its bargaining position with employers in the future.

The distribution of improvements secured in bargaining in 1982 is set out in table 11.4, which is drawn from the BNA sample. It has been argued elsewhere that the most pressing concern for unions in this recent period has been job security (Davis 1983). Indeed, one might have expected more explicit job guarantees. A recent survey reported by Mills (1983), for example, notes that at least in their bargaining demands unions were overwhelmingly concerned with gaining job security in return for labor-cost concessions. Resistance from employers appears to explain why explicit guarantees were not more common.

Table 11.4
Types of union improvements (distribution across all improvements)

Equality of sacrifice	3%
Gainsharing:	
Profit sharing	10
Stock investment	5
Bonds	1
Product discounts	2
Contingent compensation	8
Job security:	
Implicit commitment	15
Explicit commitment	
Closing notice, rights	5
Severance, SUB's	9
Retraining/placement	3
Say in business decisions	10
Union organizational gains	5
Firm information	7

Source: Tabulation derived from Bureau of National Affairs data base.

The *Business Week* poll found that only 2% of the firms surveyed were willing to give unions explicit employment guarantees in order to get concessions (*Business Week* 1982). Guarantees of this sort would bind management to potentially expensive and uncertain commitments, and there is also some doubt as to whether such guarantees could actually be enforced, particularly if the firm is in financial difficulty.

Most of the explicit guarantees in this sample are simply reversals of decisions to close plants or lay off workers, reversals that were made in return for concessions. Few guarantee employment in the future. It is not surprising, therefore, to find concerns with job security manifested through more implicit arrangements. Of the firms surveyed by *Business Week*, 42% were willing to strengthen employment security indirectly through promises to keep plants open and maintain production levels— promises that could be reversed if circumstances worsened.

The acceptance of gain sharing and contingent compensation arrangements reflects not only acceptance by management (85% of the *Business Week* respondents were willing to improve future pay levels in return for concessions) but also similar interest from the unions. It is important for the union not just to get back something in return for concessions but to get back something that looks a lot like that which was given up. Contingent compensation fills that role. It also places an ostensible limit on the duration of the concessions (for instance, until business picks up), making them seem temporary and less permanent. For management, these contingent arrangements buy time now and cost money only if conditions improve—an advantageous trade for firms currently facing a crisis. They also establish a useful precedent by tying compensation more closely to circumstances in individual plants.

Perhaps the most important point about these improvements or quid pro quos is that they have allowed the unions to salvage some gains from the otherwise disastrous circumstances associated with concession bargaining. In some cases these improvements provide a way for the unions to address fundamental problems that would otherwise be outside the bargaining agenda. Union security and automatic recognition arrangements, for example, directly address the lack of organizing success that is the basic problem facing unions in many industries and is a problem outside of the normal scope of collective bargaining.

In virtually all cases concession agreements have expanded the range of issues over which the parties negotiate, giving the unions additional influence over important business decisions that affect the security and conditions of future union employment. It is important to note, however, that unions have been able to secure these improvements only at the corporate level and that unions representing large numbers of workers (perhaps in coalitions) are more likely to win them. Some of these improvements, such as contingent compensation, provide integrative goals where the parties have common interests, but it would be unrealistic to think that these changes would fundamentally alter the basic bargaining positions of the parties. At best, these gains might make the unions better informed about the firm's situation and the two sides more willing and able to pursue negotiated solutions to their respective problems.

The fact that improvements of this sort are being written into contracts suggests that they will continue to be a factor at least for the next few years, but the question remains as to how they will change union-management relations. Contingent compensation plans, for example, bring with them a number of changes because they shift some aspects of business risks from the firm onto workers. As a result, pay levels are likely to be more variable in the future. The experience with profit sharing plans suggests that contingent pay plans will not run themselves

(Aussieker 1982). Unions will be forced to become involved in the detailed administration and interpretation of these plans, and these efforts will demand new skills and expertise on the part of the unions.

Concerns with future employment security and contingent pay arrangements are likely to focus union interests more clearly on business decisions that affect the long-run position of the firm. In air transport, for example, pilots at certain carriers have agreed to take a significant share of their earnings in company stock. As a result of their interest in the long-run value of that stock, they have tried to influence and (to their mind) improve the market strategy of their carriers. Stock-ownership arrangements give unions a clear mechanism for exerting influence on the firm and its business decisions. They also will force the union to develop additional areas of expertise if that influence is to be used effectively. The steelworkers union, for example, has recently been called on to advise members who acquired stock in return for concessions about proxy votes.

Longer-run Significance of Concession Bargaining

Many people are wondering what the long-run effects of this intense period of adjustment will be on the terms and conditions of employment. Are these changes simply a temporary gain for management that will be reversed as soon as economic conditions return to normal, or has there been a permanent shift in the economics and process of collective bargaining? The answer to this question depends upon the extent to which economic pressure has come from temporary, cyclical pressures or from long-term, structural shifts. We believe that there has been enough structural change in the bargaining environment to suggest that bargaining will never return to the stable system that we knew during the 1960s and 70s.

There is every reason to believe that the stability associated with the "core" unionized industries in the economy has been eroded for the forseeable future. The oligopolistic pricing and production arrangements in steel, autos, rubber, and other manufacturing operations has been shattered, perhaps permanently, by foreign competition. Deregulation in trucking and airlines has had a similar effect. One would expect economic forces in these industries to be much more volatile in the future and pressures to adjust costs and employment to remain more intense. It will be correspondingly more difficult for unions to take wages out of competition, and as a result bargaining will continue to be more sensitive to the needs of individual firms and plants.

This new economic environment will confront unions with a number of short-run dilemmas. The threats to employment security and the pressures to adjust labor costs will continue even if unions decide in principle to forgo concessions. The dilemma for union leaders will continue to be knowing when to draw the line on concessions: How far can wage and benefit levels be adjusted to changing economic conditions before the benefits of unionization disappear? Another dilemma exists with respect to potential remedies for these competitive pressures. Various forms of protectionism, currently presented as an alternative to these adjustments, offer the prospect of short-term improvements but potential costs to the economy in the long run.

One may wonder what effects these pressures will have on bargaining structure. The current round of concession bargaining has led to considerable fragmentation and decentralization of bargaining structure. It is likely that some of this decentralization will wane as marginal plants close and excess capacity is adjusted. Given the importance to unions of taking their wages out of competition, one might expect unions to make an effort to rebuild bargaining structures to achieve that effect, possibly with more room for adjustments at the local level.

The current round of concession bargaining can also be expected to leave its mark on future bargaining topics. In forthcoming negotiations, we expect that employers will continue to press for more flexible work rules, especially on manning levels and deployment, largely because of continued uncertainty and volatility in product markets. Because of this, some items that add uncertainty to contract arrangements, such as COLA's, will be more difficult for unions to secure in the future.

From the union side, many of the quid pro quos secured in exchange for concessions are likely to remain on the bargaining table for some time. Once issues are brought into negotiations, they have a tendency to stay there in the future. Some of these bargaining issues are likely to involve the union more deeply in the business decisions of the firm, and others may help unions address particular problems affecting them as organizations.

It is even possible that concession bargaining may have enhanced the future potential for union organizing. In some cases, unions have been getting good press for being flexible and helping firms solve their problems, particularly with respect to foreign competition (for example, at Ford). In cases where employers have pressed for concessions that were not necessary, when conditions improve there may be a backlash that may benefit the union movement (especially in nonunion operations). These developments would be analogous to the influence that the Depression had on worker attitudes in the 1940s and 1950s. In other cases the experience with layoffs and wage cuts may convince unorganized workers that they need union protection. The equality-of-sacrifice provisions secured by the UAW at GM apparently had this effect on some white-collar workers.

In general, we expect these developments to make bargaining in the future an increasingly technical operation where the role of information becomes especially important. The wider range of issues requires a wider range of information, particularly concerning the consequences of potential agreements, and unions will have to develop additional areas of expertise in order to meet that need. There is little reason, though, to expect these developments to change the attitudes of the parties in a fundamental manner; a new era of cooperation is not at hand. We might expect the changes associated with concession bargaining to increase the awareness of the parties to each other's needs, however. In many cases, the bargaining agenda has widened, and the parties have shown a willingness to experiment and seek innovative solutions to their specific problems. These conclusions parallel those concerning the introduction of productivity bargaining a decade ago (McKersie and Hunter 1973). Whether these experiments lead to continuing cooperation will depend on whether arrangements are established to provide for joint problem solving in the future. Union participation on the shop floor and in strategic business decisions provides one such arrangement and is explored later in this volume.

Note

1. We are in the process of studying the connection between actual or threatened plant shutdown and the onset of concession bargaining activity. In rough terms it appears that during the year 1982 approximately 600 plant shutdowns were threatened, with half of these proceeding into some type of concession bargaining discussions. Ultimately about half of these discussions (in other words, about 150) resulted in agreements. Quite significantly, about 40 of these concession agreements did not "save the day" and the plants ultimately closed. On the other side of the picture, there were approximately 100 concession negotiations that commenced without the immediate threat of plant shutdown (no doubt, in these situations some concern about the viability of the plant existed, given various types of "spillover" pressures).

References

Aussieker, William. "Creative Collective Bargaining Revised: The Kaiser Long-Range Sharing Plan." *Proceedings of the Industrial Relations Research Association*, Winter 1982.

Bureau of National Affairs Special Report. "White-collar Layoffs and Cutbacks." August 13, 1982.

"Concession Bargaining." *Business Week*, July 14, 1982. [unpublished survey results].

Cappelli, Peter. "Concession Bargaining and the National Economy," *Proceedings of the Industrial Relations Research Association*, Winter 1982.

Cappelli, Peter. "Plant-level Concession Bargaining and the Shutdown Threat." Massachusetts Institute of Technology, 1983. Mimeographed.

Davis, William M. "Collective Bargaining in 1983: A Crowded Agenda." *Monthly Labor Review* (January 1983).

"Executive Givebacks," *Dun's Business Month.* July 1982.

Henle, Peter. "Reverse Collective Bargaining? A Look at Some Union Concession Situations." *Industrial and Labor Relations Review* (October 1973).

Juris, Hervey. "Union Crisis Wage Decisions." *Industrial Relations* (1969).

Kochan, Thomas A., and Peter Cappelli. "The Transformation of the Industrial Relations/Human Resource Function." In *Internal Labor Markets*, edited by Paul Osterman. Cambridge: MIT Press, 1983.

McKelvey, Jean Carol. "Trade-Union Interest In Production." Ph.D. diss., Radcliffe College, 1933.

McKersie, Robert B., and Lawrence C. Hunter. *Pay, Productivity and Collective Bargaining.* London: Macmillan, 1973.

Mills, D. Quinn. "When Employees Make Concessions." *Harvard Business Review* (May–June 1983).

Shultz, George P., and Charles A. Myers. "Union Wage Decisions and Employment." *American Economic Review* (June 1950).

Richard Prosten: Harry Katz describes a process of "innovative bargaining"—his euphemism for a process that has seen some unions in some situations agreeing to contractual alterations that in some cases included some steps away from past gains. This process has not occurred everywhere. Traditional "nonconcessionary" bargaining has continued as in the past in many cases.

Katz makes it sound as though the concessions produced by this process are a desirable innovation and that past approaches and practices are perhaps bad. I find this to be an unfortunate construction. Some commentators say that unions are responsible for screwing things up and they should now give back what they have taken. While this process has, in some cases, eased specific situations, it is difficult to conclude that this process will become the model for industrial unions.

Even the more popular term, "concession bargaining," does not fit every case. The UAW uses the phrase "mid-term modifications" to describe much of its recent activity in this field.

As is frequently the case in industrial relations, what appears to be a new process turns out, on examination, to be not quite so revolutionary. The UAW, for example, negotiated deviations from the basic auto pattern at American Motors for many years. It did so because American Motors was assessed to be a company in trouble.

However, things are different now—current instances of innovative bargaining have occurred within the framework of major master agreements. They frequently affect not just marginal producers but most or all of an industry. Contracts in meat-packing and autos were traditionally among the pacesetters in industrial contracts—looked up to by many for over twenty years. Because of that historic significance, the impact of concessions in these basic industries took on in the public eye more significance than the concessions involved were due.

In the wake of contractual modifications in these major industries, a wild rash of requests for concessions started appearing. Many of the requests were clearly not justified. Many were motivated by no definable business problem other than a national tradition of corporate greed. Heads of companies no doubt went to their industrial relations departments complaining that "everybody else is getting concessions, why can't we?" At the same time, there were situations where companies were able to use local newspapers and Chambers of Commerce to convince working people that *they* were the problem—that it was employee greed that had created difficulties for the companies.

Cappelli and McKersie point to a probable tapering off in concession bargaining. It has, from our data, already happened. International unions had a lot to do with this. The slowed pace of concessions, at least after the first wave of such activity, was due at least in part to increased involvement by "headquarters." In many international unions, bargaining is a local activity. In some cases where the international was not kept adequately informed, companies were able to pull fast deals. The extent of joblessness is such that people were legitimately frightened about job security and were dragged into the process without much resistance. Once unions found out what was happening, much of this changed dramatically, as processes for assessing the legitimacy of companies' pleas were established. Unions held conferences to train their people on how to ask companies for economic details—not just standard annual-report kinds of things but the intricate details that allow unions to pursue the specifics of a company's plea for concessions. In many cases, as soon as the union responded to a request for concessions with a demand for financial information, the company dropped its request. Locals knew they could call on their international. When they did, many company requests were found to be unjustified.

Also, legal questions came to the fore—for example, management's tactic of threatening a plant with closure because employees didn't give something back *during* a contract. The case of Illinois Spring ("We're closing this facility and transferring production since you won't agree to concessions and we're moving") is a case in point. The UAW challenged the legality of this tactic in court and won. [Editorial note: The NLRB reversed its decision in this case after this discussion took place.]

The value of substantial union involvement at the national level is pointed out by the results of bargaining between the UAW and Ford or the United Steelworkers and the basic steel industry. In exchange for modifications, unions have won new job security provisions, such as the limits on outsourcing in autos.

I am also concerned about some areas of management "take-backs" that have not been mentioned. A large number of firms are attempting to take back the *future* security of workers, specifically pension funds that have been accumulated over time as workers deferred current income into the future. Frequently, company approaches to taking back the money are glossed over in such a way as to make them sound as if nobody is going to lose anything. For example, the management people at A&P had a pension fund that A&P reclaimed. Since it was "overfunded," A&P shut it down, bought annuities covering the vested portion, and in the process $200 million "reverted" to the company. The nonunion employees who had taken less pay over the years to build up the fund were the losers in this deal.

Where will the process of concessions and modifications go from here? It seems to me that we are looking at a mixed bag. Cappelli and McKersie talk about twenty-two rubber plants that closed after concessions were negotiated. When things like that happen, people start to ask questions—the obvious one being, what is the value of concessions?

It is hard to predict future activity in this area but I suspect that the downward slope of the Cappelli-McKersie concession curve will continue. People will be looking more closely at concessions before agreeing to them. However, it seems clear that to the extent job security can be improved through "innovative" agreements, the process will continue— if job security is not improved, the concessions will be viewed as senseless.

Rudy Oswald: Three things bother me about the concession bargaining study. First, it doesn't look at the question of the consequences of concessions on workers (except in rubber plants). Second, it fails to analyze whether wage concessions are related to the problems of these industries. Often concessions may not be related to the problem that is causing the financial distress. Third, there seems to be an attempt to foster a view in the country that the problem in the smokestack industries is that wages are too high. If we were to look honestly at the situation, we would discover that unions have not achieved big increases in the last ten years. Some complain that certain groups of workers have kept even with the rapid rise in the cost of living. Sad to say, few academics defend the notion that workers should be able to maintain their standard of living. Instead, the trade union movement is urged to accept the notion that it would be fine for workers to be paid the minimum wage, or even a lower wage rate. Yet this analysis points out that the financial pressures on firms are external and have little to do with wage changes.

McKersie: One thing that has fed that concern is COLA.

Oswald: Part of the concern is based on poor analysis. The big layoffs in steel and autos have meant the *average* hourly labor rates moved up substantially because it's the more senior workers (with higher wage rates) who are still working. The total compensation-cost package is spread across a smaller number of workers, thus raising average hourly labor costs more than the wage increases actually achieved by the workers still employed. The averages, therefore, have moved substantially differently in different situations.

Donald Ephlin: The impression is that "those bums in the auto industry" are given $20 an hour, but no other nations speak of hourly costs. We compare apples and oranges. For example, the Japanese have public health care while we have to count these costs as part of compensation.

I'm not sure how you define concession bargaining—in our case, we consider it to be a good strategy, not concessionary. I was one of the first to advocate going to the bargaining table early. First, we needed to stop outsourcing as soon as possible, because once work is gone, it's gone forever, and second, we were very concerned about General Motors. Come September 14 [the normal contract expiration date], GM would have dictated the terms of their new agreement; they'd decide what items would be eliminated. Going in when you have the bargaining power is better than waiting. We haven't solved our problems, but we've made significant progress, particularly in outsourcing. We can have a voice in where it's going, to a union manufacturer. Katz's summary mentions compensation-level reductions, but we had no decrease in pay.

In America, there's no question that there's an impression that we're way ahead of the pack. Rudy's right—others didn't get enough, we didn't get too much. The gap that's created is a political one. Because of that false impression we go to Washington and get no sympathy at all. People were delighted that the autoworkers and the company were in trouble. But we're getting some credit for an innovative agreement. The number one issue in labor is reducing work time. We gave up this goal for now (by agreeing to give up seven paid personal holidays per year) because it was the easiest to give up. We were too far up front—Japan was talking about decreasing one hour a week, and we were talking about a four-day workweek. Some folks have had no choice and have made real wage concessions. In the auto industry I think it worked out well. What we got in exchange for what we gave up was great. To think the labor movement is backtracking is the wrong impression. We've made inroads that will be there forever. I think we ought to explore it for what it's worth.

Some of these so-called give-backs were not justified. We took the biggest cuts in the plants outside of autos that already were far below the pattern. One important thing we did do on pay was to prepare for the future. We should have learned our lesson long ago. It's better to give up the annual improvement factor than COLA—to protect against inflation rather than have a wage increase.

You have to recognize that it's not all the same bargaining—meat-packing's is completely different from ours. I think we should distinguish between where the union had input in strategy and where the union was bludgeoned by companies. A correction—domestic outsourcing did have a negative effect—it caused a Ford plant to close. And we did preserve pattern bargaining, but some people don't understand our bargaining strategy. We got a commitment from Ford that they'd reopen a small plant of sixty people. Then we got GM to meet this "pattern" and in doing so saved four much larger plants. That's a real pattern bargaining strategy.

Michael Bennett: At my level in the auto industry, if you go back and look at my view in 1981, there was a lot of turmoil in the UAW. I like the term "innovative bargaining." Concession bargaining is a media term with a negative connotation that gravitates only to the economic isues. We've got to move away from it. The membership doesn't like it. Innovative bargaining meant that management was interested in expanding the bargaining arena—shifting the emphasis from economic to noneconomic issues, generally directed toward job security, and remaining competitive.

Now I would like to describe the changes we negotiated at our local level. The GM agreement was ratified by 7,000 votes—less than 2%. But in Flint, Michigan, we carried the vote with a margin of 12,000 votes out of 60,000. The city of Flint, Michigan, played a major role in changing the UAW from a total adversarial role to that of a dual relationship—adversarial, and yet we had input at different levels.

For example, the total cost savings for GM from the master contract was $1.50 an hour over a one- to two-year period. The average GM car sells for $11,400. Using GM figures of $20 an hour and their estimate of 155 average hours of labor to produce a car, we could calculate that if an autoworker worked for nothing, the average GM car would cost $7,800, which is absurd. We had input in areas at the national that signaled inputs from the local level. Legal services were provided, better communication, interest in increasing the quality of the product, profit sharing, joint decision making, and so forth. Locally, unions addressed issues that should have been addressed earlier. At some of our GM plants some eight-hour jobs could be completed in two-and-a-half to three hours. There was an interest by management in increasing productivity by 20%. Two plants stepped up to that commitment and others followed. More emphasis was put on job security, inverse seniority, and reducing the number of classifications and changing some work rules. The corporation estimated our local productivity improvements saved an additional $4.53 an hour in labor costs. When we add this to the $1.50 an hour from the national contract, in our opinion we made significant inroads to the alleged $8 an hour difference between Japan and the United States. We hope that in the long run that will make us more competitive and get back more of our market share and thereby create more jobs for our workers.

Sam Camens: We [steelworkers] did negotiate a concessionary agreement, we admit it—we're different from autos. It was a conscious decision on our part. We do not kid about it. We were very serious. Otherwise, a lot of suspicion would develop.

I want to add one thing to the pressures Harry Katz noted that were affecting the steel industry—domestic nonunion mini-mill competition. It's over 10% of steel production, and it's a threat to the basic steel industry.

One thing about concession bargaining has to be understood. Negotiations in both autos and steel were not just that the company asked and we gave. They were much more serious than that. I felt we did a better job in these negotiations than in the last three rounds. The company threatened us, and we had to get an agreement. Every union needs to know what they have to lose and evaluate it. During the time of negotiations the contract wasn't up, and the company said, "In August [end of the agreement] if we don't get what we need to exist in worldwide competition, you'll face a strike—and no electricity, shanties, or heat will be furnished to the pickets as in past strikes. We have enough on layoff that we'll open these plants if you agree or not. You'll be in a real war." So we had to make an evaluation. We ran a survey during the negotiations with the presidents of the locals, and we were absolutely amazed and taken aback with the answers. We made an evaluation and estimated that in August 1983 [when the contract was due to expire] steel production wouldn't be much higher than 50% of capacity. The actual consensus of the local presidents was that after two weeks of a strike we'd be in serious trouble. We made the determination as leaders that we think we're better off to get an agreement early—one that the membership will accept—than face the danger of a disastrous strike.

Arthur Gundershein: In the study there was no looking at situations where there were no concessions, in industries where there are still pressures, that is, there is no control group. Also no one has looked at the nonunion sector to see how much was unilaterally taken away from these employees. We know what's happening in terms of take-back, but not what the unions did relative to holding back.

Prosten: When a union does something, it's immediately conveyed to the public by the media in a superficial and mostly negative way. I think the academics should help us correct that image to the rest of the world.

Jack Golodner: Aren't we being schizophrenic, though? Do we want to say we're in concession bargaining or not? On the one hand we want to portray an image of being responsible and making adjustments where needed or warranted to save jobs or save a company. On the other hand we want to portray an image of being tough and strong and making gains.

VI

Unions and Quality-of-Work-Life Programs

12

Codetermination,
Collective Bargaining, and
Worker Participation in
the Construction Industry

John T. Joyce

The United States has a form of codetermination—collective bargaining; it is of limited scope but within its allotted area it has major practical significance.

Through collective bargaining, unions and management in the United States jointly determine wages, hours, terms, and conditions of work for the employer's labor force. Moreover, in many cases the parties, through collective bargaining, have established joint programs to provide for apprenticeship and training; pensions; medical and hospital care benefits; unemployment benefits; life insurance; disability, sickness, and accident insurance; vacation, holiday, and severance benefits; scholarships; child care; and legal services.

On these subjects collective bargaining in the United States has probably created a more comprehensive system of private law jointly developed by management and labor than in any other country. Indeed, until recently there were only two industrial relations systems in the United States—one in which employers were legally free to set terms as they saw fit except in the narrowest circumstances and one in which the only restraining rules were those set in a collective bargaining system. There is now far more public law concerning the employer-employee relationship, but for employees represented by unions public law is still a secondary factor.

Despite its importance, I have for three reasons called collective bargaining a limited form of codetermination. The first is that collective bargaining does not cover enough U.S. workers. The second is that management retains entire control over such strategic entrepreneurial decisions as product research and development, pricing, investment in plant and equipment, and overall industrial planning. The third is that collective bargaining is not based on a utopian injunction that the parties are to recognize their joint interests and reason together; it is an adversary system in which in the final analysis disagreements are settled on the basis of economic power.

The present system of industrial relations in the United States has persisted with relatively little change since the end of World War II. Yet under the best of circumstances such a system is inherently unstable. A relationship in which two adversaries have interests that are in common, as well as in conflict, either grows into a relationship of broader cooperation or deteriorates into a relationship of total enmity in which each party concludes that his survival depends on the destruction of the other.

From the perspective of maintaining a collective bargaining system, the present circumstances are not the best. The climate of U.S. labor-management relations is worse than it was ten or twenty years ago. While there are many signs of a hardening of position, attitude, and ideology, the labor law reform "battle" of 1977–78 is perhaps the single episode that most clearly symbolizes the growing polarization. The issue raised by the reform effort was "just how difficult should it be for workers to organize?" Management's harsh, doctrinaire, and almost universal answer was that self-organization should be as difficult as possible.

This led one highly respected senior official of the AFL-CIO's Industrial Union Department to observe, "For a number of years now I have believed there can be an accommodation and cooperative attitude between labor and management. But I don't believe that any more. The labor law reform effort has showed me beyond the shadow of doubt that we are enemies."

This increase in the level of antagonism is, of course, related to the difficult economic situation faced by the United States. Increased international competition, a high rate of American investment overseas, high interest rates, high prices for necessities—particularly energy—a record number of entrants into the work force and into retirement all combine to cause inflation, falling real wages, and slow growth. With the best will in the world, these would be enormously difficult problems to solve. Against a background of factionalism, the task of creative adaptation appears all but impossible. Thus the very value of collective bargaining—the only form of labor-management cooperation on a basis of equality the United States has evolved—has been put in doubt.

Both extremes of the political spectrum want to discard the collective bargaining process. But the problem with collective bargaining in the United States is not that it is of too little value in meeting present difficulties, but that it has been put to too little use in dealing with those difficulties. The potential of collective bargaining is not exhausted. That potential will only be realized, however, when collective bargaining is more universally employed and when it is understood and accepted that collective bargaining can and should be extended to all the factors that shape the industrial environment.

To extend collective bargaining to more U.S. workers requires intensifying the AFL-CIO's important new focus on its role as catalyst and coordinator of organizing efforts by affiliated national unions. It also requires that U.S. public action—on the part of the courts and government agencies—must more nearly conform to U.S. public policy as explicitly expressed in the National Labor Relations Act: To encourage the practice and procedure of collective bargaining.

This means, among other things, removing the legal roadblocks to effective organizing that the law creates, or permits businesses to create, speeding up the representation election and certification process, and dropping the artificial distinction between "mandatory" and "permissive" subjects of bargaining. In a free society labor and management should be free to bargain to an impasse on any subject of mutual interest that is not clearly contrary to the public interest.

In each industry, labor and management must also address those background factors that determine the degree of success that can be achieved at the bargaining table. Rather than beginning when labor and management sit down to negotiate wages and other employment conditions and ending when they get up, collective bargaining must be extended to all matters of legitimate joint concern. With collective bargaining as its core, worker participation can be extended on one side to the question of how to improve the quality of work life and on the other side to the strategic questions that determine whether a given plant, firm, or industry will stay in business and at what level of activity.

That there is both a need for, and value to, such an extension is revealed by an anecdote told recently by a former U.S. Secretary of Labor. As a participant in basic steel discussions, the secretary asked the head of a major company why the corporation had not invested past profits in expanding and revitalizing its plants in an effort to become more competitive internationally. Why, the secretary inquired, were they so much more interested in diversification into other businesses? The executive replied that he was interested in making money, not steel.

Fair enough, if his interest were the only one at stake. But it isn't. In an environment that includes greater worker participation, an executive's response to the secretary's question could not be so one-dimensional. Workers are interested in the health of the industry that they serve and in the stability of their jobs and their community for a very fundamental reason: they have heavily invested, not money, but themselves in all three. Workers therefore have a vital stake in strategic industrial decisions, and that interest—as the workers determine it— has a fundamental right to be represented. An extension of worker participation to the strategic level will not, of course, solve our economic problems. But in a highly industrialized society, it is essential that this "human factor" be added to the equation. American trade unionists understand this need.

In this pragmatic sense codetermination is not alien to the United States, nor does labor in the United States oppose it. We are, to be sure, skeptical of the new psychotechnicians of industry who seek to increase "worker satisfaction" without giving workers the means to meet with their employers on an equal footing. Without the hard muscle of collective bargaining and union representation, quality-of-work-life projects are inherently manipulative and participation in policy-making forums is at best an opportunity to exchange views and information. U.S. labor organizations are determined that, when it comes to participation, our members will get the steak, not just the sizzle.

Participation at the job site/shop floor—"quality-of-work-life"— level, and at the strategic decision—"boardroom"—level must, to be sure, have a certain degree of insulation from the particular kind of adversarial confrontation common to negotiating sessions at the level of collective bargaining. But employer-employee relationships at all three levels must be an integral part of the same process. When you move from "wages" and "working conditions" into other parts of the codetermination spectrum—into such matters as production, marketing and sales, financial management, and so on—you move from the adversarial approach traditional to the rule-making mode of codetermination and other approaches begin to appear. Such other approaches become more suitable because, in one sense, you are not then talking about how to divide profits and benefits, but how to create them.

Codetermination—defined not by one, or even by many applications, but most simply as the joint determination by two parties, labor and management, of all or a portion of the affairs of a project, company, or industry—will in different societies and countries, indeed in different industries in the same country, take varying forms. Some of these forms will be transferable—but then only as analogues—from their native habitats, while others will not. There is, however, one constant: genuine, meaningful worker participation must have collective bargaining at its core.

Worker Participation in Construction

In the United States there is a growing body of research and professional and popular literature on the subject of worker participation. In light of the industrial successes of West Germany and Japan, much of the material focuses on those countries, but there is a substantial amount on experiments and initial experiences in a wide range of U.S. situations.

Curiously, there appears to be almost no material on worker participation in the construction industry. "Curious," because in terms of gross annual product as well as in number of workers employed, construction is the largest single industry in the United States.

For American construction unions, the issue of worker participation in management is laden with ironies. The advocates of worker participation are among the more visionary thinkers in the labor movement; yet for U.S. building craftsmen, many of their ideas are "old hat." The building trade unions are often viewed as the most conservative section of the American labor movement, yet they have historically been the strongest force in our society for direct worker control of the work process. And while academics and management experts have devoted considerable energy to the study of the concepts of worker participation in other countries, construction craft unions have been, in an unselfconscious way, innovative practitioners of these concepts in the United States. In part, this flows from the nature of construction work. In part, it flows from the traditions of the industry, which, of course, are in turn based on the nature of the work as it has evolved over the centuries.

Craft traditions shaped by the medieval guilds spanned an ocean in the seventeenth century to become firmly and aptly implanted in North America. In terms of codetermination, the guild not only brought together the building craftsman, the contractor and the architect/engineer in the same organization, but the contractor/designer functions were combined in one person—the master mason.

The Renaissance brought with it increased specialization—without which, no doubt, we could not have achieved spectacular technological progress—and the roles of craftsman, contractor, architect, engineer grew farther apart. But the degree of codetermination that still existed in the Renaissance construction industry is suggested by the fact that the stonemasons of fifteenth-century Florence jailed Brunelleschi, the city's foremost architect, for eleven days, in their own jail, for violating craft rules.

In the United States, the earliest worker organizations in construction sought to achieve control over their working conditions, through direct action rather than negotiation. In contrast to manufacturing industries, where recent worker-participation programs attempt to limit the power of management to act unilaterally, early construction trades unionists attempted to establish unilateral worker control over wages, hours, and working conditions. For example, in 1833, the bricklayers of Baltimore called a meeting of the city's building tradesmen. They decided that, as of April 1, no building tradesmen would start work earlier than six o'clock in the morning nor work later than six o'clock in the evening, reserving two hours for meals. Thus the ten-hour day was at least temporarily achieved in Baltimore, through a decision rendered by the workers themselves.

Similarly, the Bricklayers and Plasterers Protective Association of New York gave notice to employers in 1850 the "Commencing on the first day of March up to the 13th day of November inclusive, wages will be $2.00 per day; for the balance of the year $1.75 and no three-quarter days allowed except where men are prevented from working by inclement weather, or any other justifiable cause." These and other proclamations of early construction unions were not an invitation to employers to open negotiations; they were unilateral declarations issued by the workers, whose terms in a tight labor market the employers were forced to accept in order to obtain skilled labor.

As the building trades unions developed and grew in the later years of the nineteenth century, this tradition of decentralized worker control over working conditions was strengthened and institutionalized. Each of the local construction trades unions adopted in its constitution or bylaws an array of work rules. Even after the development of national and international craft unions, these work rules continued to be specified in the local union constitutions, thus giving the workers in each locality immediate control over the conditions that affected their work. Today such rules, to the extent they are agreed to by the employer, are reflected in the local's collective bargaining agreement.

A major purpose of these work rules has always been to preserve the integrity of the crafts. As with the rapidly expanding manufacturing concerns, large construction employers repeatedly attempted to break the work process up into discrete repetitive tasks that required little or no skill. For example, as Robert A. Christie notes in *Empire in Wood*, large contractors divided the carpenter's trade into "door-hanging," "floor-laying," "stair-building," "window-setting," "shingle-installing," and a score of other special tasks that could be performed by virtually unskilled workers. In essence, the major contractors sought to reduce the construction workers to the status of the unskilled operative in a modern factory. The trade unions resisted this trend, asserting the workers' pride in their skills and insisting that fully skilled craftsmen provided the industry with a more flexible work force. Through their assertion of craft integrity and worker control of the work process, the craft unionists largely protected construction workers from the degradation of skills and resultant alienation that affected workers in other industries.

One consequence of this is that unionized construction workers have always been highly productive. This point is particularly important because management association representatives frequently allege that specific construction union work rules are outrageously nonproductive. Yet every research study of actual productivity has found union construction workers more productive than nonunion construction workers. This is so primarily for two reasons. First, contrary to popular myth, construction unions typically do *not* resist technological improvements; and second, when workers work to rules they have shaped, or helped shape, their satisfaction in their work is considerably greater.

The mid-nineteenth-century practice of unilateral determination by the union of wages, hours, and conditions did not prove to be effective, however. It takes an extraordinary, sustained effort to maintain the solidarity necessary to preserve such a system, particularly in the face of unemployment. Thus as a practical matter the unilaterally determined union terms were often enforceable only during peak construction periods. As work improved, so did wages and working conditions.

As work declined, so did union wages and conditions. This instability proved harmful to both sides and to industry as well. Contract construction, particularly on a large scale, requires known costs. And family needs do not expand and contract with the building cycle. Consequently, construction unions and contractors began to see the value of negotiating contracts for a fixed period of time. By leveling out increases in wages and the costs of conditions, negotiated agreements provided a badly needed measure of stability to the industry. Such contracts are still negotiated by each craft at the local level and cover all work performed by all signatory contractors within a given geographic area. This decentralized approach conforms to the reality that there is no national construction market. It is also very responsive to current worker needs and allows for great flexibility in decision making.

Furthermore, construction bargaining, in common with U.S. and Canadian bargaining generally, has always aimed at giving workers a share in shop floor/job site decision making. Agreement terms cover in considerable detail the essentials of wages, hours, and working conditions. Virtually all contracts call for mediation of worker disputes or grievances by the job steward or local business agent with the contractor's foreman or supervisor. Issues not resolved in this way are adjudicated through a formal grievance procedure held before a joint arbitration committee of local contractors and workers. Incidentally, each construction job, no matter how small, has a working steward for each craft. On very large projects, some crafts may have one or more stewards who attend full time to worker problems, but stewards are almost never authorized to call for work stoppages. The quid pro quo for arbitration of grievances is usually a provision that there shall be no work stoppage or lockout during the course of a contract. Most construction projects are rather small, but even on large projects construction workers usually work in small craft crews or teams. These teams make work decisions on scheduling, inspection, and discipline. Each member of the craft team can, because he is highly trained, perform a wide variety of tasks with a minimum of supervision.

On all but the relatively few giant projects the number of workers within a given craft is usually small enough, and job site variations considerable enough, that there is a good deal of interaction as to who will do what task and what is the best way to do it. Even on the very large projects, work assignments are generally reviewed at prejob conferences.

Most construction jobs, therefore, have many of the essential elements associated with "quality-of-work-life" projects, and in fact, a significant number of contractors use "quality circle" and "autonomous team" techniques without realizing they are doing more than following common sense. Of course common sense is not, in fact, common, and many, if not most, contractors fail to recognize the potential they have to increase both productivity and worker satisfaction.

Manpower supply is handled, in many construction locals, through a union-administered hiring hall or referral system and even where there is no formal referral system, the local construction union has a much greater role in hiring procedures than its industrial union counterpart. Indeed, the selection and training of craftsmen is a joint labor-management effort through apprenticeship committees.

Each craft has health care insurance programs jointly operated by labor and management as are the craft pension programs and all other employee benefit programs. These programs are of vital importance in the United States because public programs in these benefit areas are either nonexistent or inadequate. In heavy manufacturing industries such as steel and auto, these programs, including the investment of fund reserves, are run solely by the employer. In construction, as well as much of the clothing and food industries, worker representatives play an equal role with management in designing benefits, determining eligibility rules, administering claims, and making investment decisions.

So much for the good news. As you might expect of the largest industry in a huge, sprawling, heterogeneous, and now troubled economy, construction has a number of enormously difficult problems—the highest accidental death and injury rates; the highest unemployment and underemployment rates; gross and chronic maldistribution of manpower; gross and chronic maldistribution of materials; and wildly erratic wage patterns.

The perpetually troubled state of the construction industry and the high hourly wage rates of construction workers tend to obscure the profound problems faced by those workers. U.S. construction workers typically work by the hour and "hire and fire" practices can be almost brutal. Construction workers average only 1,200 to 1,400 hours of employment in "good" years. In addition to time lost due to weather and seasonal and economic cycles, U.S. construction workers are typically hired only for a given construction project. Therefore, except in periods of intense construction activity, a substantial number of employment hours are lost as workers seek their next jobs.

Unemployment problems become more severe as workers advance in years. Employers not only tend to feel (erroneously) that younger workers are more productive, but the accumulated damage of years of hard work in exposed weather conditions tends to increase the incidence of back and limb disabilities. As a consequence, the relatively high hourly wage rate does not average out to high annual or, and this is more important, high lifetime earnings. Construction hourly wage rates could be substantially lower if construction workers did not lose so much time due to frictional, seasonal, economic, and industrial health and injury factors.

The situation could be dramatically improved if we were permitted to act on the basis of what we know. For we know how to considerably ameliorate, if not totally solve, these problems. But in fact we are not capable of significant progress because U.S. government fiscal and monetary policies aimed at regulating or stabilizing the national economy keep the construction economy highly unstable. Such government policies are the direct cause of many problems in construction and the indirect cause of others because the extreme volatility of construction activity resulting from such policies has thus far rendered it virtually impossible to build the lasting industry structures necessary to develop solutions. As it is, joint labor-management industry committees have played the major role in keeping those problems beneath the chaos level.

Collective Bargaining in the Current Setting

I believe that in the United States collective bargaining is the core of the codetermination process, that the construction industry is and has for many years been at the forefront with regard to worker participation, but that the present collective bargaining system is inherently unstable and is under great stress in general and in construction in particular. It is likely, therefore, that the coming decade will determine whether the collective bargaining system will provide the base for broader labor-management cooperation or whether we will return to the law of the jungle.

American labor will adapt to either situation. The regressive course means a return to the "industrial unrest," as it is euphemistically described in many textbooks, which culminated in the 1930s with the passage of the Wagner [National Labor Relations] Act. To refight those battles, however, is not necessarily to arrive at the same result. It is, for example, very probable that when we next re-emerge from the jungle, American labor will have shed its century-long commitment— unique among labor movements in industrialized countries—to the concept of private enterprise.

While we cannot, and would not want to, reestablish the tight economic integration of the guilds, we can and must reduce the compartmentalization that currently exists. Specialization in construction has passed the point of diminishing returns and we, and the general public, are now paying a heavy price for the fragmentation forced upon us.

But we have yet to exhaust the potential of collective bargaining, and I think there is ample evidence within the construction industry alone to support that view. We have, for example, seen in recent years the emergence of committees at the metropolitan and regional level—the PRIDE program in St. Louis, the IMAGE program in southern Illinois, the UNION JACK program in Colorado, to name only three—which attempt to bring together the entire construction community (labor, management, and design professionals) with the principal construction users in a community or area in an effort to identify and resolve common problems. While these regional programs are relatively new, they have produced some impressive results, not the least of which is a growing recognition that labor-management difficulties are a symptom rather than a cause of the industry's problems.

Union Involvement at the Industry Level

At the national level, construction unions are increasing both their involvement and the formal nature of their involvement in strategic planning for the industry. One of the earliest, and still the most comprehensive, labor-management program is the Council on Industrial Relations established by the electrical workers and union contractors. Labor and management in the plumbing and sheet-metal trades have similar, if not quite as comprehensive, joint labor-management relations programs. The plumbers have probably the most sophisticated apprenticeship program in the country. And the sheet-metal workers, through one of their joint committees, have established one of the most innovative national programs, the Stabilization Agreement for the Sheet Metal Industry. Funded by collectively bargained employer payments on a cents-per-hour basis, this program—which provides benefits available to workers who relocate from an area of high unemployment to an area suffering from manpower shortages—constitutes the only national public or private attempt to resolve the chronic and severe mobility problem in construction. The battery of benefits available from the plan reduces the impediments to, and increases the incentives for, relocation.

In another recent development of major significance, the Building Trades Department of the AFL-CIO was instrumental in creating a multiindustry labor-management committee, the National Coordinating

Committee for Multi-Employer Plans, to cope with and help shape a mind-boggling array of government regulations covering joint labor-management pension funds. While the subject, pension regulation, is terribly important, it is a relatively narrow one and the major significance of this multimillion-dollar effort headed by the Building Trades Department rests in the technique used: isolate one of the major priority problem areas that are beyond the resources of any one craft or industry to solve; enlist labor and management allies; assemble a multidisciplinary task force staff with the competence and expertise needed to handle that problem; develop a step-by-step solution; and fully fund the effort through major financial contributions from the affected parties. Having gained the experience in how to successfully pull together such an effort, labor and management must now apply the same approach to other, even more important, areas.

One major roadblock to establishing joint programs on a collectively bargained basis was removed by the passage of the Labor-Management Cooperation Act of 1978. This measure encourages, as a matter of national policy, the formation of labor-management problem-solving groups. It also amends the Taft-Hartley Act to permit such joint programs to be funded by employer payments made pursuant to a collective bargaining agreement. On the basis of a language problem in Taft-Hartley, U.S. courts had barred unions from comanagement of such funds.

The Bricklayers Union and the Mason Contractors Association of America have been the first to establish a national effort under the Labor-Management Cooperation Act. Funded through local collective bargaining agrements on the basis of four cents for each hour worked by bricklayers, we have established the International Masonry Institute, a labor-management trust, to operate programs in four strategic areas: labor-management relations; masonry research and development; apprenticeship and training; and market development. In other words, through IMI, worker representatives and employer representatives seek to develop strategies to ensure the long-term growth and stability of the masonry industry. Of particular interest is the fact that we have, in the labor-management relations program, begun to explore the possibility of "quality-of-work-life" programs in masonry construction. We also plan to establish improved arbitration and mediation procedures, develop new mechanisms for coordinating bargaining by our locals, and hope to address the area of worker mobility.

The structure of IMI, created through the collective bargaining process rather than through legislation, avoids some of the potential pitfalls of other codetermination systems. Because IMI is operated under a joint labor-management board of trustees, the worker representatives are not integrated into an existing management hierarchy. By remaining completely independent of the management hierarchy, the bricklayers representatives on IMI are less open to the danger of cooptation that arises when worker representatives are added to existing corporate boards of directors. In the United States, where there is no legislation mandating codetermination, this independence also avoids potential legal problems associated with worker representation on corporate boards.

Perhaps most important, IMI ensures that the bricklayers representatives have equal access to information *and* an equal role in decisions related to the gathering of information. As many observers have noted, a worker representative on a corporation's board of directors is in many ways a captive of management; without independent access to information, the worker representative is in no position to offer intelligent alternatives to management's policy proposals. In the context of a joint labor-management forum such as IMI, both sides have equal access to the research and data developed by the Institute. Thus worker representatives are able to represent the workers' interests more effectively and more realistically.

Increasingly then, construction unions are participating in the strategic planning for their industry. In a labor-intensive industry such as construction, the union can be one of the most unified and powerful forces influencing decision making. These decisions center on manpower questions, market development activities, government liaison efforts, and pension fund capital investment decisions. By 1995, the U.S. Labor Department estimates that construction pension funds will total about $300 billion. The negotiated hourly payment system can be a primary tool for implementing programs. Construction thus far lacks any large corporations with a dominant industry position and a large number of permanent employees. To secure representation on a corporate board in construction would therefore be of little value even if it were practical to do so. But in a broad sense unions in the construction industry have novel and highly effective means for participating in decision making at the top level.

This drive for worker representation in the industry's decision-making process comes not from any ideological commitment to codetermination but rather from the practical commitment to protecting and advancing worker interests which has traditionally characterized building trades unions.

The central lesson to be drawn from the building trades experience with worker participation is that such participation is meaningful only when it arises from the workers' own self-organization; without strong, vital trade unions to express the workers' needs, one can have the appearance, but not the substance, of worker involvement. In the context of modern industrial relations, substantive worker involvement can only arise from the collective bargaining process.

And against the background of the troubled U.S. economy, perhaps the real question for management to ponder is not whether to tolerate trade unions but whether industry problems are in fact soluble without an organized work force sharing responsibility for the solution.

13   Worker Participation and American Unions

Thomas A. Kochan,
Harry C. Katz, and
Nancy R. Mower

The growth of quality-of-work-life (QWL) programs, related forms of worker participation, and experiments with new forms of work organization have posed both challenges and opportunities to the American labor movement. On the one hand, these informal mechanisms require union leaders and managers to modify their traditional roles and relationships in significant ways. On the other hand, they open new channels for direct worker involvement, and possibly, for greater worker and union influence. These developments have generated a vigorous debate among leaders concerning whether QWL and related participation processes will, in the long run, have positive or negative effects on the interests of labor unions and the workers they represent. Yet, the debate has, to date, largely taken place in a vacuum. While strong and convincing rhetorical or philosophical arguments have been presented by both the supporters and the critics of worker-participation processes, little direct examination of union experiences with these processes has informed the discussions.

In early 1982, however, a group of labor leaders meeting under the auspices of the Labor Policy Institute agreed to commission an independent study of the experiences of unions with worker-participation processes. These processes operate under a variety of labels in addition to QWL, such as Quality Circles (QC), Employee Involvement (EI), Labor-Management Participation Teams (LMPT), sociotechnical work systems, and others. Their common characteristics are that they involve small groups of union members and/or officers in informal participation processes at the workplace as supplements to the formal collective bargaining negotiations and grievance-handling procedures. Some also modify the way jobs and work are structured and organized at the workplace. Here we summarize the results of that study and outline its implications for the labor movement. A more detailed report may be found in Kochan, Katz, and Mower (1984).

The Sample

Survey data were collected from more than nine hundred union members from five local unions and over a hundred officers and activists from another five locals. These data were supplemented by interview and case-study data from these and several other worker-participation experiments and by an analysis of the written statements and speeches of leaders of various national unions of the AFL-CIO.

The five cases for which rank-and-file survey data are available span the range of relevant worker-participation programs and employer-union relationships needed to make useful comparisons and, with appropriate caution, some limited generalizations. With the help of our advisory committee we identified local unions and employers where some form of worker-participation activity was under way. We then discussed our research interests with representatives of these locals. A decision to conduct a survey of rank-and-file workers was then made if:

(1) sufficient time had elapsed under the worker-participation project to allow for a meaningful assessment of worker views of their experiences;

(2) some basis existed for comparing workers who were covered or actively involved in a worker-participation process with similar workers who were not covered or actively involved;

(3) both the union and the employer representatives agreed to cooperate with a survey;

(4) the group added diversity to the sample.

A brief description of each case is provided below. The actual names of firms and local unions are disguised in accordance with our agreement with each party.

Case 1: Local 1 and APEX Corporation
This case involves a large, highly skilled blue-collar bargaining unit in a large manufacturing facility of a Fortune 500 firm. The union and the company began a jointly administered QWL program in late 1980 after a clause authorizing experimentation with such a program was included in their 1980 bargaining agreement. Survey data were collected from a sample of 387 out of a bargaining unit of approximately 4,000 workers. The data were collected during the summer of 1982, approximately twenty months after the start-up of the QWL project. In this case the union is a full joint sponsor and sits with representatives of management on all of the various QWL steering and oversight com-

mittees. The actual participation process resembles a Quality Circle (QC) program. After receiving forty hours of training in problem-solving techniques, workers and supervisors meet in work teams for approximately one hour per week to identify problems and suggest solutions.

Case 2: Local 2 and the Uniform Piston Corporation
This is a bargaining unit of approximately 300 semiskilled and unskilled workers in a small manufacturing plant. The structure of the participation process again resembles a QC program. In this case the union is less centrally involved in the different stages of the process and adopts more of a watchdog, rather than a joint sponsor, role. The program had been in effect for approximately two years before the survey was conducted in the autumn of 1982. Data were collected by mail survey from 69 workers.

Case 3: Local 3 and the Communication Services Corporation
This is a large bargaining unit of blue-collar workers covering a wide range of skills employed in a facility of a large communications services firm. The QWL process in this firm is only in the early stages of development. It had been in place less than one year before our survey in late 1982. The process is part of a nationwide program that has been under way since the signing of a national agreement in 1980 in which the union and the company agreed to jointly develop a QWL program in its various locations. The union and management serve as joint sponsors of the process that is similar to a QC program. This unit provided 170 responses.

Case 4: Local 4 and the APS Company
This is a large bargaining unit of approximately 9,000 workers employed by a major parts supplier in the auto industry. Data were collected from 104 workers in various adjacent plants of a large manufacturing complex. This case serves as our longest-running QWL process in the sample. Discussions of joint activities between the union and the firm date back to 1977 and formal QWL activities have been under way since 1978. The primary union objective in this program from the outset was to save jobs in this location. In addition, this case provides data from union members in a QWL process that has gone beyond the QC stage by experimenting with autonomous work groups and work team organizations. The local union has been a full joint partner in developing and administering the participation activities since 1977.

Case 5: Local 5 and the Metro Newspaper Corporation
These data were collected from two units in the same local of the Newspaper Guild (NG) located in a large metropolitan area. One of the units is covered by a labor-management committee called the Worker Participation Committee (WPC). The WPC grew out of a 1972 bargaining agreement between this local and the Newspaper Corporation. It is a joint union-management committee that discusses a wide range of topics including working conditions, new technology, systems for performance appraisal, the selection of assistant editors, and the like. Thus, this case provides both a different type of participation structure (a labor-management committee as opposed to direct involvement of individuals and small work teams) and a white-collar professional employee group as opposed to blue-collar manufacturing or service workers. Because

Table 13.1
Demographic profile

	Total sample $N=931$	Participants $N=446$	Nonparticipants $N=485$
Age (years)	39.3	39.2	39.3
Sex (% female)	30.7	28.2	33.1
Race (% nonwhite)	12.3	10.4	14.0
Education (% high school or beyond)	94.5	94.4	94.6
Company seniority (years)	12.5	11.7[a]	13.3[a]
Hourly wage rate ($/hr.)	11.80	12.20	11.50
Union steward (%)	3.5	4.1	3.0
Member of a union committee (%)	6.2	9.7[c]	3.0[c]
Member of union executive board (%)	3.0	3.1	2.8
Local union officer (%)	1.8	1.2	2.4
Attended a meeting in last year (%)	48.2	54.4[b]	42.6[b]
Voted in last union election (%)	85.3	90.1[c]	80.1[c]
Ran for union office (%)	6.2	7.2	5.3
Called union office in last year (%)	62.2	63.9	60.6

a. Indicates a significant difference at a 10% confidence level.
b. Indicates a significant difference at a 5% confidence level.
c. Indicates a significant difference at a 1% confidence level.

this unit and its participation program differ in these ways from the others, it will be treated separately in many of the statistical analyses that follow.

Demographic Characteristics

Table 13.1 provides a demographic profile of the union members included in these cases. Overall survey data are available from 931 workers of whom 446 are currently participating in or covered by a worker-participation process and 485 are nonparticipants. (The exact sample size varies in the analyses that follow because some questions were not answered.)

The average worker in the sample is thirty-nine years old, earns approximately $11.80 per hour and has thirteen years of seniority with his or her employer. Thirty-one percent of the sample are female and 12% are members of a minority group. Six percent of the sample have less than a high school education, 94% completed high school, 29% have some college or post–high school experience, and 20% have a college degree. As the data in table 13.1 indicate, there are few significant differences in the characteristics of the participants and nonparticipants. Participants have, on average, two years more seniority with the company and are less likely to be members of a minority group than are nonparticipants. Although these average differences appear to be relatively insignificant, in the analyses to follow we will control for variations in these characteristics as we attempt to estimate the net effects of these worker-participation processes.

Participants, on average, have a history of being slightly more active in union affairs than nonparticipants. (See table 13.1.) For example, participants were more likely to be members of union committees, to have attended union meetings, and to have voted in union elections. While these differences are not large, they do indicate that those who get involved in worker-participation processes tend to be the same individuals who have higher-than-average rates of participation in union affairs.

The Worker Surveys

Is There Worker Interest in QWL Issues?

The first question asked was whether union members are sufficiently interested in QWL issues to warrant union leaders' attention. The degree of interest expressed in QWL, more traditional bread-and-butter issues, and strategic issues normally reserved to management, is reported in table 13.2. The numbers are the percentages of respondents reporting they want "some" or "a lot" of say over these issues.

A strong majority—four out of five workers—want to have some or a lot of say over the issues typically associated with QC or QWL processes, namely, the way work is done and the quality of the work produced. When these responses are compared to the degree of interest expressed in gaining a say over bread-and-butter and strategic issues, it is clear that QWL issues rank high enough in workers' priorities to warrant attention from union leaders.[1] Interest does taper off somewhat, however, over issues more directly associated with autonomous work-group processes. For example, 70–85% report an interest in influencing

Table 13.2
Interest in participation by areas of concern
Total sample (% of respondents agreeing they want "some say" or "a lot of say")

	Case 1 $N=387$	Case 2 $N=60$	Case 3 $N=170$	Case 4 $N=101$	Case 5 $N=213$
QWL concerns					
The way the work is done—methods and procedures	83	83	91	87	95
The level of quality of work	83	78	88	87	96
How fast the work should be done—the work rate	72	70	81	76	85
How much work people should do in a day	55	43	64	61	70
Who should do what job in your group or section	46	57	51	63	61
Bread-and-butter concerns					
When the work day begins and ends	50	33	63	65	76
Pay scales or wages	67	78	82	73	92
Who should be fired if they do a bad job or don't come to work	39	38	39	35	42
Who should be hired into your work group	35	23	32	37	45
Handling complaints or grievances	67	70	72	59	79
Who gets promoted	39	27	42	41	48
Strategic concerns					
The use of new technology on your job	69	70	68	77	79
Management salaries	27	22	13	41	22
Hiring or promotions to upper management	27	8	25	31	44
The selection of your supervisor	42	18	39	52	58
Plant expansions, closings, or new locations	45	22	51	70	40
The way the company invests its profits or spends its money	46	52	41	43	32

the speed of work; 43–70% want to influence the amount of work performed; and 46–63% are interested in influencing work assignments.

Does Participation Increase Worker Interest?

It is often claimed by QWL advocates that even if there is no strong interest in QWL issues before workers have had actual experience with a program, once workers have been exposed to or involved in a participation process, their interest will escalate. The data in table 13.3 test this hypothesis by comparing the degree of interest in gaining a say in QWL (and other) issues reported by those workers currently participating in QWL activities and by those not participating. While on average, union members who are currently participating in a QWL process reported a higher degree of interest, the differences were not large and varied considerably from case to case in our sample. More surprising, however, was the fact that participants expressed a greater degree of interest in several strategic issues such as the use of new technology and in several issues directly affecting their work group. Further analysis (using a regression equation that estimated the degree of interest associated with being a QWL participant after controlling for demographic characteristics of age, seniority, sex, race, wage level, and education) showed that while some of the differences were due to predispositions of the employees before they joined the QWL process, a significant amount of the remaining differences appears attributable to their participation in the QWl process.[2] There appears to be a marginal increase in the desire for gaining a say over QWL and selected other workplace issues that results from experience in a worker-participation process.

Does QWL Increase Actual Influence?

If one objective of worker participation is to increase the amount of say or influence individuals have over their work, is there any evidence that this actually occurs in these QWL processes? The evidence on this is reported in table 13.4. In four of the five cases there was no evidence that workers participating in these QWL processes actually experienced greater say or influence over these workplace issues than did nonparticipants. A significant difference was observed between participants and nonparticipants in the one case in which the local union was a full joint partner in an autonomous work-group or work-team project.[3]

Table 13.3
Interest in participation by areas of concern: Participants (*P*) and nonparticipants (*NP*)
(% of respondents agreeing they want "some say" or "a lot of say")

	Case 1		Case 2		Case 3		Case 4		Case 5	
	P $N=218$	NP $N=169$	P $N=15$	NP $N=45$	P $N=31$	NP $N=139$	P $N=52$	NP $N=49$	P $N=130$	NP $N=83$
QWL concerns										
The way the work is done—methods and procedures	87	79	67[b]	91[b]	87	92	96[b]	78[b]	96	94
The level of quality of work	85	79	80	81	94	87	92	82	96	96
How fast the work should be done—the work rate	80	68	67	71	84	81	77	76	88	81
How much work people should do in a day	59	50	47	43	63	65	64	59	72	66
Who should do what job in your group or section	52[a]	39[a]	73	51	42	53	69	56	63	57
Bread-and-butter concerns										
When the work day begins and ends	52	48	33	33	74	60	62	69	77	74
Pay scales or wages	70	64	73	80	74	84	73	74	93	90
Who should be fired if they do a bad job or don't come to work	38	40	33	40	42	38	44[a]	25[a]	52[c]	27[c]

Who should be hired into your work group	39	30	20	24	29	33	42	31	52[b]	35[b]
Handling complaints or grievances	66	67	60	73	71	72	62	57	83	74
Who gets promoted	43	35	27	27	36	43	44	37	54[a]	40[a]
Strategic concerns										
The use of new technology on your job	73[a]	63[a]	80[a]	67[a]	65	69	85	69	82	77
Management salaries	29	24	20	22	3[a]	15[a]	39	43	27[b]	15[b]
Hiring or promotions to upper management	38[a]	23[a]	7	9	23	26	27	35	52[c]	30[c]
The selection of your supervisor	50[a]	30[a]	20	18	36	40	56	47	63[b]	49[b]
Plant expansions, closings, or new locations	47	43	13	24	48	52	67	74	42	39
The way the company invests its profits or spends its money	48	44	53	51	36	42	49	38	36	27

a. Indicates a significant difference at a 10% confidence level.
b. Indicates a significant difference at a 5% confidence level.
c. Indicates a significant difference at a 1% confidence level.

Table 13.4
Perception of actual influence by areas of concern: Participants (P) and Nonparticipants (NP)
(% of respondents agreeing they have "some say" or "a lot of say")

	Case 1		Case 2		Case 3		Case 4		Case 5	
	P	NP	P	NP	P	NP	P	NP	P	NP
QWL concerns										
The way the work is done—methods and procedures	31	38	40	26	32	28	35	25	58	47
The level of quality of work	43	42	47	47	36	40	50	34	57	57
How fast the work should be done—the work rate	17	16	13	26	23	24	14	10	32	28
How much work people should do in a day	11	9	0	5	3	11	6	8	17	19
Who should do what job in your group or section	8	9	20	19	7	7	36[c]	10[c]	18	22
Bread-and-butter concerns										
When the work day begins and ends	9	9	7	16	16	13	12	4	33[a]	45[a]
Pay scales or wages	11	13	53[a]	30[a]	10	8	12	10	54	47
Who should be fired if they do a bad job or don't come to work	3	6	7	7	0	1	4	0	8	10

Who should be hired into your work group	3	4	2	0	0	1	4	2	2	5
Handling complaints or grievances	14[c]	22[c]	40	40	13	18	12	2	40	37
Who gets promoted	2	4	0	0	0	1	4	0	6	4
Strategic concerns										
The use of new technology on your job	18	22	20	17	7	12	22	14	16	13
Management salaries	2	2	0	0	0	0	2	0	1	1
Hiring or promotions to upper management	3	2	0	0	0	0	4	0	2	1
The selection of your supervisor	4	4	0	2	0	1	6	0	7	2
Plant expansions, closings, or new locations	3	4	0	2	0	3	8	2	0	0
The way the company invests its profits or spends its money	4	4	0	0	0	4	4	0	0	0

Note: Sample sizes are the same as in table 13.1.
a. Indicates a significant difference at a 10% confidence level.
b. Indicates a significant difference at a 5% confidence level.
c. Indicates a significant difference at a 1% confidence level.

Does QWL Improve the Content of Workers' Jobs?

QWL processes are often viewed as strategies for allowing workers to learn new skills, increase their freedom on the job, provide more control over the pace and content of their work, and provide more information on how their work fits into the overall production process.[4] Table 13.5 presents the data from our survey that tests whether these results occurred in these cases. On average, participants in QWL processes did evaluate the content of their jobs on these dimensions more favorably than did nonparticipants. However, only in the case in which the union was involved as a joint partner in the work team/autonomous work-group processes were these differences consistently large and significant. Thus, there is some evidence to support this claim of QWL advocates, although the result is neither uniformly positive nor extremely large.

Does QWL Strengthen or Undermine Workers' Views of Their Union?

One of the most important and hotly debated issues within the labor movement pertains to the effects that union participation in these QWL programs will have on members' views of their union. Advocates claim that union involvement will strengthen union performance and members' perceptions of the union, while critics fear support for the union will be undermined. The data in table 13.6 report the evaluations of union performance of the participants and nonparticipants in these five cases. Four points stand out. First, overall, workers rated the performance of their union lower on QWL issues than on bread-and-butter issues regardless of whether or not they were involved in a QWL process. Second, there is no evidence, except in case 2, that participants evaluated their union *lower* than nonparticipants did. Case 2 is one in which the union is not serving as a full joint partner with management but rather has taken a watchdog role. Third, when an average is computed across the cases, participants rated their unions higher on QWL issues than did nonparticipants. This difference remained significant after controlling for differences in demographic characteristics. Fourth, this difference was strongest for the union in the work team/autonomous work-group project.

Table 13.5
Worker views of the job: Participants (P) and nonparticipants (NP)
(% of respondents who "agree" or "strongly agree")

	Case 1		Case 2		Case 3		Case 4		Case 5	
	P	NP	P	NP	P	NP	P	NP	P	NP
My job requires that I keep learning new things.	77	69	87	71	94	86	75[b]	51[b]	89	92
I have the freedom to decide what I do on my job.	41	41	67	47	61	51	39[b]	19[b]	62	64
I get to do a number of different things on my job.	82	84	100[b]	76[b]	87	86	83[a]	65[a]	91	93
My job lets me use my skills and abilities.	66[a]	58[s]	60	76	71	70	45[a]	27[a]	85	86
Most of the time I know what I have to do on my job.	96	95	93[a]	100[a]	90	96	100	92	98	94
I never seem to have enough time to get everything done on my job.	38	40	33	29	48	42	23	25	48	42
I determine the speed at which I work.	65	67	93	98	61[a]	76[a]	35[a]	18[a]	59	58
It is hard to tell what impact my work makes on the product or service.	54[a]	44[a]	20	29	39	34	23[c]	56[c]	37[b]	23[b]
The work I do on my job is meaningful to me.	80	75	87	78	84	80	79[c]	52[c]	87	87

Table 13.5 (Continued)

	Case 1		Case 2		Case 3		Case 4		Case 5	
	P	NP	P	NP	P	NP	P	NP	P	NP
I feel personally responsible for the work I do on my job.	94	92	87	96	90	94	94[a]	81[a]	98	95
My job has rules and regulations concerning everything I might do or say.	58	57	47	56	74	68	54	53	21	17

Note: Sample sizes are the same as in table 13.3.
a. Indicates a significant difference at a 10% confidence level.
b. Indicates a significant difference at a 5% confidence leve.
c. Indicates a significant difference at a 1% confidence level.

Table 13.6
Perceptions of union performance by areas of concern: participants (P) and nonparticipants (NP)
(% of respondents rating the union as doing a "good" or "very good job")

	Case 1		Case 2		Case 3		Case 4		Case 5	
	P	NP	P	NP	P	NP	P	NP	P	NP
QWL issues										
Getting workers a say in how they do their jobs	39	37	33	50	32	20	62[a]	43[a]	58[c]	29[c]
Helping make jobs more interesting	20	23	7	24	13	15	58[c]	25[a]	28[b]	16[b]
Making this a better place to work	55	52	43	53	45	49	81[c]	49[c]	69	70
Helping improve productivity	40	41	27	38	30	28	85[c]	57[c]	33	23
Getting management to listen to workers' suggestions	51	52	47	32	36	32	69[c]	39[c]	77[c]	36[c]
Bread-and-butter issues										
Protecting members against unfair treatment	80[c]	68[c]	53[c]	89[c]	55	53	87[c]	50[c]	85	84
Getting good wages	89	87	67	82	84	83	83	71	97	98
Getting good fringe benefits	87	82	67	76	81	80	77[a]	57[a]	86[c]	67[c]
Improving job security	45	45	53	67	45	41	75[c]	41[c]	82	88

Table 13.6 (Continued)

	Case 1		Case 2		Case 3		Case 4		Case 5	
	P	NP	P	NP	P	NP	P	NP	P	NP
Handling grievances	73[a]	64[a]	73	87	45	42	85[c]	49[c]	85	86
Improving safety and health	68	66	60	80	58	62	83[c]	55[c]	82[c]	42[c]
Strategic issues										
Getting workers a say in the business	30[b]	16[b]	13	23	26	15	52[c]	20[c]	57[c]	16[c]
Representing worker interests in management decision making	36	30	36	40	19	24	64[c]	33[c]	78[c]	46[c]
Challenging management policies that are harmful to workers' interests	59[b]	45[b]	60	40	36	41	77[c]	35[c]	77	76
Union administration issues										
Giving members a say in how the union is run	35	31	53	73	29[a]	47[a]	54[c]	25[c]	80	75
Telling members what the local union is doing	32	34	53	65	29[a]	45[a]	65[a]	45[a]	83	81

Overall union satisfaction									
Percent "satisfied" or "very satisfied" with the union	55	49	67	84	37	45	75[c]	31[c]	84	81

Note: Sample sizes are the same as in table 13.3.
a. Indicates a significant difference at a 10% confidence level.
b. Indicates a significant difference at a 5% confidence level.
c. Indicates a significant difference at a 1% confidence level.

Do Nonparticipating Workers Want to Join the QWL Process?

The final question addressed in the survey was whether those not currently participating were interested in getting involved in the QWL process. Overall, 35% of the nonparticipants expressed an interest in joining the QWL process under way in the organization, but there were wide variations in interest across the cases. For example, only 15% in case 2 and 25% in case 1 wanted to get involved, compared to 55% in case 4 and 63% in case 3. The low rates of interest in cases 1 and 2 were probably due to the layoffs that were occurring in both cases during the time of the survey. Concern for job security was compounded in case 2 by the movement of jobs out of this bargaining unit to a new nonunion plant of the company. In case 4, on the other hand, the union had approached the QWL process right from the start as a strategy for saving jobs and was quite successful in doing so. In case 3, the QWL process was still in the very early stages of development (approximately nine months old) and therefore there was still a good deal of initial interest in the process and a number of groups waiting to start training for the program.

Overall, the survey data suggest that real improvements in workers' views of their jobs and of their union's performance have resulted from some worker-participation programs but not from others. Those experiencing improvements were ones in which

1. the union served as a visible joint partner in the process;

2. the participation process led to actual changes in work organization that enhanced the security of the labor force and the economic performance of the firm;

3. union leaders linked their support for QWL to their larger collective bargaining and representational strategies, and;

4. sufficient time had passed for the union's contribution to improving the QWL experiences of its members to be seen while the union continued to deal effectively with members' bread-and-butter concerns.

Local Union Officers' and Activists' Views

The surveys of rank-and-file workers were supplemented with surveys and interviews with local union officers and activists (union committee members, stewards, and executive board members). (See Kochan, Katz, and Mower 1984 for a full discussion of these data.) A brief summary of the views expressed by the officers and activists suggests that these individuals hold the following views of worker-participation programs.

1. Worker-participation programs have strong positive effects on union officer–plant management relationships, worker-supervisor relations, product quality, and productivity.

2. There is a mixed effect on the local union. A majority think that overall the programs will strengthen the local union. However, a significant minority is concerned about the interaction between traditional bargaining processes and the participation programs. In addition, there is no strong evidence of an increase in either member satisfaction with the union or member participation in local union affairs resulting from the programs. Union leaders also find that members do not seem to perceive or appreciate the local union's role in the participation program.

3. A new intermediary union role of participation "coordinator" or "facilitator" has arisen that emphasizes training, communication, and problem-solving skills. This coordinator often is the union representative who must mediate any tensions between the participation process and traditional bargaining procedures.

4. The biggest problems inhibiting the expansion of participation programs are layoffs, management efforts to change work rules, and supervisory resistance.

5. Two divergent views surfaced concerning the future course of participation programs. One group of union activists foresaw a limited role for their programs as a complement to traditional collective bargaining. Another group envisioned the possible expansion of the participation process to the point that workers will carry out many of the responsibilities now held by management.

Dynamics of Worker Participation Processes

In addition to the surveys, qualitative case studies of participation programs in the cases described above and additional cases in the steel, auto, and retail food industries were conducted. Each of the case studies provided different insights into the diversity of paths that worker-participation programs can take. (A full discussion of these case studies can be found in Kochan, Katz, and Mower 1984.) The main conclusions we draw from these cases are summarized thus:

1. Workers and union officers are initially quite skeptical of the merits of QWL or other worker participation processes. This initial skepticism

can generally be overcome if key local union leaders strongly support the idea of experimenting with the process.

2. In the early stages of a participation experiment, this initial skepticism among workers is replaced by generally positive responses among those who volunteer to get involved. Skepticism may, however, remain relatively high among nonparticipants unless the union and the employer keep nonparticipating workers adequately informed about what is occurring within the participation process.

3. There is a tendency for support among the participants to flatten out or decline over time as various problems or obstacles to the continuity of the process arise in the larger bargaining relationship. Among the obstacles that led to the decline of support of workers and/or local union representatives in the cases studied were:

(a) layoffs of bargaining unit members, especially where these layoffs were handled in a way that was viewed by workers and union officers as inconsistent with the consultation and problem-solving ethic that was being encouraged within the participation process;

(b) employer actions or strategy decisions that were viewed as being inconsistent with the high level of trust encouraged in the participation process. Examples of this included the opening of a nonunion plant by the employer and the shifting of bargaining unit work to this plant; unilateral management decisions to consolidate job classifications over the objection of the local union, and announcement of the decision to close a part of an operation without any advance consultation with union officials.

4. Those cases that successfully overcame the decline in worker and/ or union officer support noted in item 3 were ones in which:

(a) the employer was able to achieve tangible improvements in economic performance through the participation process. Examples of this were a case where the worker-participation process led to a new way of reorganizing work and lowering the costs of operations that otherwise would have been subcontracted to outside vendors; the case of a steel company that used the problem-solving processes developed within the worker-participation process to structure and implement an organizationwide cost-improvement program; and the case of an auto parts firm that worked jointly with the union to save jobs and to open new plants under a work team/autonomous work-group design.

(b) the union was able to link its role in the worker-participation process to its broader bargaining and other strategies for representing not only its members' interests on QWL issues but also their interests on bread-and-butter and broader strategic issues. The examples cited above serve as successful examples of this.

5. Local unions and their members were more likely to benefit from a worker-participation process when they played the role of a full joint partner in all phases of the development and administration of the program rather than adopt the role of a watchdog or secondary party. Indeed, there are clear dangers that a QWL program will narrow the role of the union and will fail to forge an adequate linkage with the larger collective bargaining process or the employer's larger business strategies if the union is not involved as an active joint partner.

The major implication of these case studies is that for worker-participation processes to survive the economic and political obstacles that they encounter over time, each party must see them as contributing to their separate economic and organizational interests. While improvements in the psychological rewards workers derive from their day-to-day job experiences may be a necessary condition for a successful participation program, psychological rewards alone do not appear to be sufficient to maintain the commitment of management, the union and its leaders, and, indeed as the rank-and-file survey demonstrated, the workers themselves.

National Union Policies

Four different national union policies toward worker-participation processes were identified in our review of activities at this level of the labor movement.

1. *General Opposition*: The national union leaders clearly state their generalized opposition to worker participation as it is currently being practiced and discourage (but do not prevent) local unions from participating in them. At present, the International Association of Machinists is one union that fits this description.

2. *Decentralized Neutrality*: National union leaders take neither a blanket stand for or against worker participation, leave the decision up to the local unions, possibly offer suggested guidelines on how to approach employer overtures about QC or QWL programs, but do not provide significant staff support or leadership to local unions that get involved in such programs. At present, probably most national unions fit this description.

3. *Decentralized Policy with National Union Support*: Specific national union officials other than the president are strong advocates of worker participation and lend their support and expertise to locals that indicate an interest in the concept. At present, perhaps only two unions, the United Steelworkers and the United Auto Workers, fit this description.

4. *Support from the President*: The president of the union publicly advocates the diffusion of worker-participation processes as a part of the basic strategy of the union for representing current and future members. Staff support is provided to study and plan for the evolution of worker-participation efforts, to assist and train local officers, and integrate the worker-participation processes with collective bargaining and other union activities. At present only one union, the Communications Workers of America, fits this description.

Despite these differences in national union policies, there appears to be unanimous agreement among labor leaders that the single biggest obstacle to the more general acceptance of cooperative strategies and experimentation at the workplace is the opposition to union organizing efforts within the American management community.

Implications for the Labor Movement

The findings summarized above suggest that there is no single best policy toward worker-participation processes that fits all situations. This implies that rather than adopting a uniform position for or against worker participation on some philosophical ground, union leaders need to think strategically about whether worker participation is in the interests of their members as well as that of the union as a whole and can be linked to the union's broader strategies for improving the effectiveness of its bargaining relationship.

We believe that the following implications for the labor movement can be drawn from this study and from our related research on developments at the workplace. These comments should not be interpreted as a blanket endorsement of a union strategy of support for or opposition to worker participation. Rather, we present what we see as the major factors for unions to consider in shaping a strategy that fits their particular circumstances.

Local Union Leaders

The ultimate choice of whether or not to actively support the development of a worker-participation process in a specific plant, office, or work site can best be made by local union leaders, based on a consideration of the need for change in their bargaining relationship and the viability of some form of worker participation as a partial solution to their problems. The pressures for change may arise from two sources: (1) external pressures to improve the economic performance of the employer and the job security of their members, or (2) internal demands from rank-and-file members for changes in their day-to-day job experiences and in the relationships between workers and managers. In the current period of high unemployment, intense competition, and general concern for productivity and product quality, the external pressures appear to dominate. However, this could easily be reversed during periods of tighter labor markets when the workers typically become more vocal and assertive in expressing their preferences. The survey data clearly demonstrate that interest in gaining greater influence over selected workplace decisions is widely shared among union members.

It is also clear, however, that if there is neither sufficient external nor internal pressure to modify the collective bargaining relationship, there is little incentive on the part of either unions or employers to embark on a worker-participation process. In many cases the collective bargaining process may have already produced sufficient flexibility in work organization, and workers may have the individual autonomy or decision-making responsibility they desire. In these cases, the effort and resources needed to foster small-group problem solving, organization of work into teams, or other forms of organizational change may not be warranted.

In cases where either external or internal pressures are driving the parties to search for ways to improve their bargaining relationship, union leaders still need to decide, before endorsing this strategy, whether a participation process is likely to succeed and is in the interests of their members and the union. While a variety of factors will influence the probability of success, there are at least three necessary conditions for union support: (1) employer acceptance of unions, (2) deep managerial commitment to the worker-participation process, and (3) a viable economic context.

Management Acceptance of Unions

Clearly, if union leaders believe the employer is intent on using the participation process to undermine the support for the union, and if the employer is unwilling to accept the legitimacy of the union, it makes little sense to cooperate with a worker-participation process. To support or endorse a participation process under these circumstances is tantamount to the local union participating in its own slow demise.

The more difficult case, however, is one where *local management* accepts the legitimacy of the union in *one particular plant*, but higher corporate management uses union-avoidance strategies to keep unions out of other new or existing sites. Local union opposition to QWL and other participation processes under those circumstances would appear to be a necessary step toward implementing the strategy that is favored by most national union leaders, namely, to force employers to make a choice between (1) acceptance of unions and the potential growth of worker-participation and other joint union-management efforts, or (2) continued low trust/high conflict arms-length relationships.

Management Commitment

Union leaders need to assess the depth of commitment to the participation process among the various managers at different levels of the firm who have the power to support or discourage the process over time. Without a deep managerial commitment to supporting a participation process over an extended period of time, neither union commitment nor rank-and-file enthusiasm for the process can make a worker-participation process succeed.

Management commitment needs to be assessed not only on verbal statements of philosophy but on the willingness of management to adjust its strategies and behaviors in ways that support worker participation. This means, among other things, the willingness to allocate resources to support participation efforts and to maintain the commitment of resources through periods of short-term economic crisis. Management (and union) commitment also is likely to be severely tested at various points during the evolution of the process as inconsistencies arise between other company (or union) strategies and objectives and the worker-participation process. Thus, the depth of commitment can not be estimated at the outset of a participation program. The real tests come later when hard decisions and trade-offs must be made between maintaining support for the process and pursuing other strategic objectives.

Economic Viability

Worker-participation programs cannot be a panacea in the face of economic problems that lie beyond the control of the local union, the employer, or the workers. In those cases, a worker-participation process may simply serve to divert attention for a short period of time from the more basic problems and will eventually lead to disenchantment among the rank and file as the problems worsen. Sometimes participation programs can be combined productively with steps such as compensation concessions. But unless the economic foundation upon which the worker-participation process will rest is itself viable, the union's efforts might better be put to other uses.

This is perhaps the hardest condition to assess before the start of a participation effort. In addition to the general uncertainty involved in forecasting the economic future of a plant or firm, employers have some discretion over the allocation of resources needed to maintain a viable concern. Thus, an analysis of the economic viability of the enterprise must consider both the external or uncontrollable economic factors that affect the survival of the business and the investment plans of the employer. The need for the employer to link the worker-participation process to its larger business strategy and to communicate this linkage to the union is the counterpoint to the union's need to embed its support for worker-participation efforts in its broader collective bargaining strategies.

Linkages to Collective Bargaining

Where local union leaders are convinced that the conditions necessary for a potentially viable worker-participation process exist, their next task is to think about how this process will fit into their overall bargaining and representational strategies. For unions and their members to benefit from the process, union leaders must do more than react to the employer's or the consultant's vision or expectations for worker participation. Instead, union leaders need to anticipate how the process will evolve over time and to consider what part they want it to play in their collective bargaining relationship and in the union's role in the workplace. As the case studies clearly point out, over time a total separation of worker participation from collective bargaining is neither possible nor desirable; it is important to recognize this at the outset.

One of the greatest challenges to the traditional role of the union that a successful participation process will produce is increased variability in practices and conditions within the bargaining unit. Three different sources of variation may cause problems for the union leadership.

First, because worker-participation processes diffuse slowly through an organization, for a long time there will be a group of "participants" and "nonparticipants." Even after the process is widely diffused, there are likely to be some individuals who prefer to not get involved in group activities and problem-solving processes. The existence of these two groups provides a fertile ground for rumors, competition, and internal political conflicts within the union. Since participants are likely to be introducing changes into the practices in their work areas, there will be a natural tendency for nonparticipants to rationalize their non-involvement by voicing skepticism toward the QWL process.

Second, introducing changes in work practices based on the ideas generated in the worker-participation process has a general decentralizing effect on the collective bargaining relationship. Proposals to modify established customs and practices, if not formal collective bargaining agreement provisions, are likely to arise. This has the effect of reducing the "common rule" strategy that American unions have used to limit competition and standardize conditions among individuals and groups within their bargaining units. The standardization of practices and rules established through the collective bargaining agreement and enforced through the contract-administration process by shop stewards has historically served as a basic source of worker security and internal union control.

A third change is the shift away from detailed job and associated contractual rules in work-reorganization experiments that broaden out job responsibilities. In the more advanced cases, such as work-team arrangements, the concept of an individual job description or assignment is replaced with a set of tasks that lie within the general responsibility of the group. The movement toward work teams, pay-for-knowledge compensation systems, job rotation, and semiautonomous work groups therefore all require workers and their local unions to partially abandon their historic strategies for maximizing job control through enforcement of detailed rules governing specific, narrowly defined jobs. In return, the workers receive greater training in a variety of job responsibilities and more control over how the group organizes itself to conduct its tasks. Workers and their union representatives also gain more information about the work and its contribution to the overall production process and the economic performance of the enterprise. In short, all of these changes reduce the reliance on strict rules governing individual worker job rights and responsibilities and increase the variation in practices and flexibility in the use of human resources. The shift away from standardized and tightly detailed jobs also increases the variability across and within workplaces. Managing this variability and flexibility without increasing divisiveness and competition among its members will become a major new role for the local union.

Although our findings stress the need to link worker-participation processes to the larger collective bargaining efforts on a strategic level, this does not necessarily imply a total integration or merger of the participation process with the *procedures* for resolving grievances and negotiating collective bargaining agreements. Issues of contract interpretation or alleged violations of individual worker rights that are best suited to resolution through the established grievance procedure will continue to occur. Likewise, basic differences in economic interests will continue to exist between workers and their employers; these will require hard bargaining at periodic intervals. The key challenge to union leaders and management representatives is to manage these "mixed-motive" relationships such that cooperative problem-solving efforts can comfortably coexist with hard bargaining and the formal adjudication of disputes.

In some cases the union and management representatives may be successful in carrying over problem-solving processes to their collective bargaining negotiations process, while in others the styles of interaction and the decision-making processes between these two activities may continue to differ. Whatever the mixture of styles and processes, the key to their successful management lies in the ability of the parties to prevent the episodes of more intensive conflict from driving out the high levels of trust needed to continue the problem-solving processes. Union leaders and employer representatives will continue to experience periodic conflicts that pose threats, or as one union official put it, "shocks to the system." Maintaining trust and commitment to the participation process through these periodic conflicts or adversarial shocks will be a skill required of those who want to maintain the continuity of the worker-participation process. Eventually, the ability to do so successfully will be viewed as a sign of the maturity of the parties and of the participation process.

The survey data clearly show that union members will not radically transform their views of what they expect from their local unions once a QWL or other worker-participation process is under way. Unions will continue to be evaluated by members on their performance in handling traditional collective bargaining responsibilities as well as their performance on QWL issues. This suggests that union leaders will need to devote time, energy, and organizational resources to providing both sets of services. Internally, therefore, this means recruiting, training, and developing both union stewards and union facilitators of QWL processes; finding volunteers to staff both traditional internal union committees and those union-management committees that support the participation process; and, most important, coordinating these dual sets of activities. All of this adds additional complexity to the task of local union administration.

Strategies for National Unions

Even though worker-participation processes are carried out through local unions, national union officers and staff have important roles to play in the development and implementation of a coherent union strategy toward worker participation. Indeed, given the interest that now exists among many employer and local union officials, QWL and other forms of worker participation will continue to develop. Unless national unions develop a clear policy and take the necessary steps to implement it at local levels, these processes will proceed without national union guidance.

Given the diversity of employers with whom the different locals of most national unions deal, neither blanket endorsement nor blanket opposition of worker participation by national union leaders makes sense. Instead, national union leaders might do better to communicate their views on the conditions under which they believe participation processes are viable and the conditions under which they would advise against union endorsement and involvement. Beyond articulating a clear policy position, however, there are a number of important functions that national union leaders and staff professionals can carry out that will help implement a strategy of supporting worker participation in those bargaining relationships where they are deemed appropriate, and discouraging them where these conditions are not met.

Leadership Development
One of the most positive by-products of QWL experiments is the emergence of a talented group of new local labor leaders who have been trained in group dynamics, problem solving, and team building. Through their roles as QWL facilitators these local union representatives are also

gaining a greater exposure to and serving a much wider cross section of union members than most shop stewards or grievance committee members. These individuals represent a rich pool of potential future union leaders.

Along with these facilitators stand the elected local leaders who have taken the political risks associated with supporting a QWL process. Together, these elected leaders and QWL facilitators represent a highly committed group that believes deeply in the need for strong unions as well as in the value of worker participation. One of the most important contributions that a national union can make toward strengthening the role of worker participation within the union and diffusing the process to a wider spectrum of union members is to reinforce, support, and draw on the talents and experiences of these individuals. Failure to provide career opportunities within their unions for these local activists risks losing many of them to management positions or underusing them if they fade back into a less active rank-and-file status. Taking advantage of their training and experience by, for example, using them in educational and training conferences, not only will help others to learn from their experiences but also will provide the support and reinforcement needed to encourage them to continue to be active in their union. In short, as one member of our project advisory committee noted, these experienced local leaders represent a pool of largely untapped resources from which the labor movement can draw in training and educating other members.

Worker Participation Training
In addition to the career and leadership development efforts for those already experienced with worker participation, there is a major role for national unions in educating other local leaders and national staff representatives about these processes. With a few notable exceptions, most of the training and education of the union leaders about QWL and related participation programs has heretofore been organized and run by management, academic, or consulting organizations. While these programs have been useful in exposing union representatives to the concepts, philosophies, and procedures of QWL, they are not likely to be useful in helping unions develop their own ideas of what worker participation can do for their organizations and how it fits into their larger bargaining and representational strategies. For the labor movement to develop its own vision of where worker-participation processes

will take their organizations, it is essential that national unions take the initiative in training their local representatives.

This training need not necessarily be completely separate from that provided by employers and QWL consultants. Indeed, there is merit in jointly designed and conducted training processes where the consultants, union representatives, and management professionals share their experiences and expertise and provide skills training for union and management facilitators. Regardless of whether training is joint or separate, national unions need to develop specialists who can serve as trainers of local officials. By doing so, national unions can ensure that local union leaders will understand where the QWL process fits into the broader strategies of the union.

Monitoring and Supporting Local Union Activities
If a national union wishes to implement a policy of supporting worker participation under appropriate conditions, and have this policy consistently implemented at local levels, it will need to (1) develop experts on its national staff who can participate in the national networks of QWL professionals, (2) provide staff assistance to local unions that are considering the question of whether or not to get involved in a participating process, (3) monitor developments at the local level as they unfold, and (4) engage in the types of "firefighting" activities that are necessary to help see these processes through times of crisis. A few unions have developed this type of expertise on their national staffs or have individuals who regularly represent their unions in the many public forums and conferences devoted to QWL and related topics. More active union involvement in this professional network can help to shape the thinking of the consultants and management professionals who now dominate those groups and influence the evolution of ideas about worker participation. Union involvement will help to educate the consultants and other ardent advocates of what must be done to make these processes acceptable to the labor movement. Having expertise in the national office of the union will also be essential for any union that seeks to know what is happening within its local unions and to influence the course of development of worker participation. Our case analyses also demonstrate that representatives of the national union can take some of the pressure off innovative local leaders and show workers the connection between participation programs and other national union activities.

The Role for the Top: The AFL-CIO and Its Departments

While there is no expectation that the AFL-CIO, the Industrial Union Department, or any other unit at the federation level will or should deviate from the approach of leaving policies regarding worker participation to their constituent unions, there are several critical functions that can be served by leaders at this level consistent with their role in the structure of the labor movement. These functions are: (1) foster dialogue on this issue among national union leaders and with representatives of business and government, (2) convey to the larger public the labor movement's views and strategies for relating worker participation to collective bargaining and broader national economic and labor policies, and (3) encourage experimentation with worker-participation efforts that operate under appropriate conditions.

Clearly, there will remain a range of views about the viability of worker-participation efforts and their appropriate role within broader labor-movement strategies. While it may be neither possible nor desirable to press for a consensus on these issues across the various national unions and their leaders, it is clear that the issue of how the worker-participation efforts fit within the larger collective bargaining and public policy agenda of the labor movement needs to be moved to a higher level of priority and to be more actively debated at the highest levels of the labor movement. Bringing together national union leaders with different views and experiences to discuss actual experiences with worker-participation processes and to debate their implications can best be done by the federation and its departments and affiliates. Out of these discussions may emerge a clearer picture of what the labor movement's model for QWL and related processes should be—a limited supplement to collective bargaining or an evolving step toward an American brand of shop floor industrial democracy that is an integral part of the collective bargaining process.

Labor movement leaders have an important role in shaping the image of unions in the eyes of workers, employers, and the larger society. If, under appropriate conditions, worker participation is seen as an integral component of the broader strategies for strengthening the roles and effectiveness of unions at the workplace and supplementing their collective bargaining activities, then the task of the top leaders will be to convey this view to all of these audiences. The message currently conveyed from the top of the movement is one of cautious skepticism and neutrality. One can envision, however, a different message that specifies the conditions that must be present, but then conveys enthusiastic support for experimentation with alternative types of worker participation. This shift in the message communicated would again help challenge management for the initiative on worker-participation efforts and would serve to further legitimate and support the activities that are under way within the various national unions.

Finally, the experience of this project suggests that the federation has a unique role in fostering research that takes advantage of the many natural experiments currently under way within the various national and local unions. This research has only begun to tap the diversity of experiences that will be playing themselves out over time. From this diversity generalizations can be drawn about what conditions produce successes and failures with greater objectivity than can be expected from research conducted by parties who have a direct political stake in the outcomes of these efforts. Furthermore, like high-level management executives who have difficulty getting objective information from their QWL staffs about potential problems that may be brewing below the surface, union leaders may have difficulty acknowledging problems with programs that they have supported. Yet it is from problems or failures that we often learn the most important lessons.

Likewise, where there are success stories to be told, the stories have more credibility if told by people who have less of a political stake in promoting them. Important lessons can be learned from the successful cases by probing the reasons that lie behind the successes. Thus, a major role for the federation should be to continue to support to research on these topics, to debate the implications of the results of the research produced, and to disseminate these results and their implications as widely as possible within the labor movement and among the larger community of interested management, government, and third-party representatives.

Implications for the U.S. Industrial Relations System

Integrating worker-participation efforts into the broader bargaining and public policy strategies of the labor movement could potentially lead to a number of important changes for the larger U.S. industrial relations system. We will now outline a number of those implications that can be readily identified.

Impact on Job-Control Unionism

The most direct effect of expanded worker-participation efforts, especially those that involve work reorganization, is a movement away from the detailed job-control form of unionism characteristic of U.S. collective bargaining. This does not mean that the collective bargaining agreement will no longer govern the terms and conditions of employment. However, it does imply that the detailed specification of contractual rules may give way to a more flexible and varied form of work organization at the plant level. This implies a major change in the roles of the local union, supervisors, and higher levels of management.

For the union, this requires relinquishing one of its traditional bases of power and security in return for greater information and perhaps influence over a wider array of issues that traditionally have been reserved to management. It implies that the traditional principle that "management acts and workers grieve" will have to give way to more joint planning and consultation at the workplace.

For the worker, this new arrangement means exposure to a wider variety of tasks and more advanced training, and, therefore, wider opportunities for skill acquisition and enhancement. On the other hand, it also implies greater responsibility for decisions that would otherwise have been left to a supervisor or low-level manager.

For management, this development implies a trade of some of its traditional prerogatives and a redesign of the role of the first-line supervisor in return for greater flexibility in human resource management and a reduction in the detailed rules governing job definitions and assignments. In summary, for all the parties, it implies a movement toward a more proactive form of labor-management relations based around more joint research and analysis, planning, and consultation.

Effects on Labor Law

Over time, the expansion of this form of organization and participation may lead to a breakdown in the legal line of demarcation between "labor" and "management." In particular, it places the role of the supervisor in an even more nebulous status than before. This, in turn, should call into question provisions in the National Labor Relations Act (NLRA) used to determine who is a worker covered under the act and who is a supervisor, to be excluded from the act. It also challenges the relevance of the NLRA's scope of bargaining doctrines as interpreted by the National Labor Relations Board. If work teams and union representatives are to get more deeply involved in sharing information, consulting, or perhaps even effectively deciding issues that lie outside the issues of wages, hours, and working conditions, the distinction between mandatory and permissive subjects of collective bargaining becomes increasingly blurred and less relevant.

One more potential outgrowth of these participation efforts may eventually be the development of some form of "works council" arrangement at the plant level. In a sense, a form of this already exists in the joint labor-management steering committees that oversee many of the QWL participation processes.

Linkages to National Labor and Economic Policies

At a higher level, one might ask whether worker participation has an important role in the larger labor, human resource development, and economic policies of the country. Should worker participation, along with the other changes in industrial relations set in motion by these projects, be viewed as part of a larger national strategy for reforming labor policy and enhancing human capital investment and development? Can it be part of the debate over the adequacy of the public policies governing not only union recognition and collective bargaining but the entire range of labor and human resource policies and their linkages to national industrial and economic policy?

We believe a strong case can be made for treating these practices, forms of work organization, and the labor-management relationships as the micro foundation for a new industrial and human resources development policy. Furthermore, it may be desirable for public policy debates over trade or tax policies targeted on particular industries to consider the state of labor-management relations (and joint efforts to improve them) in those industries.

These are questions that the labor movement and others concerned about the future of the U.S. industrial relations system must grapple with in the years ahead. Perhaps the analysis here will stimulate the dialogue needed to move this debate closer to center stage.

Notes

This paper is drawn from a larger study carried out with the support and cooperation of the Labor Policy Institute and the Industrial Union Department,

AFL-CIO. The complete study is found in our book *Worker Participation and American Unions: Threat or Opportunity?* (Kalamazoo, Mich.: The W. E. Upjohn Institute for Employment Research, 1984). Financial support was also received from the Alfred P. Sloan and the Sidney Harmon Foundations. The views expressed are our own and should not be interpreted as the official views of the sponsoring organizations or of M.I.T. We wish to thank Howard Samuel and Richard Prosten for their encouragement and assistance throughout all stages of this work and the union leaders who served on our advisory committee and have commented on the final report. We also wish to express our appreciation to the many union and employer representatives and workers who provided the data contained in this work.

1. The degree of interest expressed here is consistent with the results of similar surveys of blue-collar workers. See, for example, Kochan, Lipsky, and Dyer (1974) or Kochan (1979) or Quinn and Staines (1979). For a study that also demonstrates that workers assign a higher priority to gaining influence over issues that directly affect their immediate job-related experiences than over the broader strategic issues normally reserved to management, see Witte (1980). For further evidence of this from samples of workers from twelve countries, see IDRT, *Industrial Democracy in Europe* (1980).

2. All regression equations referred to here include these demographic characteristics plus a set of dummy variables that control for other unmeasured characteristics of the local unions. The complete regression results are reported in the appendix to chapter 4 of Kochan, Katz, and Mower 1984.

3. Ideally, one would prefer to measure differences in perceived influence of the same workers before and after participating in a QWL process. While this was not possible in this study, results reported here using cross-sectional comparisons of participants and nonparticipants are consistent with panel studies showing little or no significant change in actual influence. See Witte (1980).

4. These questions are taken from the Job Diagnostic Survey, an instrument designed to measure the content of jobs and their motivational potential. See Hackman and Oldham (1981).

References

Hackman, J. Richard, and Greg R. Oldham. *Work Redesign*. Reading, Mass.: Addison-Wesley, 1981.

Industrial Democracy Research Team. *Industrial Democracy in Europe*. Oxford: Oxford University Press, 1980.

Kochan, Thomas A. "How American Workers View Labor Unions." *Monthly Labor Review* 102 (April 1979): 15–22.

Kochan, Thomas A., Harry C. Katz, and Nancy Mower. *Worker Participation and American Unions: Threat or Opportunity?*. Kalamazoo, Mich.: The W. E. Upjohn Institute for Employment Research, 1984.

Kochan, Thomas A., David B. Lipsky, and Lee Dyer. "Collective Bargaining and the Quality of Work: The Views of Local Union Activists," *Proceedings of the Industrial Relations Research Association,* 1974: 150–162.

Quinn, Robert P., and Graham L. Staines. *The 1977 Quality of Employment Survey.* Ann Arbor: Institute for Social Research, 1979.

Witte, John F. *Democracy, Authority, and Alienation to Work.* Chicago: University of Chicago Press, 1980.

Discussion, Part VI

Rudy Oswald: Three items: first, in terms of necessary conditions for union support, Kochan mentioned employer acceptance of unions. Many employers see QWL as a way of keeping unions out, rather than accepting them. A number of employers do use QWL to undermine unions. It's an hour per week to tell their employees, "You don't need unions," like the 1920s employee committees. Unions have always been interested in a voice through collective bargaining, in what's now given the new label of QWL. Second, in terms of managerial commitment, it's much easier for the union than for management to go through a democratic process. Management is essentially hierarchical and QWL affects management's structure. Some Quality Circles only talk about peripheral issues, but in many cases first-line supervisors are threatened—there is an attempt to undercut their basic role. Third is a gray area—Taylorism or job control—the interrelation between job structure and wages. Wages are determined through formal procedures. For instance, less supervision means higher wages, more responsibility means higher wages, and the more narrowly defined and more repetitive the job is, the lower the wages. But what do you do with pay in QWL? That's a very crucial issue. We haven't established a new wage-setting arrangement to accompany QWL. We're doing things on one side without creating a mechanism on the other side. How do you share the benefits of an increase in productivity?

Leslie Calder: Our union was part of Kochan's study. Like autos and steel we were faced with foreign competition. In 1982 the Japanese came out with approximately twenty-five new models of copying machines. With a survival rate of 20%, five out of twenty-five would create a very serious threat. In 1980 we got into the QWL process, not out of pressures from the company but out of a desire to be involved. I had seen articles from the UAW's Bluestone [former Vice-President of the UAW] and I thought we should try it as an experiment. So in 1980 we had a meeting with the top executives and agreed to try it at least. A year later we ran into serious problems of Japanese competition, profitability decreased at a rapid rate and costs increased. The implication was that in three to five years we might not be in business—a clear indication of trouble. Fortunately, the process gave us a format for meeting with top management of the company. We've had that going on for some time and today we meet once a quarter. But we were able to survive, or at least stem the tide, because not only within the work force but within management itself, we were shocked out of our complacency. Management was fat, and when the competition came they didn't know how to face it.

I use the term "employee involvement," since employees are involved directly in decision making, and I'd say for the last three years it's been a pleasant one for us. Oswald raised some good questions but so far things are looking up for us. I think the QWL or employee-involvement program contributed to that. The quality of our product is far superior to what it was five or six years ago and I think there's a great amount of awareness of that on the part of the workers. Employee involvement provided the opportunity to communicate with those people and about those things that are not possible through collective bargaining.

In 1981 we had a wiring harness problem—the operation was much cheaper in Mexico and in nonunion U.S. firms and we were faced with the possibility of subcontracting. Union officers and company representatives got together to try to do something about it. There were 200 people in the department and we were asked to cut their costs by $3.2 million. We agreed to engage workers from the department as a committee of six, and they were assigned to come up with a solution in three months. They were afforded the opportunity to investigate all areas, including financial data, overhead figures, and visiting the competitors' sites. Before the recommended solutions, we had sixteen supervisors over those 200 people. We had an allocation for $400,000 for training in that department—training they haven't done in five years. We found that maintenance was allocating a good part of its budget to that department, and that management support in terms of overhead was being allocated far beyond the support actually being given. We found we could get along with four supervisors instead of sixteen. We made the $3.2 million reduction and we saved the department.

That taught us a lesson—we can make a serious attempt to solve a problem if we get cooperation from management. We had an alliance unique in the labor relations field. That gives us the opportunity to look at these areas and try to work together and if the results are successful, employees can take pride in it. It's my judgement that we can't sit by—we have to react in some way. This is probably one answer; in this case it works. We're moving now into the autonomous work-group area. That will be an even greater challenge and the union will have to be more involved in job restructuring, increasing skills, and so forth; how to address those issues is our challenge today.

John Carmichael: We were also in the study. In 1972 we started a project initiated by the union, not management, that was negotiated at the bargaining table. We had reached the point where half of all our grievances were not covered by the contract, but we were running into all kinds of problems and we needed another forum. The project handled a lot of problems, including the redesigning of a newspaper from top to bottom in three months. We felt all the apprehensions Oswald mentioned, but we went ahead. None of those apprehensions turned into reality. We didn't have to deal with any of them because they didn't appear.

William Stevenson: In worker-participation programs the biggest part is job satisfaction, job enhancement, so I don't see how we can feel threatened by it. We should be working more diligently to redefine our role, and the first-line committeeman—what will he become? We must stop worrying about the threat participation might pose and realize that this is a human resources thing we've been trying to deal with for years.

Thomas St. George: It's true, the current wage structure is an outgrowth of Taylorism. We have become committed to a wage structure that may no longer serve our interests. We should go back to our basic philosophy and goals and see whether or not that wage structure really meets those goals.

"Quality Circles" is such a broad term—I agree they're not risky to a certain extent, but when the employee gets that power, the risk is there to a lot of people, including union and management. Bluestone got into it not as a savior to GM and its economic woes, but to address the blue-collar blues. And though it's developed over the years to be an economic producer, it still started from the social aspect.

It's the most militant unions that are getting involved in it that are having the largest successes. The following are what I think are the major considerations for QWL: (1) The role of the floor rep and the first-line supervisor is imperative. You have to spend time working with them and have an agreement to disagree. (2) The folks on the floor must understand the rules. (3) QWL cannot be held for political ransom. You can't say "cut out the committees until you get the grievances solved, or worked out," and it has to be equally administered right down the line. You need a tremendous amount of education for company reps and union reps. (4) A balance between the union-management relationships and the level of QWL can exist. If you have a good, open, honest relationship, you can get involved in a more comprehensive process. You can't if trust isn't there—then the union won't take the risk to get involved.

Richard Balzar: We have to put where we are today in historical perspective. The year 1973 marked the first joint QWL program in the United States and in 1977 we were still very unsure. What's remarkable is the leadership role of the unions. The local union is getting more sophisticated. They have gone beyond the point of asking "Does it work?" or "What's the payoff?" Now they are saying, "How do we get what we want out of it?" and exploring the nature of work and pay implications. Kochan had some good strong points—the union has to be married to it. I think we don't spend enough time worrying about the union reps. But the real issue is, it's only been ten years, and extraordinary gains have been made.

John Flynn: From everything I've heard here, I gather one of our major goals has to be to take wages out of competition, and the strategy mentioned has been legislation. If the hoped-for remedy is based entirely on success at the ballot box—we better have a back-up position.

The building trades have had legislation as a strategy for thirty years. We thought situs picketing would solve the problems created by non-union encroachment into our business. We were promised by six presidents, Republican and Democratic, that they would sign the Situs Picketing Bill if we could get it through Congress. During most of those years, both the House and Senate were controlled by the Democratic party, but we do not have a Situs Picketing law today. We then thought labor law reform would help bring the needed relief—and we do not have labor law reform. So, again, rather than put all our strategy into legislation, we ought to have a back-up position.

I suggest we look inward—perhaps we are part of the problem. To the extent we are not productive, we must have the guts to correct this problem. Our unions may require some restructuring. Building trades unions, in particular, suffer from too much local autonomy.

Possibly, QWL can be used under the right circumstances to help reach our goal. Joyce has expressed in writing some interesting ideas that should be looked at.

We should see to it that what comes out of these conferences is communicated to the membership. I suggest a massive education program—a massive communication program so that the rank-and-file members are fully aware of the problems faced by *their* unions. This should be part of our strategy. Also, unless unions embark on a massive organizing effort, unions are going to continue to lose political clout. The more we lose control of our jurisdiction, the less likely a legislative strategy is to succeed.

If democracy requires an enlightened electorate, the labor movement certainly requires an enlightened membership to survive.

VII

A Comparative View

14 Labor Movements in
Canada and the United
States

Noah M. Meltz

Historically union membership as a percent of the number of paid
workers has followed similar trends in Canada and the United States;
this similarity ended in the early 1960s. The percentage of workers in
Canada unionized in 1980 was, according to some measures, almost
twice that in the United States. Are the labor movements really that
different? The answer suggested in this chapter is "yes and no." While
there are great similarities between the labor movements as such, what
is particularly different are the laws and enforcement mechanisms and
underlying factors that combine to create a generally more favorable
climate for the labor movement in Canada.

Five considerations are dealt with here: first, a comparison of overall
trends in union membership growth; second, an examination of the
patterns of change in the percentage of unionized workers by industry
sector; third, the primary reasons for the diverging trends from the
mid-1960s; fourth, possible underlying factors which may contribute
to these differences; fifth, implications arising from this analysis.

**Trends in Trade Union Membership in Canada and the United
States**

In both Canada and the United States there are different ways of measuring the number of trade union members and different bases can be
used to estimate the extent of unionization of the labor force.[1] The
most important consideration in measuring the number of union members is whether unaffiliated associations of professional employees and
unaffiliated organizations of government employees that engage in
collective bargaining are included or not. I present both series here.

The extent of unionization depends on which measure of the labor
force is used. Here the number of union members is compared with
the number of nonagricultural paid workers, for two reasons. In North

America unionization has traditionally been very low among agricultural and self-employed workers. Since the number of workers in both these sectors has declined precipitously in the past half-century, a more accurate reflection of the extent of unionization is provided by excluding them. The second reason is more pragmatic: this is the longest historical series available for the two countries (Bain and Price 1980).

Figure 14.1 shows the actual number of union members for the past seventy years. The sharp rates of growth in the teens, late thirties, forties, and early fifties are familiar to students of the labor movement, as are the declines in the twenties, early thirties, and late fifties. The most recent growth period was the late 1960s and early 1970s. In the United States the peak was reached in 1974 with subsequent downs and a few ups. In Canada there were continual increases up to 1982.

When the size of the labor force is taken into consideration, dramatic differences can be seen in the extent of unionization in the two countries since the early 1960s. As figure 14.2 shows, American union membership as a percent of nonagricultural paid workers declined almost steadily from 1954, no matter which measure is used. By contrast, the Labour Canada series shows a major reversal after 1964 that brought the percent unionized in Canada to historic heights (39% of nonagricultural paid workers in 1982). While the Bain-Price series[2] shows a high and relatively unchanging union membership percentage in Canada, the same widening gap is shown between the figures for the two countries, no matter which series is used. Both Canadian series also show that for more than half of the past sixty years of relatively comparable data, the extent of unionization in Canada has been greater than that in the United States.

Two other general points will complete the overview of trends in the labor movements. The percentages of female union members were identical in 1980 at 30%. Canada had caught up to the United States after lagging behind. Second, the Canadian labor movement has become increasingly nationally based. Before 1975 a majority of Canadian trade unionists were members of international unions (with head offices in the United States). By 1982 the international figure was 44.2%. The latter development in particular has a bearing on the differences in the labor movements.

Whichever measure is used, Canada appears to have relatively more trade union members than the United States and the gap is widening. An increasing part of this gap is contributed by members of national (Canadian-based) unions.

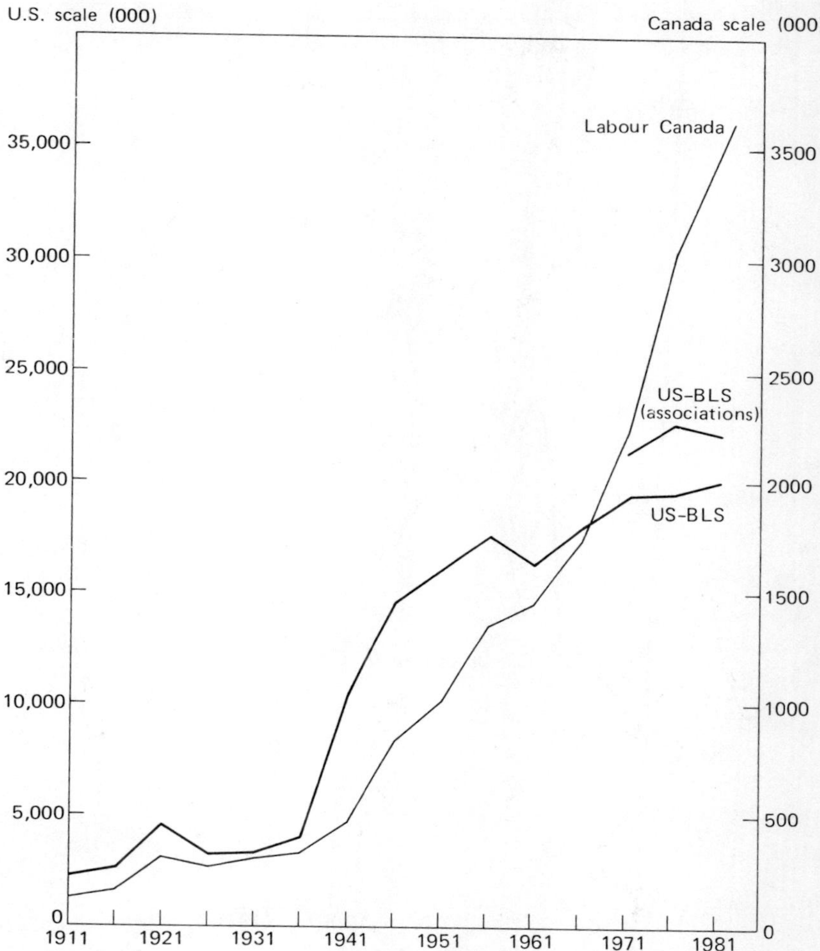

Figure 14.1 Total union membership in Canada and the United States, 1911–1982. Note: U.S. excludes Canadian membership in international unions. Source: Labour Canada (1967, 1982), Bain and Price (1980), and Gifford (1982).

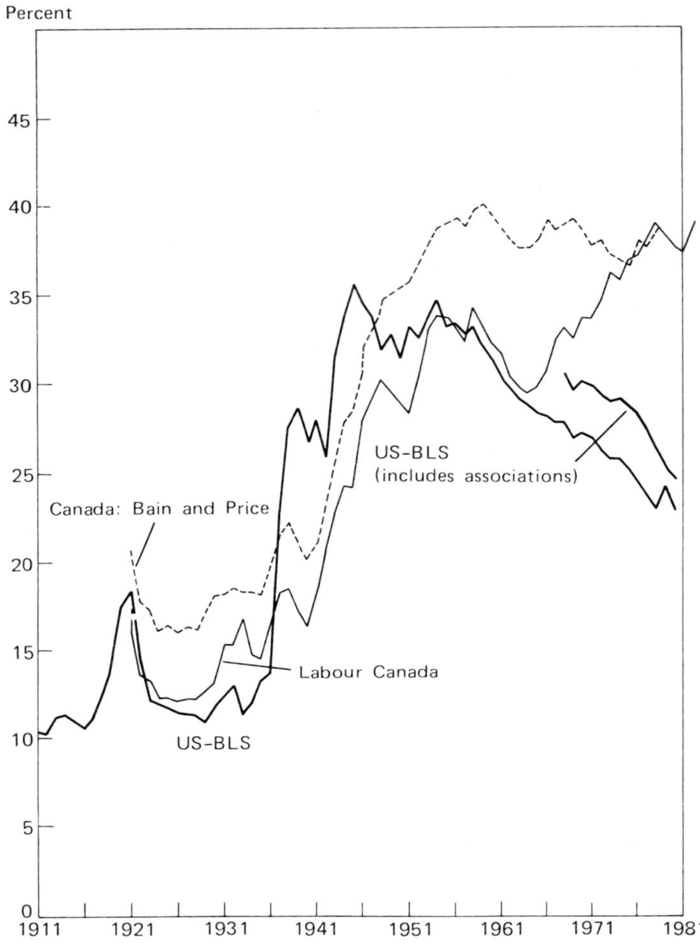

Figure 14.2 Union membership as a percent of nonagricultural paid workers: Canada and the United States, 1911–1982. Source: Labour Canada (1982), Bain and Price (1980), and Gifford (1982).

Union Membership by Industry

A ready explanation for the differences in union membership between the two countries is the more rapid growth in public-sector unionization. While the growth of public-sector unions is certainly an important factor there are other differences as well.

Table 14.1 presents union membership by industry sector from 1966 to 1980. Comparisons by sector between the countries are only approximate, since there may be differences in the classification of industries.

In both Canada and the United States there was a twofold increase in public-sector (government) unionization. The difference is that Canada started from a higher base. In 1980 Canadian government employees had double the rate of unionization of their American colleagues. In fact, all broad industry sectors were more highly unionized in Canada in 1980 than in the United States.[3] This was not the case in 1966, when construction as well as transportation, communication, and public utilities had a higher unionization rate in the United States.

Over the fourteen-year period the extent of organization of American workers decreased in all sectors except trade, finance and service, and government. In Canada, except for mining, there was either growth or stability (aside from a slight decrease in transportation).

The overall rate of unionization can also be affected by changes in the distribution of the labor force among industry sectors, even if each industry's union percentage does not change. Between 1966 and 1980 both countries saw shifts in the industrial composition of employment, as shown in table 14.2. In both cases there was a major decrease in the proportion of the employed who worked in manufacturing and an increase of those in trade, finance, and service industries. Because of differences in the bases used for estimating employment in each country one has to be cautious in comparing the actual numbers. What can be done is to examine the impact of the changes in distribution within each country and how it affected the overall rate of unionization.

In both countries, had there been no other changes, the shift in employment toward trade, finance, and service employees would have lowered overall rates of unionization. A decrease did not occur in Canada because membership rates grew in these industries and remained unchanged in the others. A net decline occurred in the United States because the growth of unionization in trade, finance, service, and gov-

Table 14.1

Union membership by industry sector in Canada and the United States, 1966–1980 as a percent of nonagricultural employed

	Canada				U.S.[c]				
	1966	1968	1974	1980	1966	1968[a]	1974[a]	1980a	1980b
Mining	51.4	50.9	44.6	32.5	43.5	47.6	47.2	32.1	28.0
Manufacturing	43.3	43.7	43.8	43.2	42.5	43.3	42.2	32.3	33.4
Construction	47.2	55.0	62.9	57.6	69.3	71.0	62.9	31.6	35.8
Transportation, communication and public utilities	57.3	57.0	49.5	53.2	75.1	71.4	65.0	48.0	56.4
Trade, finance, insurance and service	9.2	14.3	14.9	16.7	8.9	8.7	8.6	13.7	15.4
Public administration (Government)									
Bain & Price	37.2	52.6	67.9		15.8	32.4	37.5	33.8	25.1
Calura	68.3	61.4	70.4	67.8					
Total[b]	32.6	33.2	33.2	32.6	27.9	30.3[a]	28.9[a]	23.0	24.7[a]

Source: George S. Bain and Robert Price, *Profiles of Union Growth, A Comparative Statistical Portrait of Eight Countries* (Oxford: Blackwell, 1980).

Courtney D. Gifford, *Directory of U.S. Labor Organizations* 1982–83 Edition (Washington, D.C.: Bureau of National Affairs, 1982).

Statistics Canada, *Corporations and Labour Unions Returns Act, Reports for 1966, 1968, 1974, 1980,* Part II—Labour Unions, Ottawa, Canada: 1968, p. 86; 1971, pp. 75–76; 1976, p. 71; 1982, p. 65.

1980a taken from Gifford (1982)

1980b based on the number of union numbers (Gifford 1982) and the number of employed wage and salary workers by industry taken from the *Monthly Labour Review* 104, no. 12 (December 1981), p. 75. "Government union members" includes the 2,271,000 difference between membership totals in tables 2 and 3 of Gifford (1982), presumed to be an estimate of the number of persons in employee associations.

Note: The industry classifications are those of each country and are not necessarily comparable.

a. Includes professional and state government employee associations.

b. Excludes agricultural, forestry and fishing.

c. Excluding membership in Canada.

Table 14.2
Distribution of nonagricultural employed by industry sector 1966–80

	Canada				U.S.			
	1966	1968	1974	1980	1966	1968	1974	1980
Mining	2.1	1.8	1.5	2.1	1.0	0.9	0.9	1.1
Manufacturing	30.2	27.1	24.7	21.8	30.0	29.1	25.6	22.4
Construction	7.4	6.2	5.7	5.1	5.1	4.9	5.0	4.9
Transportation, communication and utilities	10.3	10.1	10.0	8.8	6.5	6.3	6.0	5.7
Trade, finance and service	42.5	47.5	50.7	54.3	40.5	41.4	44.4	48.0
Public administration	7.4	7.3	7.4	7.9	16.9	17.4	18.1	17.9
Total (excludes agricultural, forestry and fishing workers)	100.0	100.0	100.0	100.0	100.0	100.0	100.0	100.0
Number of persons (thousands)	5,643	6,312	7,961	9,397	63,995	67,961	78,412	90,564

Source: See table 14.1 for all except U.S. 1980 which is taken from *Monthly Labor Review*, December 1981, table 8, p. 75.
Note: The industry classifications are those of each country and are not necessarily comparable.

ernment was not sufficient to offset the declining rates of organization in the other sectors.[4]

A final consideration is the impact of the difference between the industrial distribution of employment between the two countries. If the distribution of employment in Canada in 1980 had been the same as that in the United States, and if the rates of union organization were the ones that actually existed, the overall union rate would have been even higher than it was in 1980 by approximately 10%. The difference in industrial distribution of employment between the two countries is thus not a factor in the higher membership rate in Canada. In fact if Canada were more like the United States in its employment distribution there would be a greater difference in the overall rates of organization.

The major characteristic distinguishing the two countries is that in Canada more workers are organized within virtually every industry sector and in particular within government, manufacturing, and construction.

What Are the Reasons for the Divergence in Union Membership Growth?

The divergence in union membership growth resulted from a more rapid increase in public-sector unionization in Canada (government, teaching, health) and from the limited erosion of membership share in other industries. Two factors can be identified for these developments: federal (Canada) and provincial legislation which supported and often encouraged the organization of public-sector workers and legislation plus vigorous labor relations boards' enforcement of regulations against antiunion practices.

Labor legislation in Canada is for the most part a provincial responsibility. The British North America Act (1867), which was the Canadian Constitution up to 1982, was interpreted as giving the federal government limited responsibility in this field (such as transportation, communication, banks, and grain elevators). Less than 10% of the Canadian labor force is subject to federal legislation. Provincial involvement has meant comparisons among jurisdictions. When combined with other factors, the result has been legislation generally supportive of unions.

The major developments in legislation occurred from the mid-1960s to the mid-1970s. Probably the most dramatic change was the Public Service Staff Relations Act (PSSRA) of 1967 which gave almost all federal civil servants the right to organize, bargain collectively, and strike (Kruger 1971). On January 1, 1967, the Public Service Alliance of Canada (PSAC), formerly the Civil Service Association of Canada, became affiliated with the Canadian Labour Congress and was counted as being a union. Its 92,800 members ranked third in Canada in 1967, behind the United Steelworkers (130,000) and the Canadian Union of Public Employees (106,100) (Labour Canada 1967).

PSSRA was followed by legislation granting bargaining rights and the right to strike in a number of other provinces in 1973: British Columbia, Newfoundland, New Brunswick, and Manitoba. Before PSSRA, Saskatchewan had given these rights to its public employees in 1944; Quebec was next in 1964 with provision for the right to strike by provincial civil servants, hospital employees, and teachers (Kruger 1971).

By the time of PSSRA (1967), nurses, teachers, and other public servants were becoming more militant, perhaps encouraged by the results obtained by workers under generous government-sanctioned settlements in 1966 and changing levels of education and expectations (Crispo and Arthurs 1968, Nault 1969). In addition, municipal employee unionization was enhanced by the formation of the Canadian Union of Public Employees (CUPE) through an amalgamation which by 1975 had become Canada's largest single union.

In those provinces where public servants were not granted the right to strike (Alberta, Ontario, Nova Scotia, Prince Edward Island), collective bargaining procedures were introduced with provisions for compulsory arbitration of the terms of collective agreements in the event of an impasse. Later, even in some of these provinces groups were given the right to strike, such as primary and secondary schoolteachers in Ontario in 1975. This followed a series of illegal strikes in 1974 and early 1975 (Kervin 1977).

There is a general consensus that legislation in Canada has assisted and in many cases (such as teachers in Ontario, where membership is compulsory) promoted unions in government and other public services (Carter 1982, Chaisson 1982). In recent years legislation has continued to support unionization through a number of pioneering reforms—in British Columbia with the provision for the imposition of first agreements in the event of an inability to agree on a first contract (Weiler 1980); in Quebec an anti-strike-breaking law; and in Ontario the imposition of compulsory dues checkoff for union members and nonmembers (Carter 1982).

These last items of legislation are examples of aspects that also relate to the second consideration, provisions of enforcement of legislation, that facilitate union organization and continuation in Canada. These aspects would seem to be factors underlying the limited erosion of trade unions among non-public-sector employees in Canada.

Perhaps the single most important factor is the provision in virtually all jurisdictions in Canada for the granting of representation rights without a vote where the appropriate labor relations board is convinced that the union membership is a majority of workers in the bargaining unit (over 55% in Ontario and over 50% under federal legislation). In the United States unions have been winning less than half of recent representation votes (Kochan 1980). In Ontario, the largest labor jurisdiction in Canada, a majority of representation votes in 1981–82 were lost by unions (96 out of 176). However in 636 cases certification was given automatically, raising the unions' overall certification rate to 76% (Ontario Labour Relations Board 1982). Halliday also reached the same conclusion in his comparison of the effects of legislation on trade unionism in Canada and the United States, and he found that Canadian boards have also been much speedier in dealing with certification applications (Halliday 1982).

A third factor in the more favorable treatment of unions in Canada has been the extent to which LRBs have cracked down on unfair labor practices by management. Two notable recent examples are the *Radio Shack* case (1979) and the *Securicor* case (1983). The Radio Shack case is particularly relevant since Radio Shack is known in the United States as an antiunion firm that attempted to export its labor-relations philosophy to its Canadian subsidiary. After a long and bitter strike over the issue of dues checkoff in a first agreement with the Steelworkers, the Ontario Labour Relations Board found that Radio Shack had bargained in bad faith (Cavalluzzo 1979). The board ordered the company to compensate employees $180,000 for wages and benefits lost because of the company's violations of the Labour Relations Act. The Steelworkers' union was reimbursed $131,000 for organizing expenses and $19,000 for legal costs. The strike also led to the passage of Bill 89 that instituted mandatory dues checkoff in Ontario (*Steelabour* 1981).

In the *Securicor* case the Ontario Labour Relations Board ruled that Securicor, hired by Automotive Hardware Limited during what became a six-month strike by the Steelworkers, violated the Labour Relations Act because "its undercover agent, posing as a striker, secretly supplied information about union strategy and morale to company officials"

(Tenszen 1983). Securicor was ordered to pay $422,000 in wages and benefits to 380 workers for the time it was deemed to have prolonged the strike. The firm was also ordered to refrain from infiltrating unions to spy on them before or during any strike or lockout. In late May 1983, the firm was appealing the case.

In the United States, decisions of the National Labor Relations Board are frequently challenged, and, in fact, provision is made for court tests. In Canada, the legislation gives LRBs final decision power and challenges can only be made on a point of law. This difference in approach does not provide Canadian management with the delaying tactics available in the United States that can act to undermine union organizing efforts (Halliday 1982, Kochan 1980, Bain 1978).

The combination of supportive legislation and strong enforcement of provisions forbidding antiunion (as well as antimanagement) practices seem to be significant factors in the diverging union growth patterns.

Given the nature of the unionization process, there is a complex of interacting factors in addition to the legislation and its enforcement. The striking differences between the two countries in these respects suggest that they must play a role in the higher Canadian unionization figure, particularly in sectors such as manufacturing where there is a large number of firms to be organized.

Underlying Factors Behind the Divergent Membership Trends

The underlying factors behind the divergent membership trends can be divided into two groups: factors that have always existed, and factors that merged in the early 1960s.

The labor relations environment in Canada has always been distinguished from that in the United States by a number of factors: a tradition of greater government involvement in the economic life of the country; a history of tripartite boards; a parliamentary as opposed to a congressional system; and socialist political parties in both Canadian federal and provincial legislatures. These factors combine to explain why the percentage of workers organized by unions in Canada was higher than in the United States before the Wagner Act of 1935 and after the late 1950s (see fig. 14.2).

The federal government played a direct role in the economic development of Canada and the acceptance of government involvement has persisted (Easterbrook and Aitken 1958). Examples are a publicly owned airline (Air Canada); a publicly owned broadcasting system

(CBC); a publicly owned oil company (PetroCanada); numerous other Crown (government-owned) corporations; and a national health system. This acceptance of government also relates to the long-standing practice of tripartite boards in labor relations matters. At the turn of the century, Canada's first Deputy Minister of Labour (and later Prime Minister) William Lyon Mackenzie King introduced the concept of a tripartite (representing labor, management, and the public) board to inquire into labor disputes and to report the results and recommend solutions in the Industrial Disputes Investigation Act of 1907. While the board was investigating the dispute, there was to be a compulsory cooling-off period during which there could be no strike or lockout (Morton 1980). King's principles still form a strand in labor-management relations in Canada, although the tripartite principle is more in evidence in grievance arbitration and government councils and commissions than in the certification procedure itself. The King principles also carry with them an implicit recognition of the role of unions, at least in certain contexts.

The parliamentary system seems to be more supportive of third and even fourth parties than the congressional system. In Canada this has meant the existence for five decades of a socialist and later a socialist-labor party. The Cooperative Commonwealth Federation (CCF), formed in 1933, became the government of the province of Saskatchewan in 1944 and introduced many programs favorable to labor, including the right of civil servants to bargain collectively and strike (1944).

In addition to these general factors, there were specific developments beginning in the early 1960s that tended to enhance the position of organized labor in Canada. These included the formation of new political parties, the existence of a sizable amount of interunion competition, increased nationalism, the lack of the equivalent of antiunion "sunbelt states," and increased public-sector militancy.

A major development was the formation of the New Democratic Party (NDP) in 1961 through an alliance of the CCF with the Canadian Labour Congress. The NDP has formed governments in Manitoba (where it is presently in power), Saskatchewan, and British Columbia, and has sizable strength in Ontario and in the federal parliament. NDP governments or NDP goading of governments has been an important factor in raising labor issues or providing a threat to the other parties to make them stress labor issues for fear of losing voters to the NDP. It seems to be more than a coincidence that the 1960s and 1970s have seen a series of labor-supportive legislation, as was the passage of

PC1003 [Canada's Wagner Act] after labor-related parties won three of four by-elections in 1943 (Morton 1980, 183).

It might, on the other hand, be argued that the general wage restraint under the Anti-Inflation Board (1975 to 1978) and the limitation on wage increases and the right to strike by federal and many provincial public servants (1982 to 1984) represents a move away from a labor-supportive approach. This remains to be seen.

In Quebec, the Parti Quebecois (PQ) was strongly supported by and identified with the labor movement in its 1976 election. Subsequent legislation followed, including the anti-strike-breaking (antiscab) bill. Although the government has had a falling-out with the Quebec labor movement in 1982–83, the links that did exist showed significant support for labor for a time. Extreme economic difficulties appear to have forced a weakening of the link.[5]

Other factors that are different in Canada underlie the divergent union trends. A most important difference is the existence of a significant amount of competition within the Canadian labor movement—much more competition than would appear to be the case in the United States. The merger of the AFL with the CIO in 1955 seems, from a vantage point across the 49th parallel, to have reduced competition among labor groups in the United States. While the Teamsters, the National Education Association and others, such as the Mineworkers, are independent of the AFL-CIO, the federation still represents 68% of organized labor. In Canada the Canadian Labour Congress formed in 1956 by a merger of AFL and CIO affiliates, represented two million members and 58% of Canadian labor in 1982. In addition to the long-existing Quebec-based Confederation of National Trade Unions (CNTU), other and smaller federations were formed (the Central des Syndicats Democratiques and the Confederation of Canadian Unions). In 1982, the construction trades affiliated with the AFL-CIO left the CLC over a question of jurisdiction in Quebec to form the Canadian Federation of Labour with 200,000 members, roughly equivalent in size to the CNTU and one-tenth of the now-smaller CLC.

A major factor in competition in Canada has come from national unions, that is, unions that charter locals only in Canada. The national unions are based in the public sector and have been the primary beneficiaries of both the strong demand-led increase in employment as well as legislation fostering trade union organization (see Chaisson and Rose 1981). In 1982 international unions represented 44% of Canadian organized labor, down from approximately 70% in the mid-1960s and

95% as far back as 1905. There was an earlier decline in the proportion of international unions to a low of 57% in 1934 but it rose again through the wave of CIO-led organization through the affiliated Canadian Congress of Labour (Chaisson 1982).

Not only have national unions been active but nationalism has played a role with a move for greater Canadian autonomy within international unions and the breaking away of some Canadian branches to form national unions such as the Canadian Papermakers Union (CLC)[6] and the Energy and Chemical Workers Union (CLC).[7] In both of these cases the parting of the ways was amicable; however, independent and fiercely nationalist unions such as the Canadian Association of Industrial, Mechanical, and Allied Workers (affiliated with the CCU) have mounted aggressive raiding attacks on the Steelworkers and the Mineworkers.

Another difference is that Canada has no equivalent of the U.S. sunbelt states, that have not only grown rapidly in employment but have been covertly or overtly antiunion with "right-to-work" laws. In Canada, the most rapid growth areas, Alberta, British Columbia, and Ontario, have largely or very explicitly been supportive of unions. British Columbia has the second highest percentage of union workers in Canada and has been innovative in labor laws. Ontario has roughly the national average of percentage of membership and has been innovative as well. While Alberta has the lowest rate of organization of the three, 24.2% in 1979 (Wood and Kumar 1982), it has accepted the general approaches to labor law prevailing in other provinces.

There is a much narrower range in the rate of unionization in Canada as compared with the United States. Newfoundland, the most unionized province in Canada in 1980, had less than twice the membership rate of Alberta, the least organized (42.6% versus 23.1%). In the United States, the most organized state, New York, had five times the rate of the least organized, South Carolina (38.8% versus 7.8%).

The single most notable case of a gesture designed to stifle union growth was that of the Michelin Bill in Nova Scotia in 1980. Special legislation was passed to require that "if an employer had more than one plant within the jurisdiction that any petition for certification must be made by a bargaining agent representing employees in an appropriate bargaining unit across all plants" (Anderson 1982). It is alleged that the Michelin Tire Company threatened to close its existing two plants and not build a third one if any of its plants was unionized. This bill is such an exception in Canada that it seems to prove the rule. In spite of this one piece of legislation, firms have not been flocking to Nova Scotia.

A final factor, beginning in the mid-1960s, was the increased militancy of public-sector employees, including seaway workers, postal workers, nurses, and teachers. Crispo and Arthurs (1968) and Nault (1969) present possible reasons for the militancy while Rose (1983) examines the long-run growth of unions in the public sector. The muscle-flexing was important in the chain of events that led to the granting of collective bargaining and the right to strike in most jurisdictions.[8]

Implications

We began with the question: are the Canadian and American labor movements really that different? The answer is "yes and no." The movements are not different in their basic structure, functions, and general method of operation (see Kruger 1971 and Anderson 1982). But they are different in the context in which they are operating, especially the political environment and to some extent the social environment. The result has been that Canadian society, on balance, appears to have been more supportive of trade unions and collective bargaining than the United States.

It is possible that some brakes may be put on legislative support for unions. In July 1983 the government of British Columbia, fresh from an election victory over the NDP, introduced an unprecedented series of bills that will produce a significant rightward shift in the economic climate of the province. The bills (proposed legislation) include the elimination of both the Employment Standards Board and the Human Rights Commission. (The latter is to be replaced by a council to adjudicate disputes.) The Public Sector Labour Relations Amendment Act gives the government sweeping control over recruitment and work assignments. Another act permits public-sector employers to terminate employees without cause when the existing collective bargaining agreement has expired. The provision of greater flexibility in the management of human resources is predicated on the view that it will increase productivity in the provincial economy. Labor has reacted with shock and anger and at the end of July 1983 was attempting to coordinate action in their opposition to the legislation. It is too early to predict the ultimate effect of this legislation or its impact on the degree of union organization in this second most highly unionized province (after Newfoundland). Clearly, other provinces will be watching the events.

Whether there will be a general shift away from the days of prounion atmosphere is yet to be seen. It is possible, since as we have seen here, legislation and its application are crucial factors underlying union growth.

Are there lessons for the U.S. and Canadian labor movements? I would like to indicate three things that seem to be suggested by the preceding discussion.

First, political pressure, operating directly or indirectly through socialist or social democratic parties, in a parliamentary system where the provinces play a major role, has led to legislation and strong enforcement of labor laws that have supported the growth of trade unions. Second, there has been a long tradition in Canada of tripartite boards and general government involvement, which would tend to support collective bargaining and implicit recognition of unions. While Canada may lag behind Europe, and in particular a country like Sweden, it would appear to be ahead of the United States in this respect.

Third, the significant amount of competition within the Canadian labor movement has probably also been a factor in the growth of trade unions, although likely less than the legislation and vigilant labor board enforcement of fair treatment of unions.

Will Canada and the United States continue to see diverging patterns of union membership growth? The answer to this question depends on developments within both countries. At the beginning of the 1970s it appeared that Canadian union growth would slow down (Williams 1971), yet it boomed. The key will be in the trade, finance, and insurance sectors. In Canada the banks are under federal jurisdiction (the Canada Labour Code). In 1977 the Canada Labour Relations Board ruled that a branch of a bank is an appropriate bargaining unit. It was believed that this would enable unions to grow in the banking sector, but after a brief and limited flurry, organization virtually stopped (Lowe 1980).

The sharp recession of 1981–83 probably produced some decline in union membership and a cautious approach by workers. This caution may dampen union organizing efforts in the initial stages of the economic recovery. However, when better times reappear, workers may be more receptive to unions both as protection against future downturns in the economy and as a collective means to deal with the threats of microtechnology that have been thoroughly aired by the media. This could lead to a renewed growth of union membership in Canada.

On the other hand, there are forces that could lead to less union membership growth. On the surface, Canadian management seems to be more accommodating and less openly confrontational than American management (Aaron 1979). Is this a reaction to the Canadian environment in which unions have been relatively more accepted than in the United States? Is this the result of a much higher level of union organization and the lack of alternative locations in Canada to escape from unions? If a factor underlying union growth was acceptability due to favorable legislation, then will the changes in British Columbia legislation in the summer of 1983 be a harbinger of general Canadian restriction on trade unions and thereby lead to less union growth? Which way things develop in Canada and how they compare with the United States will depend on the complex interaction of factors that characterizes industrial relations.

Notes

The author would like to thank Morley Gunderson, Arthur Kruger, and Robert Davies for their detailed comments and suggestions. Other helpful comments were received from John Crispo, Desmond Morton, and Joseph Rose and from Ray Hainsworth.

1. For summaries of discussion of trends in union membership in the two countries, see Bain (1978) and Kochan (1980). For discussions of the inter-relationship see Swidinsky (1974), Chaisson and Rose (1981), and Halliday (1982).

2. The Bain-Price (1980) series includes as union members all persons in professional and government associations who eventually came to bargain collectively with their employers.

3. The detailed industry data for 1980 show slightly higher U.S. figures in trade (10.1%, versus 8.9% in Canada) and finance, insurance and real estate (3.7%, versus 2.5% in Canada). For sources see table 14.1.

4. Caution has to be exercised in comparing the 1980 membership rates by industry in the United States with the estimates for 1974 and earlier years. Nevertheless there still seem to be long-term trends of a decrease in the percentage organized in manufacturing and an increase in the percentage organized in public administration. Gifford (1982) shows a decrease in the percent organized in manufacturing from 38.8 in 1973 to 32.3 in 1980, and an increase in the percentage organized in public administration from 27.8 in 1973 to 33.8 in 1980.

5. In the fall of 1982 the Quebec government passed wage-cutback laws that reduced the salaries of public workers (civil servants, teachers) by as much as 20% for a three-month period at the beginning of 1983. The cutback was intended to save the Quebec government over $500 million. On May 30, 1983 the cutbacks were ruled unconstitutional because the annexes that accompanied the legislation were not written in both English and French, the official languages.

6. The Canadian Papermakers Union was formed in 1974 by a merger of Canadian branches of the International Brotherhood of Pulp, Sulphite, and Paper Mill Workers and the United Papermakers and Paperworkers. A few locals of the latter union did not join the merger and remain in independent existence.

7. In 1980 the Canadian sections of the Oil, Chemical, and Atomic Workers International Union (AFL-CIO/CLC) merged with the Canadian Chemical Workers Union (Ind.).

8. In the case of the postal workers, the Public Service Staff Relations Act, even with its strike option, did not lead to a settling down of their industrial relations. Major technological changes and divided federal government responsibility led to the creation of a Crown Corporation, Canada Post, in 1981, which removed it from PSSRA and placed the corporation under the Canada Labour Code, that is, under legislation less restrictive than PSSRA.

References

Aaron, Benjamin. "New Tensions in the Relationship between Management and Labor in the United States." Toronto: Centre for Industrial Relations, University of Toronto, 1979.

Anderson, John. "The Structure of Collective Bargaining." In *Union-Management Relations in Canada*, edited by John Anderson and Morley Gunderson, 173–195. Don Mills, Ontario: Addison-Wesley, 1982.

Bain, George Sayers. *Union Growth and Public Policy in Canada*. Hull, Quebec: Labour Canada, 1978.

Bain, George Sayers, and Robert Price. *Profiles of Union Growth*. Oxford: Blackwell, 1980.

Carter, Donald D. "Collective-Bargaining Legislation in Canada." In *Union-Management Relations in Canada*, edited by John Anderson and Morley Gunderson, 29–45. Don Mills, Ontario: Addison-Wesley, 1982.

Cavalluzzo, Paul J., ed. *Levgold Current Labour Developments*. Toronto, Ontario: Golden and Levinson, 1979.

Chaison, Gary N. "Unions: Growth, Structure and Internal Dynamics." In *Union-Management Relations in Canada*, edited by John Anderson and Morley Gunderson, 147–170. Don Mills, Ontario: Addison-Wesley, 1982.

Chaison, Gary N., and Joseph B. Rose. "The Structure and Growth of the Canadian National Unions." *Relations Industrielles/Industrial Relations* 36, no. 3 (1981): 530–551.

Crispo, J. H. G., and H. W. Arthurs. "Industrial Unrest in Canada: A Diagnosis of Recent Experience." *Relations Industrielles/Industrial Relations* 23, no. 2 (1968): 237–264.

Easterbrook, W. T., and Hugh G. Aitken. *Canadian Economic History*. Toronto: Macmillan, 1958.

Gifford, Courtney D. *Directory of U.S. Labor Organizations*, 1982–83 Edition. Washington, D.C.: Bureau of National Affairs, 1982.

Halliday, Alasdair Hugh. "The Effects of Legislation on Trade Unionism in Canada and the United States." B.A. thesis, Harvard University, 1982.

Kervin, John B. *The 1975 Metro Toronto Teacher-Board Negotiations and Strike*. Toronto: Centre for Industrial Relations, University of Toronto, 1977.

Kochan, Thomas A. *Collective Bargaining and Industrial Relations from Theory to Policy to Practice*. Homewood, Ill.: Irwin, 1980.

Kruger, Arthur M. "The Direction of Unionism in Canada." In *Canadian Labour in Transition*, edited by Richard U. Miller and Fraser Isbester, 85–118. Scarborough, Ontario: Prentice-Hall of Canada, 1971.

Labour Canada. *Directory of Labour Organizations in Canada*. Hull, Quebec: Minister of Supply and Services, Canada, 1982.

Labour Canada. *Labour Organizations in Canada*. Ottawa: Queen's Printer, 1967, 1969.

Lowe, Graham S. *Bank Unionization in Canada: A Preliminary Analysis*. Toronto: Centre for Industrial Relations, University of Toronto, 1980.

Morton, Desmond, with Terry Copp. *Working People, an Illustrated History of Canadian Labour*. Ottawa: Deneau and Greenberg, 1980.

Nault, Aime. "Teachers' Militancy and the Changing Teacher-School Management Relationships." *Relations Industrielles/Industrial Relations* 24, no. 1 (1969): 167–194.

Ontario Labour Relations Board. *Annual Report 1981–82*. Toronto, 1982.

Rose, Joseph B. "Growth Patterns of Public Sector Unions." In *The Future of Public Sector Industrial Relations*, edited by Gene Swimmer and Mark Thompson. Ottawa, Ontario: Institute for Research on Public Policy, forthcoming.

Statistics Canada. *Corporations and Labour Unions Returns Act*, Report for 1980, Part II, Labour Unions. Ottawa: Minister of Supply and Services, Canada, 1982.

Steelabour. Toronto, December 1981.

Swidinsky, R. "Trade Union Growth in Canada: 1911–1970." *Relations Industrielles/Industrial Relations* 29, no. 3 (1974): 435–451.

Tenszen, Michael. "Spy's firm must pay lost wages to union," *Toronto Globe and Mail*, May 14, 1983.

Weiler, Paul. *Reconcilable Differences*. Toronto: Carswell, 1980.

Williams, C. Brian. "Trade Union Structure and Philosophy: Need for a Reappraisal." In *Canadian Labour in Transition*, edited by Richard U. Miller and Fraser Isbester, 145–172. Scarborough, Ontario: Prentice-Hall of Canada, 1971.

Wood, W. D., and Pradeep Kumar. *The Current Industrial Relations Scene in Canada 1982*. Kingston, Ontario: Industrial Relations Centre, Queen's University, 1982.

Discussion, Part VII

Lynn Williams: I think Noah Meltz's contribution is first class. It covers the ground thoroughly and makes all the points it should, but there are some interesting ironies I've observed. One of our great original pushes in the Canadian labor movement was to try to get a national labor code. We obviously failed but backed into what turned out to be a good deal. We paid a price, though. We have not established national bargaining as in the United States. One of the few examples where we did establish national bargaining was in the transportation industry, an industry which does come under the federal legislation.

At the Ontario Federation of Labour, we had a president who always wanted to propose changing the law to require a vote for union representation as in the United States including, of course, the lower membership figure in support of the application. A group of us had regularly to deter him from doing this since we much preferred the automatic provision. Of course, the automatic recognition provision is not as simple as it may sound. The automatic aspect can be challenged if, by process of resignation or change of support to another union, the strength of the application has fallen below 55%. So normally we want to sign up considerably more than 55% and then there is a lot of activity to maintain that level of support.

Most of the union leadership in Ontario liked the first contract arbitration provision of the British Columbia law, but when I was last active in the labor movement there, the conventions of that kind of arbitration procedure for contract settlement would establish a dangerous precedent.

I would view the question of the competition between the labor boards a bit differently than the way Meltz did. I would ascribe the improvements that were achieved in provincial legislation not so much to competition between the boards, as to the fact that various provincial

New Democratic Party governments were able to use their political power and improve the laws in support of labor's proposals, which would then provide the labor movement with the opportunity to go to other provinces and press for equal treatment. I would not describe the improvements as resulting as much from competition among the chairmen of the labor boards as from the reaction of their political leaders to these political pressures.

From my personal perspective all of the things Meltz mentioned are important, but I think the most important difference between Canada and the United States is that there isn't any South or Sunbelt in Canada—or in any other advanced industrial country, for that matter. The result is that employers have nowhere to hide from the labor movement. We do have one area in which wages tend to be lower— the Atlantic provinces—but it is not an unorganized area. If a new plant is established there it is likely to have ten unions knocking on its door. There is also the province of Alberta which is not so highly unionized, but which maintains relatively comparable wage rates because oil is its main industry.

I would also say that the existence of the international labor movement has been a crucial factor in Canada. It has meant that the Canadian labor movement has had a lot more clout relative to its size than any other labor movement. Canadians have had great autonomy and have also enjoyed the support of international unions so that they could deal with the major companies from a position of strength and face strikes when that has been necessary. The significant fact behind that statistic is not that there are a great many strikes but rather that there have been some long and difficult ones, with major employers, which have been of great significance in establishing more adequate recognition for the labor movement.

I would not want any of this to suggest that life is a cinch in the labor movement in Canada; it is not. Canada has its share of professional union-busters and the labor leaders don't fare any better in public opinion polls than in the United States.

John Joyce: It seems that the thrust of both Meltz's and Williams's comments are correct. But I do want to comment on some of the figures for construction contained in table 14.1. That table shows that construction industry unionization in the United States reached a high of 71% and is now down to about 36%. Our statistics indicate that the whole series from which these data are drawn is flaky. At no point did construction union membership get as high as those numbers suggest. That would be equivalent to saying that there are ten million construction workers and that is just not correct. Our figures do show a decrease in union coverage but it is not as steep as the table suggests.

Finally, regarding John Flynn's comments on strategy and politics, the union certification process is clearly in need of change [see Discussion, pt. VI]. In our industry alone, much of the growth in residential construction took place in the Sunbelt states and that has helped to contribute to a decline in our numbers. Many people believe that an election process simply is not viable in construction. But if we could get the process handled quickly in two or three days as it is done in Canada, we could have an orderly process for our industry.

Epilogue: Is a New Industrial Relations System Emerging?

The objective of the conference on which this book is based was to engage a cross section of labor leaders in intense discussion about a range of research looking at many facets of the industrial relations system in transition. The quality of the discussion speaks to the success of the conference. The purpose of this final chapter is not to summarize the papers or the discussion but to draw several conclusions of our own based on the reactions of these labor leaders to our research.

The Macro vs. the Micro as Levels for Special Attention

We introduced the conference by noting there have been many changes in the economic and political environment within which industrial relations operates, and it is unclear whether these changes portend merely a temporary setback, a permanent disaster, or the prelude to a rebirth of the labor movement and the emergence of a new system of industrial relations. What is clear, however, is that there is considerable experimentation and change taking place on the microlevel of this system. It is to this level of analysis that our research is directed, and as a result most of the discussion of the conference took place at this level.

By taking the pressures and developments in the macroeconomic and political environment as a given, we were able to concentrate on concrete developments within the system, but this emphasis left a number of conferees somewhat frustrated. They pointed out that the future success of the labor movement and industrial relations more generally depends upon the climate of public opinion and the willingness of public policy to confront issues such as labor law reform, industrial policy, and macroeconomic affairs. We are mindful of the importance of these macrodimensions and for this reason ended the conference with a consideration of the Canadian experience. The result was that most participants left the conference saying, "If only we operated north of the border, matters would be considerably different." Whether such wistfulness is justified is not clear. Certainly, the contrast between the United States and Canada developed in the chapter by Noah Meltz demonstrates the importance of differences in macro policies and societal conditions for the performance of industrial relations at the industry, firm, and individual-worker levels. An adequate analysis of these macroissues and international comparisons perhaps warrants a separate conference.

Indeed, to anticipate a theme we will come to at the end of this chapter, the changes in industrial relations we have been studying at the microlevels are not likely to produce a stable "new system" of industrial relations in the absence of supporting changes in economic policies and the political and social climate at the macrolevel. But the converse is also true. Macrochanges in labor's political influence and social acceptability will not produce a new stable system in the absence of significant changes in collective bargaining, shop floor practices, and in strategy formulation at the levels of the firm and the national union. The latter point is one of the most important, perhaps the key message derived from our research.

Having recognized the importance of linking changes in the macroenvironment and public policy to the microlevel, we can now consider some of the major themes we drew from the conference discussions.

Organizing the Unorganized

By whatever measure one examines, bringing new members into the labor movement is not going very well. Of the many comments and analyses made about the poor showing of unions in representation elections, we feel that one of the most telling points was made in Charles McDonald's description of the "sophistication gap" that has developed between management and labor in their handling of organizing campaigns. One might say that when the election method of establishing certification of unions was put into law in the 1930s it provided unions, especially in manufacturing industries, with a new and effective technique for adding members. Given the pent-up demand for collective bargaining and the availability of this new procedure, unions were able to grow very rapidly during the 1930s and 40s. Over time, however, employers learned to use and abuse the election procedures with considerable skill and today are probably more experienced and skillful at the electioneering process than are most unions.

Certainly, there are some bright spots for unions. A number of important union election victories were described along with some of the techniques used by organizers who have had high rates of success. But these are more often the exception than the rule.

What do we make of this and what can we say with respect to the future? Generalizing from the 1977 Quality of Employment Survey and the recent AFL-CIO Organizing Department survey in the high technology industry, there clearly is a general potential for unionizing. The latter survey found that close to one-half of the workers see advatages in group affiliation. The trick for unions is to tap this potential without provoking disincentives to representation because of the particular union or particular organizing techniques involved.

If we ask what produced the organizing successes in the public sector (the last area where the United States saw a major upsurge in unionization), several characteristics stand out. Among them are the important role of professional associations such as the National Education Association (NEA) during the preunion period, the key role played by specialized unions such as civil service, police, fire, and nurses' associations, and the grass-roots strategy of organizing from within with assistance from professional organizers familiar with specific problems of public-sector workers. But most important was the lack of sophisticated or aggressive management resistance to organizing in the public sector. The message seems to be that in the absence of changes in either the law, the social climate, or union tactics that can *truly* neutralize employers in organizing campaigns, the NLRB election procedures are unlikely to produce significant numbers of new union members in the foreseeable future.

Based on this analogy, substantial inroads into the service sector, white-collar occupations, and areas where women are concentrated will only take place in the presence of unions that have special portfolios and are seen as being "like us" and not like the stereotype of the labor movement generally. In examining the content of management statements, the arguments that seem to be most effective in deterring unions underscore the image of unions as being remote, as being interested in the big industries, and as fitting the image of the "labor boss" rather than the local association that is largely run by members and meets the special or specific needs of the members through group action and collective bargaining.

This emphasis argues for something approaching enterprise unionism, or at least highly decentralized local unions, where leaders focus their attention on the special characteristics of the local plant or office. Indeed, one of the conferees suggested the NEA model for organizing and bargaining in new areas.

It is also clear that more unions will need to link their organizing efforts at the bargaining unit with "corporate campaigns" or other efforts to secure a pledge of neutrality from management at the top level of the firm. The public- and private-sector experiences of the past two decades suggest management neutrality is a necessary, but perhaps not a sufficient, condition for successful organizing. Relating the campaign to the specific concerns of the employee groups and having inside or local leaders who closely reflect the characteristics and views of the workers are equally important.

The Economics of Collective Bargaining

One of the liveliest discussions of the conference took place around the question of concession bargaining, centering on the extent to which wage scales must be adapted to competitive realities versus the ability of unions to "take wages out of competition." Several major industries, such as autos and steel, figured prominently in this discussion.

Certainly in a number of industries compensation costs are higher than the costs of a U.S. manufacturer producing offshore or the landed cost of a competitor's product produced by foreign labor. But, as several participants pointed out, there has always been a difference in wage rates between U.S. workers and those in other countries. What has changed is that this difference has become *the* key competitive factor because of changes in transportation, the organization of manufacturing (making it possible to produce subcomponents at various places), and the growth and increased sophistication of many foreign companies.

The U.S. labor movement had been successful in taking wages out of competition in many manufacturing industries, but with all of the changes in the competitive environment the wage advantage becomes a key determinant of the long-run survival of the firm and the job security of union members.

What is missing at the moment is an effective strategy for again taking wages out of competition. Let us look at this question in terms of the automobile industry. Regardless of whether the gap between a typical Japanese and American automobile worker is $8, $6, or $4 an hour, the gap is of sufficient magnitude to require some type of strategic response by the UAW. Some of this gap might be met by technological change, a response that has supported higher wages in the United States over a long period of time. Some of the response might come at the national level, such as the 1982 settlement that has reduced compensation over what it might have been by $1.50 to $2.00 an hour. And some of the gap might be met by changes in the plant-level work systems or other changes in the deployment of the work force.

During the conference we heard of a number of examples in steel and automobiles where the gap was being closed, but these were primarily at the local level as workers who felt threatened joined with management to undertake a variety of programs to lower effective unit labor costs. As a result, collective bargaining is becoming more decentralized, because the strategy and the framework to support a high-wage policy are not being supplied at the national level. This is another version of the general point that we see a weakening of pattern bargaining and that collective bargaining for the foreseeable future is going to become much more decentralized, with wage and compensation arrangements tailored to the particular economic exigencies faced by the plant in question. It is unlikely, however, that plant-level productivity improvements and wage moderation in collective bargaining can completely close the labor-cost gap. Solutions that involve restructuring policies and practices at all levels of the bargaining relationship will be required.

Unions in key manufacturing sectors might look to the model of unions like the ILGWU and the Amalgamated Clothing and Textile Workers Union that have by necessity helped shape strategies or what might be called private industrial policies for the industries in which they represent workers. Because of the long-standing pressure from imports, the garment and small-goods industries have always been living at the margin. Consequently, the unions just mentioned have operated at the political level by lobbying for tariffs and import arrangements, at the industry level by supporting research and application programs for new technology and modernization, and at the collective bargaining level by fashioning wage and fringe benefits on a company, and indeed sometimes on a plant-by-plant, basis to reflect the economics of the particular product line in question. Academics who concentrate on understanding union wage policies have not paid enough attention to the behavior of unions and industries that have experienced economic restructuring as a steady and normal process.

Involvement of Unions in the New Systems of the Workplace

Ten years ago we would not have predicted that today unions would be intimately involved in programs of quality of work life and work restructuring. At that time these experiments were being conducted in unorganized plants, and where they did occur in organized plants, they were quite peripheral to the main activities of labor-management relations. In a growing number of instances, however, it is clear that these activities are becoming central to both the economic performance of the plant and the nature of the industrial relations system. The important question is whether these plants will continue to innovate and provide an interplay between the new participation programs and collective bargaining practices or whether with the passage of time there will be reversion to earlier practices.

For the moment we can note from the conference some of the very strong testimonials on behalf of what some labor leaders see as the "new era" of worker participation. A new breed of union leadership has emerged out of local-level experiences to play a key role in these programs. The health of the quality-of-work-life movement in part rests on the career progression of these individuals.

Conclusions

Can we see a new system of industrial relations emerging after reviewing our research with this group of labor leaders? If we answer in terms of current or even emergent practices observed in the field, the answer is clearly no, or at least not yet. What we have instead is a good deal of piecemeal experimentation, innovation, and some throwbacks to earlier eras of intense conflict. But if measured by the thoughts and ideas expressed by some of the union participants and by their reactions to some of the ideas and conclusions expressed in the research, our answer is more qualified. Clearly, some union leaders see the current experiments and changes as temporary adjustments from patterns they hope to return to with better economic and political times. But others have begun to think about building on the current changes to create what we would call a new industrial relations system. These visions deserve the label of a "new" industrial relations system because they challenge several or all of the traditional principles underlying collective bargaining in the post–World War II environment.

At the microlevel any new industrial relations system would have to be one that is able to live with greater variations in labor costs across firms. The inability of unions to take wages out of competition in many key industries implies the need for greater reliance on contingency forms of compensation. But collective bargaining alone will not be a sufficient form of labor-management interaction in this environment. For a stable relationship to evolve, the parties will need to move beyond collective bargaining to provide more involvement of unions in planning and decision making at the strategic level of the firm. In return, unions will need to work with employers in modifying work organization at the shop floor level to enhance productivity and flexibility for employers and career opportunities and employment security for workers.

At the macrolevel the new system would involve a greater acceptance of unions in society and meaningful labor law reform and a growth-oriented macroeconomic and industrial policy, all derived from a rebirth of the political influence of the labor movement.

But these are visions, not realistic predictions to be drawn from the conclusions of the research or from the predictions of the labor leaders. No one presented a scenario for how this or some other new system would come about in the near or even long term. Thus it is not vision or new ideas that are missing among either labor leaders or academic researchers. What is missing is a pragmatic strategy for change that would provide a transition to a new steady state in industrial relations. In the absence of such a strategy, not only the American labor movement but American management, indeed American society, will continue to live with an industrial relations system as described in the final paragraphs of chapter 1, a system caught up in a state of internal contradictions incapable of either returning to the old order or of turning the new vision into reality.

Note

This chapter was prepared by Robert McKersie, Harry Katz, Thomas Kochan, and Michael Piore.

List of Participants

Stephen Albanese
American Postal Workers Union

Richard Balzer
Consultant

Max Bazerman
Sloan School of Management, M.I.T.

Michael Bennett
United Automobile Workers

Michael Bonn
United Steel Workers

Leslie Calder
Amalgamated Clothing and Textile Workers Union

Samuel Camens
United Steel Workers

Peter Cappelli
University of Illinois

John Carmichael
Newspaper Guild

Donald Ephlin
United Automobile Workers

Peter Eritano
United Steel Workers

Hank Farber
Economics Department, M.I.T.

John Flynn
International Brotherhood of Electrical Workers

Lorel Fogel
Communications Workers of America

Richard Freeman
California Institute of Technology and Harvard University

Jack Golodner
American Federation of Labor and Congress of Industrial Organizations

Art Gundershein
Amalgamated Clothing and Textile Workers Union

Jack Joyce
International Union of Bricklayers

Harry Katz
Sloan School of Management, M.I.T.

Robert King
United Automobile Workers

Janice Klein
Harvard Business School

Thomas Kochan
Sloan School of Management, M.I.T.

Doris Lackey
International Union of Bricklayers

E. Robert Livernash
Harvard University

Charles McDonald
American Federation of Labor and Congress of Industrial Organizations

Robert McKersie
Sloan School of Management, M.I.T.

June McMahon
Service Employees International Union

Andrew Martin
Civil Engineering, M.I.T.

Noah Meltz
Center for Industrial Relations, University of Toronto

Vera Miller
Amalgamated Clothing and Textile Workers Union

Nancy Mills
Service Employees International Union

Charles Myers
Sloan School of Management, M.I.T.

Reginald Newell
International Association of Machinists and Aerospace Workers

Leslie Nulty
United Food and Commercial Workers

Joseph O'Donnell
Trade Union Program, Harvard University

Arthur Osburn
Massachusetts State Labor Council

Paul Osterman
Employment Security Task Force for Manpower Development,
Commonwealth of Massachusetts and Boston University

Rudy Oswald
American Federation of Labor and Congress of Industrial Organizations

Charles Perlik
Newspaper Guild

Michael Piore
Economics Department, M.I.T.

Lee Price
United Automobile Workers

Richard Prosten
American Federation of Labor and Congress of Industrial Organizations

Charles Sabel
Program for Science, Technology, and Society, M.I.T.

Thomas St. George
International Union of Electrical Workers

Harley Shaiken
Program for Science, Technology, and Society, M.I.T.

Abraham Siegel
Sloan School of Management, M.I.T.

John Stamm
Babson College

Herman Starobin
International Ladies Garment Workers Union

William Stevenson
United Automobile Workers

Anil Verma
University of British Columbia

Phyllis Wallace
Sloan School of Management, M.I.T.

David Wanger
Sloan School of Management, M.I.T.

Lynn Williams
United Steel Workers

Index